The Story of

Kate and Howard

by

Judith Thompson Witmer

Nan Thompson Edmunds

Jo Ellen Thompson Lorenz

The Story of Kate and Howard

ISBN 978-0-9837768-5-7

Published in the United States by Yesteryear Publishing.

Books are available at **www.amazon.com** as well as through the publisher:

Yesteryear Publishing

P.O. Box 311
Hummelstown, PA 17036

www.yesteryearpublishing.com

yesteryearpublishing@gmail.com

(717) 566-8655

Kate and Howard

Introduction to Kate and Howard

Growing up I had always been told that I resembled my father. Recently in sorting photographs, I came upon one of my mother as a young girl, one that I had seen many times before; however, this time looking at my mother's photo was like I was looking at myself at a young age. I don't have a sharp image of my father at this same age, but it would be interesting to see why people told me I looked like him. There must have been characteristics, expressions, or my demeanor that led those who knew him to say I resembled him.

Thinking about this led me to the realization that my children and grandchildren, as well as those of Jo Ellen and Nan, had not known their maternal grandfather, our father, Howard V. Thompson. Because our parents separated when I was fifteen, Jo Ellen was thirteen, and Nan only nine, we essentially grew up without a father. Further, we were homeless for two years after my mother realized she had to leave the family home and take us with her, finding places for us to live with other relatives. I had never thought of myself as a homeless person, yet we were.

We saw very little of our father after that separation and never completely understood the dynamics that situation created. Divorce was unusual in the 1950s and while there may have been a stigma of sorts, I don't believe we had any sense that there was. Everyone treated us as if everything was normal. But it was not.

Later in adulthood and particularly in my researching for the three social histories I wrote based on what it was like growing up in Curwensville in the twentieth century, I began to better understand what had happened to cause my father to change from the "Daddy" we knew from 1937 to the early 1950s. I learned that he had had a difficult childhood under his domineering father, even though his father, our paternal grandfather, was a successful businessman, owner of an electric company, then a water company and twenty-three theatres, as well as a founder of the Curwensville State Bank—and president for ten years; he also ran twice for State Senator.

Howd, or "Bubby" as our father had been called, worked for his father from the time he could remember. His 1920 Diary, written when he was fifteen, confirmed the many times he missed school to read meters throughout Centre County (they then were living in Bellefonte). His father, a self-made man, allowed no frivolities and would not allow his son to waste time playing sports (although as a young man he was a champion tennis player) or even to join the Boy Scouts. (Howd secretly bought a uniform and would wear it when his father was out of town.) Our father's protector and best friend was his mother. At her death in 1951 his world fell apart and he never recovered.

On the other hand, our mother never wavered in her devotion to us, having the courage to do what needed to be done when she felt our home was no longer safe. Kate, the middle child of her own mother's "second set" of daughters who were a decade younger than the two oldest daughters, was a quiet child, reserved and not at all adventuresome. However, she most certainly became the strongest of the five Pifer daughters, rising to all the tasks that faced her, and earning the respect of all who knew her and the unquestioning love from her children and grandchildren, forming a special bond with each of the youngsters.

Wanting my children and their cousins to know their grandparents as children, youth, and adults and to, perhaps, better understand some of the facts that led to the estrangement of their grandparents, I began the search for answers. In total, this is a quest for understanding and a record of facts of who our parents were, why our mother made the choices she did, and perhaps even why our father could not become what he might have been.

This is not a typical biography, but rather a collection of history, remembrances, experiences, explanations, and tributes to Kate. It contains the genealogies of both Kate and Howard, who they were and who they became, scenes of our childhood, unpleasant—but necessary—familial lawsuits, and, perhaps, understanding and forgiveness. Howard's 1920 Diary and excerpts from Judith's Diaries, as well as letters among family members, are inserted here just as they were written, without editing.

Judith: Archivist, Researcher, and Author
Nan: Designer, Editor, and Contributor
Jo Ellen: Proofreader and Contributor

Kate

Table of Contents

The Story of Kate

The Story of Howard begins on page 161.

Detailed paternal and maternal lineages have been prepared for Kate and Howard, available upon request.

Genealogy of Katherine Pifer Thompson

John Frederick Pifer's Maternal Lineage

(The lineage of John Pifer can be traced to William the Conqueror through his mother, Rachel Reed.)

Charles Clifford, Revolutionary patriot (b. November 10, 1730 in Hunterdon County, NJ; d. January 1, 1816 in Westmoreland County) married Jane Gordon (b. 1738; d. 1802) in 1757. James Clifford and Margaret Oliphant are the parents of Charles Clifford.

Charles Clifford moved from Bethlehem Township, Hunterdon County, NJ in the spring of 1759 and took up a homestead tract in Westmoreland County, Pennsylvania which is still in the family's possession (or was when the account cited was published).

Clifford assisted in the building of Fort Ligonier (*Frontier Forts of Pennsylvania,* Vol. II, pages 941, 244, 284). He was captured by the Indians near Fort Ligonier, April 22, 1779. A party of five all fired at him, the bullets passing through his hat and clothes, and one ball splintered his gun barrel and cut his face. (*History of Westmoreland County* by Boucher.) He served on the frontier and his name appears on the muster rolls of the third battalion. (Westmoreland County Archives, Vol. 5, pp. 653-654.) *PA Archives,* V. 4, Series 5, p. 432.

During the Revolution, Clifford served in Pennsylvania as a Private in the Westmoreland County militia. His name appears on a return of prisoners (dated Quebec, November 8, 1782) sent to the province of Quebec for exchange since the first of November 1779; this shows that he was sent September 1781 by way of Lake Champlain. (Attested to by a Mr. H. H. Shenk, Custodian of Records of the State, Harrisburg, PA, 1922 taken from the Adjutant General's Office, War Department, Washington, DC.)

Children of Charles and Jane Clifford	Born	Married
James Clifford	1758	Mary Rodgers
Thomas Clifford	1760	Catherine Lawson
Jane Clifford	1762	John Menoher
Charles Clifford	1764	Jennie Lytle
Joseph Clifford	1766	Isabel Pritchet
Edward Clifford	1768	unmarried
Mary Clifford	1771	James Whiteside
Sarah Clifford	1776	**Robert Reed, Sr.**

There is evidence of a Robert Reed, Sr. (Scotch origin) born in 1730 and who married Polly Pumroy (origin Donegal, Ireland). Robert and Polly may be the parents of the following Robert Reed, Sr., but it is odd that there would be two "Sr." Reeds. However, looking only at dates of birth, #1 is 1730, #2 is 1772 and #3 is 1804, it is possible they are the same line. That would also mean that #2 was born when his father was 42 years old.

Robert Reed, Sr. (b. 1772; d. October 17, 1848) married Sarah Clifford (b. 1776; d. November 7, 1853) on June 1, 1793. They are the parents of Robert Reed, Jr.

Robert Reed, Jr. (b. October 30, 1804; d. January 20, 1865), son of Robert and Sarah, married Leah Peoples (b. 1810; d. December 15, 1845) in 1833.

Rachel Reed (b. April 6, 1834 at Ligonier Valley, West Moreland County; d. March 9, 1901 at Brookville, Pennsylvania), daughter of Robert and Leah, married Jonas Pifer in 1859.

	Born	Married
Robert Reed, Sr. (Scotland)	*1730*	*Polly Pumroy (Donegal, Ireland)*
(child) **Robert Reed**	**1772**	**Sally Clifford**
(child) **Robert Reed, Jr.**	**1803 (04)**	**Leah Peoples**
(child) **Rachel Reed**	**1834**	**Jonas Pifer**
(child) **John F. Pifer**	**1868**	**Matilda Smith**
(child) **Katherine Pifer**	**1908**	**Howard Thompson**

John Frederick Pifer's Paternal Lineage

The Pifer ancestors came from Germany on the Pink Mary ship in 1733.

Born in 1789, John Frederick Pifer married Charlotte Fry (b. 1791; d. 1875) in 1810. John and Charlotte were two of the first settlers in Jefferson County. Two of their children were John F. Pifer (originally [John] Fredrig Peiffer) and David Pifer.

Born in 1813, John F. Pifer married Catherine Shetterly (b. 1817; d. 1889) and they had eight children, one of whom was Jonas, born in 1838 at McCalmont Township, and died at Beaver Township, Jefferson County, on July 24, 1884.

Jonas Pifer married **Rachel Reed (b. 1834)** in 1859. They are the parents of five children.

Margaret (b. 1861) (married Bert Jourdette)
>Don Jourdette

Joseph[i] (b. 1863)
>Richard[ii]
>Frank (Ottawa)
>Nora (Kansas City)
>Ruby (Topeka)
>Clara (Wellsville)
>Florence (unmarried it appears)

Hugh (b. 1865) (wife's first name was Carrie)
>Hal
>Viola
>Earl
>Don

John Fredrick[iii] (b. 1868)
>Josephine
>Ruby[iv]
>Jessie[v]
>Katherine
>Margaret Jean

Katherine/Kate (John's twin)[vi] (b. 1868)
>John
>Catherine Princetta,
>>b. September 21, 1902[vii]
>Henry

Richard (b. 1873)

John Fredrick Pifer was born on July 25, 1867/8 in Beaver Township, Jefferson County. He died at Curwensville on May 3, 1954. (His obituary gives **1868** as his date of birth and Brookville as his place of birth.)

John Fredrick Pifer married **Matilda Adeline Smith.** John and Matilda were married on June 20, 1894. Matilda died at Curwensville on May 1, 1955.

Matilda Smith Pifer's Paternal Lineage

(An earlier Matilda Smith was listed among the early citizens of Jefferson County in the 1830s).

William McElhaney, born in Donegal, Ireland, is the first ancestor of Matilda Adeline Smith to be identified. He is the father of **Andrew McElhaney** (b.1755) who married **Mary Campbell** (b.1768). The youngest daughter of Andrew and Mary was **Elizabeth Mary McElhaney** (b.1811) who married **Robert Harrison Smith** (b.1809).

It is not known if Robert Harrison and Elizabeth were married in Ireland or America. It is, however, known that their third child, **Robert B. Smith,** was born in Jefferson County, Pennsylvania on June 20, 1841. This Robert married **Mary Ann McElheney** (b. 1843). They are the parents of Matilda Adeline Smith and her siblings.

Robert's date of death is unconfirmed. Mary Ann died in 1882 (likely in childbirth) at age 39.

In the census taken on June 18, 1880 for Washington Township, Jefferson County, the following are listed as the children of Robert and Mary:

Jessie, age 15, b. 1865

Robert, Jr., age 13, b. 1867

Evelena (Lena), age 11, b. 1869

Matilda, age 8, b. 1872

Ella, age 6, b. circa 1874[xi]

Adda, age 1, b. circa 1879

Rosanna, not in census, born 1880

Ella (Nell), listed in family notes as the youngest, b. 1882

Matilda Adeline Smith was born June 2, 1872[ix] at Lane's Mills, Jefferson County. (Other information gives Matilda's place of birth as Beech Woods[x] which also is in Washington Township.)

Progeny (Six Surviving Children) of Robert and Mary Smith

Jessie married Jake Heighes

> Robert
>
> Clark (in the set of photographs in Judith's collection)
>
> Hilpa
>
> Hazel (identified in the set of photographs)
>
> Margaret

Robert is the only boy in this family of five daughters. There is no family information on him except for an entry in Matilda's Bible, "Dear Rob died July 22, 1941, Los Angeles, CA"; however, there is no confirmation as to whether or not this is her brother Robert.

Evalena (Lena, Lennie) married M. E. Heighes, Jr. and lived in Hubbard, Ohio

> Inez
>
> Margaret (married name Longwell)
>
> Helen
>
> Mary (married name Patterson; daughter Margaret)

Matilda Adeline Smith married **John Fredrick Pifer** on June 20, 1894

> Josephine Smith Pifer Hamilton (b. 1895; d. September 1972)
>
> Ruby Idora Pifer Wayne (b. 1897; d. June 1983)
>
> Jessie Beverly Pifer Hawes Mohney (b. July 9, 1905; d. June 1, 1993)
>
> **Kathryn Shields Pifer Thompson** (b. February 11, 1908; d. January 31, 1998)
>
> Margaret Jean Pifer Bloom (b. February 11, 1910; d. December 30, 1958)

Rosanna (Rosie), b. June 24, 1880; d. September 11, 1970; married Edward Stormer

> Edward, Jr., b. March 9, 1914

Ella ("Nell"), the youngest, was born in 1882 and married a Mr. Jordan.

Progeny of the Children of John and Matilda Smith Pifer

Josephine Smith Pifer Hamilton married Droz Hamilton on December 20, 1919. (b. December 21, 1887; d. August 10, 1961)

- ♦ Noel Franklin, 1934 (Wife: Karin)

Ruby Idora Pifer Wayne married Tom Wayne.

- ♦ John A., b. April 18, 1924; d. March 25, 1994 (Wife: Nanette)
  - ◦ Gregory
  - ◦ Lisa
- ♦ Thomas J., b. June 20, 1929; d. August 16, 1977 (Wife: Mary Lou)
  - ◦ Mark
  - ◦ Gary Cooper

Jessie Beverly Pifer Hawes Mohney married Harry Hawes in 1930; married John (Jack) Mohney on June 22, 1963. (John was born on June 5, 1906 and died on October 14, 1974.)

Kathryn Shields Pifer Thompson married Howard Vincent Thompson, June 27, 1927.

- ♦ Matilda Kay: November 1, 1930
  - ◦ Mavis Kim – September 2, 1952
- ♦ Judith Evelyn: March 9, 1937
  - ◦ Jean Rochelle – March 7, 1959
  - ◦ Thomas Ross – April 23, 1968
- ♦ Jo Ellen: November 6, 1938
  - ◦ Janelle Corinne – January 2, 1969
  - ◦ Eugene Kendall – April 17, 1970
- ♦ Elizabeth Nan: August 19, 1942
  - ◦ Shayne Scott – December 9, 1965
  - ◦ Jesse Joel – November 6, 1979

Margaret Jean Pifer Bloom married A. Chester Bloom circa 1926-27.

- ♦ Chester Eugene, b. 1927 (m. Mable Riddle)
  - ◦ Mark
  - ◦ Debbie
- ♦ Donald Dwight, b. 1929 (m. Kathryn Lorraine Valimont)
- ♦ Janet Lynne, b. December 1946 (m. James Carter)
  - ◦ Shelly

Dates of High School Graduation of Pifer Sisters and Their Children

Josephine Pifer Hamilton	1914
Noel	1952
Ruby Pifer Wayne	1915
John	1942
Tom	1947
Jessie Pifer Mohney	1924
Katherine Pifer Thompson	1925
Kay	1948
Judith	1955
Jo Ellen	1956
Nan	1960
Jean Pifer Bloom	1927
Eugene	1945
Don	1947
Janet Lynne	1965

Dates of High School Graduation of Thompson Sisters' Children

Mavis Kim Brunetti *(Matilda Kay Thompson Walker)*	1970
Jean Rochelle Ball *(Judith Evelyn Thompson Witmer)*	1977
Shayne Scott Edmunds *(Elizabeth Nan Thompson Edmunds)*	1984
Thomas Ross Ball *(Judith Evelyn Thompson Witmer)*	1986
Janelle Corinne Lorenz *(Jo Ellen Thompson Lorenz)*	1987
Eugene Kendall Lorenz *(Jo Ellen Thompson Lorenz)*	1988
Jesse Joel Edmunds *(Elizabeth Nan Thompson Edmunds)*	1998

High School Graduation Photographs

Kate and Howard

| Matilda Kay | Judith Evelyn | Jo Ellen | Elizabeth Nan |

| Mavis Kim Brunetti | Jean Rochelle Ball | Thomas Ross Ball | Janelle Corinne Lorenz | Eugene Kendall Lorenz | Shayne Scott Edmunds | Jesse Joel Edmunds |

Jean Ball Jacobs

Thomas R. Ball

Janelle Lorenz Wright

Shayne S. Edmunds

| Jordan Ashlee Jacobs | Jillian Rochelle Jacobs | Olivia Emerson Ball | Emily Madison Ball | Corinne Catherine Wright | Theodore Piers Wright | Aero Graham Edmunds | Iris Isadora Edmunds |

Note:

A photograph taken of the Smith sisters as adults: Jessie, Lennie, Dilly (Matilda), Rose, Ella. As was the custom, the women likely were in a line (left to right) according to age. Also, because we always were told there were five sisters in the Smith family, it is likely that the information on page 12 in italics is possibly in its first listing of Ella and that perhaps Adda did not survive childhood.

Robert Sr., their father, in a chart of the time (no exact date given) was listed as Head of Household, Jessie as doing housework, and Robert, Jr. as a Farm Laborer.

Matilda Smith Pifer had four Aunts (no clear evidence if they are all sisters and if they are all the children of Matilda's father's family or Matilda's mother's family):

- Rose (married a Logan)
- Agnes (married Will Clark; they had a son Robert Clark)
- Jessie (born in 1845)
- Hazel

Some tangible evidence:

- We have a calling card for Mrs. Andrew Logan; on the reverse side is a hand-written message, "Congratulations and best wishes (from) **Aunt Rosie** and Uncle Andy."
- **Aunt Agnes** Clark is identified (in the photo collection Judith has) as an aunt to the Smith children. Aunt Agnes sent a letter to Matilda on January 31, 1930; she was writing from Cincinnati, Ohio, and may earlier have lived in Kentucky. The letter mentions an "Orville."
- Agnes and Will (Clark) sent a post card to Jessie (Pifer) in 1918.
- There are other photographs in the mentioned collection that served as identifiers: Hilpa is identified as the daughter of Jessie (Smith).

Endnotes

i   Joe, in his 20s, left the area of Brockwayville in Jefferson County and went to Salt Lake City by way of Kansas City and then Denver. He later returned to Elk County, married, bought a farm and began raising a family. In 1910 he left again and after brief stays in Oklahoma, Texas, Arizona, and California, settled in Portland, Oregon where he was engaged in lumbering. He also was a well-driller. John and Joe, referenced in letters from John to Matilda, met, for example, in areas in the middle of the country to do well-drilling together. Joe, at age 90, visited John (then age 85) in 1953 and the event was noted in *The Clearfield Progress*.

ii   Richard married Laura Stahlman on November 21, 1896 in Brookville. Laura was born in 1880 (this information based on her obituary which gave April 13, 1950 as her date of death and her age as 70) and was reared in Jefferson County. Richard and Laura first lived in Curwensville and then in DuBois where Richard was editor of the *DuBois Express*. They later settled in Kakabeka Falls, Ontario, and in 1935 moved to Ft. William where Richard was engaged in lumbering.

iii   John named a daughter Catherine for his twin sister and his twin named her two children John and Catherine.

iv   Ruby Pifer, daughter of John, and her cousin Ruby Pifer, daughter of Joseph, likely both were named for an earlier Ruby.

v   The three younger daughters were named for their aunts.

vi   Kate Pifer married William Shields, known to the family as Uncle Will. They are the parents of two children. The Shields lived in Jefferson County and his family members were very active in their church. Aunt Katherine Pifer Shields is the name as it was signed in a gift to Jessie from John Pifer's twin sister. (There are many variations throughout of the spelling of Kathryn, Katherine, Catherine.) **Kathryn Shields Pifer** was named for her father John's twin sister, Kathryn as her first name and Shields to assure that his sister's married name also was honored.

vii   Catherine married a Mr. Bowser and died June 1, 1987 in Phoenix, Arizona. Catherine's daughter sent a memorial card to Kate Pifer Thompson (card signed by Katee/Kate Schnither [?]).

viii   Referenced in the 1930 Quinquentennial of Mt. Pleasant.

ix   DAR records give birth date as February 6 (2/6 which is the reverse of 6/2 the date I have for her), 1872.

x   DAR records give place of birth as Lanes Mills, Jefferson County.

xi   Possibly a child was born and died and the name was then used for the youngest child.

In Memoriam

Katherine Shields Pifer Thompson

The Last of the Pifer Girls

Feeding birds, sweeping porches, special treats, favorite meals, a glance out the window to the now empty cottage . . .

Walking out for a visit, seeing something at the store that would please her . . .

Experiencing an event and saying, "Won't Mother enjoy hearing this . . ."

Valentines and birthday cards, candy and flowers, a best liked tea and fudge.

Everywhere—at home, at work, shopping, traveling—we are reminded of her presence and how much our lives were intertwined.

The long talks shared at the beach, stories of the days when Kate herself was sixteen, including tales of the TDS club!

Santa's birds who watched to see if we were "being good"; Christmas Eve visits to Aunt Jean, Aunt Josephine, and Aunt Jessie; leaving cookies and milk for Santa's visit, and finding letters from Santa on Christmas morning.

The poems of Robert Louis Stevenson and Eugene Field; huddling together listening to Inner Sanctum on the radio; first run movies at the Rex Theatre; homemade caramels taken outside in the snow to harden and carried back in to be "cracked" into pieces of various sizes; penuche and doubled-decker fudge; Hershey buds; baked potatoes at the end of an evening's sledding down Schofield Street. And in the summer, Irvin Park, where she delivered picnic lunches for hungry, water-logged kids, for whom she tooted her car horn as she drove over the bridge, announcing her arrival; and the story of looking for a very young Nan in the shallow part of the river near the shore where she was expected to be when someone pointed out that "Fish Thompson" was on the diving pier in the deep part of the river.

Music lessons, bartering for dancing lessons, 4-H, Girl Scouts, Rainbow Girls, pink net gowns, dresses by Mrs. Buterbaugh, Sunday School, a horse, college — she knew the way to enrich our lives in a small town. Not having had money for

21

a Girl Scout uniform when she herself was a young girl, she nonetheless provided uniforms for us on an income that could scarcely bear additional expense. Proms, graduations, weddings, performances—she was always there with us and for us.

From singing in church as children at two years of age to excelling in school; from placing in beauty pageants in Washington DC to earning advanced degrees; from producing "near-perfect children" to being successful in our chosen careers, her standards for us were clear: "Do your best." While we did not fully realize it at the time, all of our endeavors were for her. We clearly wanted to show her and to bask in her approval. How she enjoyed our successes! And how she delighted in the reflected glory, small or large.

Like a queen holding court, among us she was secure in her position of grande dame. While never deigning to command, she liked nothing better than to have all of us "doing her bidding." She would joke that she had to be careful what she mentioned she would like, for one of us—and sometimes all of us—would make her wish our unspoken desire to please her.

A mother bird, nudging her young out to try their wings: at eighteen to DuBois Center of PSU, at seventeen to Washington, DC, and supporting her youngest's desire to go West—how difficult and how unselfish to urge us to find our own way.

Our visits back home to Curwensville where she made each of us feel special, in turn, offering each one's favorite meals and treats, especially prepared for the visit and making herself available to do whatever we wanted. And the many "care packages" that were sent back with us, respectively to our own homes.

From our first dresses, through our proms and our weddings, even to the last years of her life, she loved our bringing our purchases to show her. "Smart clothes" were important.

Janelle's loving perseverance included her grandmother in her wedding, which became Kaki's last hurrah; all of us (maybe sensing this) went to great lengths to make this event most special. Traveling nearly 500 miles roundtrip, Jean prepared and brought her entire family; cousins Tom, Shayne, and Jesse also were in attendance along with Shayne's future wife, Grace Graybill; Judith planned travel arrangements and accomodations to ensure Mother's comfort and to lessen the stress of traveling and preparing to attend the events of the wedding; Jo Ellen selected special attire

for her, and Nan devoted herself to assisting Mother with her hair, makeup and outfit. Oh, yes, Judith also ordered a half dozen dresses from which to choose one to wear to the wedding, especially to include Mother in helping select just the right dress for the occasion, just as all of us had taken selections from Brody's "on approval" many years before.

Every grandchild, in turn, has known her love, and has had a distinct relationship with her. Each, in turn, spoke or wrote about Kaki, ending with such phrases as, "... and she loves me." Change for an ice cream cone or investment in a worm farm; buying their old toys to make a game out of giving a nickel, dime, or quarter; long bus rides to accompany a grandchild on a visit; "gas money" for a teen-ager and loaning her '66 Chevy convertible; moving aside her own belongings so a music studio could be created; and a gown to make a wedding even more precious than we could have realized.

The wind beneath our wings, she was the source of laughter and private jokes; finding foibles in all but her own children; unspoken expectations for them; pride and delight in every accomplishment of her daughters and seven grandchildren; anticipation of the success of the great-granddaughters; keen of mind to the end; and, always, unconditional love.

Scarcely a week before a family celebration in honor of her birthday, she folded those wings, leaving us as she had lived: without fuss, and, as she would say, in "quiet, good taste." May we continue to honor her memory much as we have always loved her—by living good lives and devoting ourselves to our children as she did hers.

Our Kate

Daughter of
Matilda Smith Pifer
John F. Pifer

Sister of
Josephine Smith Pifer Hamilton
Ruby Idora Pifer Wayne
Jessie Beverly Pifer Mohney
Margaret Jean Pifer Bloom

Our Kaki

Grandmother of
Mavis Kim Brunetti Richards
Jean Rochelle Ball Jacobs
Shayne Scott Edmunds
Thomas Ross Ball
Janelle Corinne Lorenz Wright
Eugene Kendall Lorenz, Jr.
Jesse Joel Edmunds

Great-Grandmother of
Jordan Ashlee Jacobs
Jillian Rochelle Jacobs

Aero Graham Edmunds
Iris Isadora Edmunds

Emily Madison Ball
Olivia Emerson Ball

Corinne Catherine Wright
Theodore Piers Wright

Our Mother

Mother of
Matilda Kay Thompson Walker
Judith Evelyn Thompson Witmer
Jo Ellen Thompson Lorenz
Elizabeth Nan Thompson Edmunds

In loving memory and tribute,
Judith, Jo Ellen, and Nan

A Tribute to Kate, 1998

This tribute—which has gone through several iterations—was first written as a simple memory of things Mother had told us about her childhood. Some of the information is also found in the longer "The Story of Kate" which was written in 2014 as part of a memoir and family history for her daughters, our children, and our grandchildren.

Our Kate

Born in 1908 when Theodore Roosevelt was president, Kathryn Shields was the fourth of five daughters and the middle daughter of the "second family" of three girls, Jessie Beverly, older, and Margaret Jean, younger, born a dozen to fifteen years after the two older sisters. Kathryn's best friend was her younger sister, Margaret Jean, born exactly two years to the day after her own birth date, on February 11, 1910. That friendship was to remain steadfast until Jean's death in December 1958.

Only five years old when she entered first grade, Kate, as she was by then called by her family, was a shy child with a strong sense of fairness. She was not ready to go to school and described her young self as a "scaredy cat." She and her classmates were among the first to be taught through the newer Palmer method of writing which had recently replaced the more ornate Spencerian method (later superseded by the Peterson method in the mid-1940s). Along with learning to write, the children were occasionally permitted to "color," although in the early days of this century crayons were expensive and doled out stingily in the schoolroom. Few children had crayons at home. Perhaps this is why Kate later admonished her children to take good care of their "colors and coloring books."

The five Pifer sisters were reared by a loving, caring mother, concerned with appearances and propriety, and a stern father, typical for the early 20th century. Their mother, Matilda Smith Pifer, was also one of five sisters, although the Smith sisters had been orphaned when Matilda was but a child. Matilda's older sister reared the younger siblings and, despite hardship, all five girls finished public school, quite a feat for those times. (We Thompson sisters never knew our maternal great-grandparents and there were very few stories told of even our grandmother's early life, other than the poverty and the unlikely similarity of being one of five daughters and, later, having five daughters of her own. We don't even know how our Grandmother and Grandfather Pifer met, although we do know that they were originally from a county adjoining the one where they later resided.)

The Story of Kate

John F. Pifer was a twin. His sister Kathryn and he had other siblings, but little was ever spoken of them, except for brother Joe and sister Kate with whom John remained in touch all of his life and for whom his fourth daughter was named. In fact, John Pifer's daughter Kate bore both the Christian and the married name of her aunt, Kathryn Shields. John and his brothers began as employees of the Keystone Drilling Company in Beaver Falls, later expanding to Pifer Brothers of Brockwayville and DuBois. Once he married and began his own family, John Pifer went on his own, complete with business cards identifying him as a Drilling Contractor, specializing in water wells, pump holes and wire holes for mines. In other words, he drilled wells. His well-drilling machine, half the size of a railroad boxcar, was fired by coal. It was transported by horses on a low wagon or by the Brockway Rail Line and the Pennsylvania Railroad on a flatbed train, on a car which boasted "Westinghouse Air Breaks." His jobs took him as far west as the state of Indiana and as far north as Canada.

Matilda Smith Pifer very much enjoyed her own brood of five girls: Josephine (Josie, and later, "Juju"), the firstborn in 1895; Ruby (Rue) born in 1897; Jessie (Jebbie), 1905; Kathryn (Kate), 1908; and Margaret Jean (Jean), the baby of the family, 1910. The girls addressed their mother as "Mama" (a term we did not use with our mother, probably because our father addressed his mother as "Mother"). "Grandpa Pifer" is all we ever heard our Mother and aunts use in referring to their father when they spoke to us, but when speaking about him among themselves they referred to him as Dad. John Pifer had fairly steady employment, but money was tight. Fortunately "Mama" sewed, so the girls were always well-dressed. ("Poor, but proud" is a term we heard often to describe their upbringing.)

A three-bedroom house, with one of the rooms no larger than a nursery, was not very commodious for a family of seven, so "Mama," always industrious and inventive, carved out sleeping space in the attic. Not insulated, except where Mama had tacked cardboard between the rafters, the attic room was very cold in winter and hot in the summer. Opening the windows helped in the summer, and in the winter, Mama heated bricks and placed them in the attic beds to warm them. When all five children still lived at home, two of the girls slept in the attic; usually those two were Kate and Jean. Jessie always seemed to manage to claim the tiny single room, while the second bedroom was shared by the two older girls, Josie and Ruby. Early in the morning the girls would scurry down the stairs to the bathroom their mother had arranged to have built shortly after the family had moved to the duplex early in the century.

While they lived only a half block from Main Street, they were not permitted to go downtown, not even to the corner. Their boundary was the back porch for play and the front porch for company and for sitting quietly on a Sunday afternoon or summer evenings. While Kate and Jean were content to play on the back porch, Jessie often would find reason to deliver something to a friend in the next block or even farther away if her story were plausible enough. She also learned early on that she would be permitted during the summers to visit her married older sisters, one of whom lived in Altoona and one in Canton, Ohio. Adventuresome, she would pack a bag and travel by train to a household which would be more lenient than that of her parents.

In the fall of 1918 when Kate was only ten the Spanish influenza epidemic struck America and claimed more victims than the World War that was raging in Europe. The girls remembered the many deaths and the quarantine signs, marked with a black wreath signifying a household's loss. To make matters worse, the winter of 1918-1919 was also unforgettable with its record-breaking cold, snow, and ice.

A well-behaved child, Kate, who did not like to be noticed, admitted to not speaking out much in school, but recalled one particular incident when a teacher grabbed her by the sleeve of her blouse; the blouse tore away from her upper arm, exposing it. Out of embarrassment and indignity, she pushed or struck the teacher, resulting in her mother's having to come to school to speak with the principal.

In later years Kate talked about being a Girl Scout, but Curwensville local history indicates the Girl Scouts weren't formally organized in the town until 1933. (Perhaps she meant the Girl Guides as a photograph of Mary Alice Thompson shows her and her cousin Marjorie in such uniforms.) When scouting was re-introduced to the town forty years later, Kate shared her scouting experiences with her own daughters who all readily joined the troop (although where she found the money for the uniforms is a mystery.) More fun than the scouts, however, was the secret club formed by Kate and a small group of close friends. They made a vow that none of its members would ever reveal what the initials of the TDS Club represented.

Vivid memories during the growing-up years of Jessie, Kate, and Jean include 1920 when at age 25, Josephine became engaged and 1924 when Ruby gave birth to her first child, a son, making the other four of them aunts for the first time.

High School Years

Mama was determined that all five Pifer girls be graduated from high school—in the classes of 1914, 1915, 1924, 1925, and 1927. As a junior in high school Josephine would have been permitted on occasion to attend a movie or perhaps a live performance at the Opera House where Nat Charnas was the manager. Among the movie offerings in 1913 were a Keystone Comedy titled "Mabel's Hero," a western, "Pecos Pete in Search of a Wife," and "the greatest comedy every made," according to the program, "Heine's Resurrection." However, of greatest local interest in the spring of that year was the Junior Class Play, "Lost – A Chaperon," performed on Tuesday, May 13, with tickets priced at 25 and 35 cents. Josie had a small part in the play and her mother and sisters were all in attendance.

In Josie's Class of 1914 were only 24 graduates, most with surnames still familiar in the town. The Faculty's Farewell Reception was held on Friday Evening, April 14, in the Park House, later known as the Park Hotel. How prescient and wistful are the words on the program: "Ah me! Those joyous days are gone. I little dreamed till they had flown, How fleeting were the hours." The signature of each classmate can still be seen on Josephine's printed program, carefully saved along with other school mementos.

Ruby's exotic appearance made heads turn and those meeting her for the first time were intrigued by both her features and her name. While the date of her graduation from the Patton Graded Public Schools, Curwensville High School, is listed on her sheepskin diploma as June 15, 1915, that was so unusually late into the summer that one must wonder if the date is not in error. Almost without exception, graduations took place in Curwensville in May. Even more curious, the annual Alumni Banquet, the town's largest social event, also bears the date of June 15, 1915. Ruby, much like Josephine before her, took summer courses and began teaching the fall following her graduation from high school. Her school, only twenty miles from Curwensville, might well have been two hundred miles, because there was no way for her to live at home and "commute." In those days, teachers lived in the community or township in which they taught, with a family, or families on a rotating basis. In fact, room and board was usually part of their contracted payment. It was in this town where she first taught that she met her husband-to-be. His family had a farm near the schoolhouse, and Tom Wayne was immediately smitten by the new teacher.

Several years later in 1924, true to the style of the time, Jessie's high school graduation portrait shows a properly pouting beauty with a styled bob, double-dropped pearl earrings, a velvet or fine wool dress trimmed with marabou and,

28

as a finishing touch, a long strand of pearls. The following year, Kate's portrait reveals a shy young woman, barely seventeen at graduation, with short hair and a very simple, long-sleeved shift, probably made by her mother on her Singer treadle sewing machine. Kate's thick brunette bob (not frizzed with a curling iron like her sister's) is held in check with a plain barrette, and she is wearing the same pearl necklace earlier displayed by Jessie. Margaret Jean's graduation portrait shows a shyly smiling young woman in a hand-detailed, two-toned shirtwaist dress with small decorative buttons. Her hair is cut short but not bobbed and she wears no jewelry.

As shy and retiring as Kate was, Jessie liked to be noticed and strove to be regarded as one "to the manor born." During the days in which the two older girls were being courted by a long line of suitors, the young men would arrive at 408 Thompson Street with flowers or candy. One ardent pursuer in particular brought boxed candy, a rarity in the Pifer house. Jessie, with great largess and the recipient's permission, liked to open the box and offer a choice of the candy (one piece per person) to whichever family members were present; the lid of the box would then be firmly replaced. On one occasion, after being ceremoniously passed around, the box of candy was placed on the arm of the settee (by accident or design was forever after debated). Jessie in her haste to show the guest a photograph of his enamored, bumped into the settee, sending the candy box flying, its contents spewed on the floor. Outwardly mortified yet very cool-headed, Jean and Kate hastened to pick up the candy, ostensibly to return the pieces to their assigned positions in the sectioned box. For every two chocolates they replaced in the container, the girls pushed one piece under the settee for later retrieval.

On another occasion, a visiting friend of Jessie's — Jessie seemed to have an endless stream of friends, both male and female — found herself ready to leave as a rain shower began. There was only one large umbrella (Mama's prized possession used only in great emergency) in the house, and certainly it was not available to be loaned to a guest. Not to be abashed or deterred by fact, however, Jessie, with great poise, asked of the household, "Where is the pearl-handled one?" Fortunately, the rain abated, and there was no need for embarrassment at not being able to offer the use of an umbrella, pearl-handled notwithstanding.

Musical entertainment was limited to the movies or live performances, both of which were at hand in Curwensville. The Opera House, and later the Strand Theatre, offered both. Current movies were shown on a regular schedule with Charlie Chaplin always a favorite. Traveling theatre companies frequently were booked in the small towns. In addition, every summer a professional touring company went from town to town, much like the rainmaker or music man, and produced an annual "local talent" musical. The producer/director was in charge, casting the "show" with (one might guess) nearly everyone who auditioned. Following two weeks of rehearsals, the production culminated in a grand performance. Kate, even though she had a good singing voice, preferred the chorus, leaving the larger, and often lead, roles to her sister, Jessie.

Jessie had a voice that townspeople spoke of even years later when there were few persons left to remember. "A beautiful, crystal clear soprano, a strong voice that commanded listeners to silence," is what they said. In her late teen years, a voice teacher moved into town. All were sure that Jessie would become the star pupil, and they waited in eager anticipation to hear how such a voice could possibly be enhanced by formal singing lessons. Something dreadful happened however, and, presumably as a result of the lessons, Jessie lost her singing voice. No one can verify it, but rumor has had it all these years that the vocal teacher, jealous of this golden-voiced student, "ruined" her voice. Jessie never sang another note and, curiously, never spoke of this tragedy. One can only speculate what happened. The story has remained a mystery with no explanation except that given by the townspeople.

By May of 1924, while Jessie was eagerly anticipating graduation, Kate was told that she had completed the required number of credits to be graduated at the end of her junior year. Nonetheless, because she was only sixteen, she chose to return to high school the following year and take two classes, French and math. Although she was intuitively intelligent, she always said she had lacked the confidence to reach her full potential. (It also should be remembered just how limited opportunities were in a small town isolated from many cultural influences.) Kate was always an avid reader, her favorite poems remaining with her into her 80s. James Whittier's "Snowbound," James Russell Lowell's "The First Snowfall," Tennyson's "Charge of the Light Brigade" and "Enoch Arden" are several examples of poems she enjoyed and could recite from memory. A member of the high school Literary Society, she confessed that she was terrified of "reciting" and had joined the organization only because there were so few extra-curricular activities offered. Her oratory, "Do It to a Finish," was presented on April 15, 1925; one can only imagine her stage fright, yet her pluck in fulfilling her commitment.

The 1925 Commencement Program spelled her name "Katherine" (The inconsistency in the spelling of her name throughout every stage of her life is something we could never quite understand, yet she never seemed to be bothered by it, even when for years she spelled her name "Catherine" because that is the way her husband spelled it.) As part of the program, Kate sang in a quartette with

Mary Margaret Adams, Estella Brown, and Ruth Kephart, sister of her lifelong friend Kathryn Kephart (who had been in her class all through school, but who had enough credits and chose to graduate at the end of her junior year). Graduation was held in the Strand Theatre on Thursday evening, May 28 at 8:00 p.m. Baccalaureate had been scheduled the previous Sunday, May 24 and the Annual Senior Banquet was celebrated at the conclusion of the Commencement Program. The following Friday, May 29, the Annual Alumni Public School Picnic was held at Irvin Park.

Four of the five Pifer girls prepared to be teachers "just in case," that meaning in case they might not marry. Mama wanted to be sure her girls could support themselves. (Jean married at the end of her senior year, so that matter was settled.) Classes could be taken not far from Curwensville, either in DuBois or Altoona, and occasionally in Clearfield, although Ruby attended Grove City College for a short time. Commuting from home was not Jessie's idea of how to spend her time and she was determined to go away to college. Heaven knows how that was paid for—perhaps once Josephine and Ruby were married and there were only three daughters at home, money was more readily available. Or, knowing Jessie, perhaps she convinced the local bank to loan her the money. Mama often took bank loans, so this would not be beyond possibility.

During her senior year of high school, Jessie requested a college catalogue from Clarion State Normal School. This she studied very carefully, anticipating life on a college campus. A steamer trunk was found for her use (perhaps the same one used by Ruby nearly a decade earlier) and was quickly festooned with a label in the shape of a pennant, proclaiming "CSNS: Clarion." Remnants of her life at Clarion still cling to the tiny hidden compartments of the trunk. Jessie Beverly Pifer became a member of the Freshman Class at Clarion State Normal School in the summer of 1924 where she immediately caught the eye of the president of the Clarion High School Class of 1925 and son of a prominent family of the college town of Clarion. A photograph of the class remains, details still crisp, revealing a group of eager young people standing on the cusp of their adult life. Jessie had a good time. She was born for the life of a busy coed.

Kate, on the other hand, preferred to live with her oldest sister Josephine in order to attend teacher preparation courses at the Pennsylvania State College's branch campus in Altoona. She was not one to venture into the unknown or to live on a college campus; she wanted the safety and familiarity of family. At nearly 30 years of age, Josephine was pleased to have her little sister live with her, as her husband Droz Hamilton traveled in his business. Kate frequently went home by train on the week-ends, likely to see Bubby who was working for his father's water company in Curwensville, and also to give Josephine and her new husband some privacy when he returned on Friday evenings from his job which kept him on the road during the week.

One did not need a college degree to teach grades one through eight. All that was required was a high school diploma and the equivalent of a year of higher education which could be completed through a series of summer courses taken either at a college or through college extension courses offered in towns throughout the state. The only other eligibility requirement to be assigned a school through the county system was a letter of recommendation, verifying the character and ability of the applicant. Even before she had been graduated, Kate was provided validation by Mr. Grant Norris, Supervising Principal of Curwensville Public Schools. Katherine Pifer found herself teaching school at age 17, feeling relieved that she had not been graduated a year earlier!

Schools usually opened the day following Labor Day and closed in early May. However, vacations were very infrequent, with nothing like the number of vacation days which are found in later school calendars. County Teacher Institutes were typically scheduled for dates close to Christmas, such as December 22, 23, and 24 (Yes, Christmas Eve day.) The annual salary was approximately $800 for 7½ months of teaching. Kate admitted that while often the boys in eighth grade were much taller than she was, they were kind and respectful.

Kate lived at home, except for the times she boarded, and continued to see Bubby who was most eager to marry her. However, at ages seventeen and eighteen she was not quite ready. She had no desire to live the life of the social butterfly that Jessie enjoyed, but she did delight in the company of friends, both couples and "the gang." Bubby was an avid tennis player and when Kate had the chance she played doubles or just watched Bubby successfully compete for local trophies.

By 1927 she agreed to marry and, consequently, was no longer eligible to teach, for married women were not permitted to teach public school. Her friend Kathryn Kephart had married Mearle Smith, but her marital status was kept a secret so that she could live at home and continue to work. Kate and Bubby set up housekeeping in a second floor apartment in a private home. They later moved to an apartment in the block-long retail business part of town where she began life as a "young married," going about town, shopping and doing errands.

The Story of Kate, 2014

(An Expansion of "A Tribute to Kate, 1998")

For more detail on most of the stories of Kate's growing up,
please see *Jebbie, Vamp to Victim.*

Ancestry

July 25, 1868 is the birth date of John Fredrick Pifer, noted in no history books, but with whose lineage the story of Katherine Shields Pifer begins. As a historical reference this was the summer that reconstructed governments had been set up in eight of the eleven Southern states, and in the fall of that year Ulysses S. Grant was elected President.

John Pifer's own maternal ancestry in America may have begun with Robert Reed, Sr. who had been born in Scotland in 1730. As a young man Reed had immigrated to central Pennsylvania where he married (rather late in life at age 40) Polly Pumroy who had come to America from Donegal County, Ireland. Robert and Polly Reed's son and namesake was born in 1772. This son, Robert Reed, Jr. married Sara (Sally) Clifford and in 1803 their son was born; he, too, was named Robert Reed. It is likely this Robert Reed (III) who settled in the Brookville area and married Leah Peoples. (It is also possible that the first Robert Reed, who married Polly Pumroy, is not part of this Pifer lineage.)

The daughter of Robert and Leah is Rachel Reed [sometimes spelled "Reid"], born in 1834, who married one Jonas Pifer, three years her junior, circa 1860.

The father of "our" John Pifer is this Jonas Pifer whose paternal lineage is German-Irish. Jonas' own father, John F. Pifer, was one of the first two settlers in Jefferson County.[1] Both Jonas and John F. made a stake in what they called Paradise Settlement in what later became Henderson Township, adjoining Clearfield County. The families bought their land from the federal government at 50 cents to $1.00 an acre and the senior John F. Pifer, along with his two sons, John and Jonas, erected a small log cabin and began farming the land. They evidently were successful as it was said that "among the best cultivated farms and those with the best improvements" were the farms of David, Jonas, Isaac, and B. F. Pifer.[2]

---

1   Scott, *The History of Jefferson County*, p. 668.

2   Ibid., 669-670

The Story of Kate

Jonas Pifer married Rachel Reed; they lived in Brookville where they reared a family of four boys and two girls. Their oldest son Joseph was born in 1863, followed by Margaret, Hugh, then John (to be the father of Kate) and his twin sister Kathryn/Katherine on July 25, 1868. There is also a son Richard who is the youngest.

The town of Brookville, 165 miles from the state capitol of Harrisburg, dates from 1796, eight years prior to the establishment of Jefferson County of which it is a part. Brookville's early growth can be attributed to its strategic location along the Susquehanna River and Waterford Turnpike, a toll road completed in 1822 from the Susquehanna River in Clearfield County northwest to Waterford in Erie County. In 1830 Brookville officially was established by the county commissioners as the county seat and was laid out by them into lots. By 1832, just two years after the first town lots were sold, there were forty dwellings, a brick courthouse, four stores, and four taverns.

Prior to 1860 much of the commerce had been conducted through barter, either of goods or services. The barter system changed to a monetary system when lumber became salable. When the settlers first came to the area later to be known as Jefferson County the land had one of the finest growths of timber of any territory in the United States east of the Pacific Coast. The white pine stood thick. Many trees were more than one hundred feet from the stump to the first limbs and had a length of 25 to 40 feet at the top above the limbs. Interspersed were hemlock as well as oak, ash, maple, cherry, poplar, cucumber, beech, and other varieties.[3] Thus, many of the newcomers to the town of Brookville came because of this prosperous lumber industry. A low grade division of the Allegheny Valley Railroad opened in 1853 and trains began running regularly to Brookville, increasing business opportunities to send and receive goods.

The first school in Jefferson County, constructed of rough logs, opened in 1803. Classes were offered for only three months and the patrons of the school paid the teacher's salary. Even with a small population, Brookville provided a formal education for its children. John Pifer (to become the father of the Kate in this story) and his twin sister Kathryn presumably attended a lower school in the town and possibly spent some time in the junior high school built in 1878.

Nearby Brockwayville was home to various newspapers, one of which was *The Dubois Evening Express,* started in 1883, becoming a daily in 1893; Richard (Dick) Pifer, brother of John Pifer, served a time as editor. Another of several newspapers in this small city was *The Morning Herald,* published by Charles J. Bangert and V. King Pifer, a cousin to John Pifer.

3   Pentz, *The City of DuBois,* p. 11

Matilda Adeline Smith, later to be the wife of John Pifer and mother of Kate, was the daughter of Robert Smith and Mary McElheney of Beech Woods, a hamlet in Washington Township near Brookville. Matilda was born on June 2, 1872 (making her two years older than Winston Churchill and Robert Frost). Matilda was the fourth child (and third daughter) of her parents.

There were to be a total of seven daughters in the Robert and Mary Smith family: Jessie, born in 1865; Lena (Lennie), born in1869; Matilda (called "Dillie" by her four sisters) and born June 2, 1872; Ella (Nell), born in 1874; and Rosanna (Rosie) E., born on June 24, 1880; as well as a son, Robert, born in 1867. (There is evidence of the birth of a sixth daughter and possibly seventh prior to Rosanna; this child likely died young.) These children were orphaned when their mother died shortly following the birth of her youngest child and the second to be named Ella. The task of caring for the household and rearing the younger siblings thus fell to the older two girls, particularly Lena, from what can be determined.

Despite hardship, all five girls attended and likely completed common school (6th, 7th, or 8th grade, depending upon what the school offered). If a young man (rarely woman) wanted additional education he had to attend one of the academies scattered throughout the state. This lack of opportunity for education for females is likely the main reason for Matilda's firm determination that her own children would not only finish high school, but attend Normal School.

Perhaps because of their early difficulties to reach adulthood, as adults the five Smith sisters remained in close contact with one another despite the geographic distance between them. The sisters relied on letters as their primary means of communication. Several of them lived only twenty or thirty miles from one another, but a visit was rare.

The Smith sisters very seldom spoke about the untimely loss of their mother. In fact, the five sisters related very few stories of early life to their children, other than the poverty and the implausible similarity of Matilda's being one of five daughters and, later, having five daughters of her own, and even one of those five producing four daughters.

It is almost certain that John cut his education short (probably at around the age of sixteen, circa 1884) to join his brother Joe as an employee of the Keystone Drilling Company in Beaver Falls. A year later brother Dick joined Joe and John when they left the Keystone Company to become the Pifer Brothers Company of Brockwayville and DuBois. The three brothers remained in business together for another year. Transporting their drilling rig by train, they traveled around the nation to wherever their services were needed.

More adventuresome than his younger brothers, Joe decided he would like to try his luck further West and in 1886 he packed up and left for what was called "Oregon Country," attracted by the advertisements of the great transcontinental railroads which followed the line of the old Oregon Trail. His well drilling took him throughout the entire country and occasionally he would meet John, along with Hugh and/or Dick, for a collective well-drilling job in the country's heartland of Indiana and Ohio. Occasionally the brothers even found themselves traveling into Canada.

John and his brothers remained a team until many years later when Dick also decided to leave the area and move to Ohio. John then became an independent jobber, complete with business cards identifying him as a Drilling Contractor, specializing in "water wells, pump holes, and wire holes for mines." Like most equipment of this time, his well-drilling machine, half the size of a railroad boxcar, was fired by coal. For local jobs, the machine was guided up planks onto a low wagon that was hauled by horses. When it was necessary to travel any greater distance, the rig was transported by the Brockway Rail Line and the Pennsylvania Railroad on a flatbed train.

Curwensville and Surrounding Areas

The history of the town of Curwensville somewhat parallels that of Brookville, forty miles distant. Founded three years later than Brookville, Curwensville is situated on the West Branch of the Susquehanna River and was named for John Curwen, Sr., of Montgomery County, Pennsylvania even though this John Curwen never lived in the town which bears his name.

Like most early settlements, the area of Curwensville was appealing because of its waterways as a means of transportation and early source of potable water. By 1811 Curwensville was known as the largest upriver village on the West Branch of the Susquehanna River and the gateway to the wilderness beyond. Within a decade, following the completion of the Erie Turnpike, the village saw a rapid influx of newcomers.[4]

The river provided a natural highway across the county, traveling southward to Sunbury and Northumberland where it joined its North Branch, then on through Harrisburg and to Baltimore and Philadelphia. By 1818 a local lumber industry had begun with several small mills springing up along the river, and by 1889 there were a number of sawmills in the area so that much of the lumber could be "finished" locally rather than the logs being shipped to other points.

The first school house in Clearfield County was built in 1803, in Pike Township which surrounds Curwensville. Originally it was open only several months each year, the term beginning in November or December and ending in January or February. The school term gradually lengthened so that by the 1880s school began in mid-September and ran until April.

In the village of Curwensville itself, the first school was opened in 1812 in a private home and taught by Josiah Evans. Later the citizens built a log house for school purposes. In 1833 a school house was built through subscription on land on upper Filbert Street contributed by John Irvin. In 1854 or 1856 William H. Irvin, at his own expense, built what was known as the "Brick Schoolhouse," which he later rented to the borough.[5] In 1860 the old Methodist Episcopal Church was purchased and used as a school. The first completely public borough school was built in 1867 after the school directors were authorized to borrow money and build new schools as needed; this building cost $2,750 and was used for the next twenty years.

As this age also saw the popularity of free public high schools, the citizens began to talk of the possibility of providing a high school education, and on September 2, 1884 the cornerstone for a new school was laid, complete with Masonic ceremonies. The Honorable John Patton donated $20,000 for this school constructed of native sandstone, 62 x 71 feet, with eight classrooms, four on each floor connected by halls and two stairways. The monolithic stone

Patton Building

---

4   Ibid., p. 21
5   *Curwensville in Celebration of 200 Years*, p. 18

building became the focal point of the town and the place for many community ceremonies. The first class of five boys and five girls was graduated at the First Commencement on April 8, 1886, the same year as the dedication of what came to be known as the Statue of Liberty. In 1892 an addition was built on the back of the Patton Building, disturbing its proportions, but providing the needed space for science labs (a narrow chemistry room and a physics classroom with elevated "arena" seating) and four additional classrooms.

Winters could be harsh in the mountains of central Pennsylvania and temperatures often were near zero. Travel by horseback, carriage or, in winter, by sleigh, was not easy, but travelers could find lodging at nearly every crossroads. Most illnesses in the mid-century were treated by "home remedies" and general medicine which addressed no particular disease. Doctors could do little more than give advice and make patients more comfortable. Not even the aspirin had yet been developed.

The first telephone line in the county was built from Curwensville to Cherry Tree in 1881.[6] By January 1882 a line was constructed from Curwensville to Clearfield by picking up the line from Clearfield to Cherry Tree, but it was not until late in the century that a toll line was built through to Curwensville to connect with the Clearfield and Huntingdon Company. One telephone served the entire town of Curwensville, as was the case in DuBois. When a person wished to use the telephone he went into the pay station to have a number dialed for him; he would then wait until a messenger was sent to inform the person with whom the caller wished to converse.

1889 Johnstown Flood

1889 is referred to by historians as "A Landmark Year" in the country's history with the World Exhibition opening in Paris with its 1,056 foot high Eiffel tower; the opening of the Oklahoma Territory; and the statehood of North Dakota, South Dakota, Montana, and Washington. The best-selling book of 1889 was Edward Bellamy's *Looking Backward*, a Utopian novel about a non-Marxist socialist community in the year 2000.

Of greater interest to central Pennsylvanians in 1889, however, was something far more mundane but always of concern. The snow and high water that winter and spring was the major topic of conversation among residents, as there had been more than a hundred days of rain since mid-fall and the rivers were running high. The first sign of really serious trouble, though, was a heavy snow in April, which melted

---

6   *Curwensville High School Alumni Association 100th Anniversary, 1887–1987*, unpaginated.

almost as soon as it came down. Then in May came eleven days of rain. On the night of the 29th the U.S. Signal Service issued notices that the Middle Atlantic States should expect severe local storms. By the time the storm struck western Pennsylvania it was the worst downpour ever recorded and the most extensive rainfall of the century for so large an area.

Unaware of the siege under which its western neighbors had fallen, Curwensville residents arose on Memorial Day anticipating the holiday picnics and festivities. The weather cleared long enough on Thursday, May 30 to hold the annual Memorial Day parade just as it had been held for more than 40 years (and continued for more than another three-quarters of a century). As usual, most of the town turned out for the parade with plans to pack a picnic lunch to join family or neighbors in the outdoors. Late that evening the rain came, first fine and gentle, just a bit more than a fine mist. During the night the rain was heavier and steady and by dawn of the next morning (Friday, May 31) Anderson Creek, which divided the main section of town from South Side and Windy Hill, was bank full. During the next few hours the Susquehanna River, which also bordered the town and into which Anderson Creek empties, rose rapidly and in a short time the bottomland from Bridgeport, less than a mile to the west of Curwensville, to the "Big Mill" began to look like a lake, with what appeared to be several small islands scattered about. These islands were houses which had been surrounded by the flood.

Local losses began with the dam at Arnold's saw mill at Bridgeport. With it the flood came rolling and crushing everything in its way [with both the force of the water and the weight of the debris], instantly sweeping the Walnut Street Bridge (over Anderson Creek) on its way. A few minutes later Filbert Street Bridge crashed, and the entire mooring mass swept onward in a mad effort to crush the new railroad bridge and the Covered Bridge. The railroad bridge split and moved off its foundations before it held firm. This saved both the main span of the Covered Bridge and the $10,000 iron bridge which connected the town to Irvin Hill. The lumber, logs and drift were driven into the flat around Filbert Street, moving the railroad tracks. Trains could go no farther than the Susquehanna House and it was weeks before rail service was restored.[7]

Yet the townspeople counted themselves most fortunate, especially when news of the disaster at Johnstown reached them, an event still considered one of the worst "natural" disasters America had ever known. It would be five years before Johnstown was rebuilt. The destroyed bridges along the line of the Pennsylvania Railroad from South Fork to Johnstown were rebuilt from sandstone taken from Curwensville's Roaring Run Quarries.

---

7   "The Curwensville Review, June 1889," reported in *150th Anniversary*, p. 127.

By 1890 the railroad, the telegraph, the sewing machine, and oil or gas lighting were common. Most towns the size of Curwensville had a bank, library, high school, and theatre. General stores provided much of household needs. There were typewriters in most offices and several people had purchased one of the new Kodak "detective" cameras.

Matilda and John Pifer

In June of 1894 John F. Pifer and Matilda A. Smith were married in a small ceremony with Matilda's sisters and two of John's brothers the only persons in attendance. Matilda wore a white dress of fine muslin and lawn with leg-of-mutton sleeves and a tucked bodice. She had designed it herself and had sewn it by hand.

The newly-weds settled in Brookville where their first child was born in 1895 and named Josephine Smith Pifer, in honor of John's brother Joe and in recognition of Matilda's maiden name. By the spring of 1897, shortly after the birth of their second daughter, whom they named Ruby Idora, John decided to find an area that was growing and could support a well driller who wanted at least half his business to be local. He had considered DuBois until he learned that underground DuBois was filled with springs and many residents had only to tap into these natural sources of water without having to drill wells.

The timing was right to move as a new toll road had been built from the Jefferson County line to Curwensville. That would increase interest in Clearfield County for settlement, leading to new industries which, in turn, meant more opportunities for his business. The Pifers rented a small house and were soon settled. There, John Pifer was able to support his growing family, although not in any extra comfort. It fell to Matilda to use her ingenuity and skill to stretch the earnings of her husband. She made most of her daughters' clothing, at first by hand, and later with the aid of a treadle Singer sewing machine, her first luxury (and one of the few in her life).

Beginnings and Childhood

On July 9, 1905 the third daughter was born to Matilda and John, making Jessie Beverly ten years younger than her oldest sister Josephine. Two and a half years later, Katherine Shields (Kate) was born on February 11, 1908 and exactly two years after that, the last Pifer daughter, Margaret Jean, was born on February 11, 1910.

The five Pifer sisters were reared by their loving, though not demonstrative, mother who may have been a bit overly concerned with appearances and propriety. With their father's frequent traveling to do well-drilling, the girls' mother was the strongest influence on their young lives. Their father was stern, typical for the time. There was, in fact, little outward expression of affection in the family. One reason was the style of child-rearing (the days of working class families were so filled with chores that there was little time for personal interaction). Another reason was that Matilda Smith likely had not had expressions of maternal affection available to her, and perhaps a third reason was because of John's stoic German heritage.

Matilda did the best she could, bringing up her children to expect more from life than she had had. She almost never spoke of her own childhood, except in times of exasperation when one of the girls would complain about some chore they all found to be unpleasant. There were no stories about "when Mama was a girl," even about the poverty. Mama herself never commented on the unusualness of being one of five (or seven) daughters and then having five daughters of her own. She most identified with Jessie, as each was the middle child of a family. On the other hand, the two older girls were so many years older that Jessie was more like the oldest child of three, and, indeed, those who knew them referred to Matilda Pifer's two families.

Traveling photographers were a mainstay in small towns such as Curwensville, and Matilda somehow found the money to have formal portraits taken of her children, although this did not occur with great frequency. In a group photograph taken when Jessie, Kathryn, and Margaret Jean (known as Jean) were respectively six, four, and two, Jessie is wearing an enormous bow in her hair, at least half the size of her head, and a large, round locket, perhaps borrowed for the occasion. In contrast, Kathryn is dressed plainly, with no ornamentation (although she always confessed to acting "contrary" that day, hiding her wrist encircled by a gold bracelet and deliberately extending the unadorned arm).

A three-bedroom house, one of which being a small nursery, was not very commodious for a family of seven, so Mama, always industrious and inventive, carved out sleeping space in the attic. Not insulated, except where Mama had tacked cardboard between the rafters, the attic room was hot in the summer and very cold in winter. Opening the windows helped in the summer, and in the winter Mama heated bricks and placed them in the attic beds to warm them. When all five children still lived at home, two of the girls, usually Kathryn and Jean, slept in the attic. Early on winter mornings the girls would scurry down the stairs to dress in the warmer part of the house. During the hottest part of the summer, they begged to sleep on the back porch, but their mother did not think that was appropriate for families who lived "in town." She considered sleeping outside an indication of lacking refinement.

During the winter, the girls all wore long underwear, covered with black stockings, a petticoat, and a dress. In the summer the long underwear was shed, but the stockings and other garments remained. The Pifer girls were not allowed *ever* to go barefoot.

While the family lived only a half block from State Street the girls were not permitted to go "downtown," not even to the corner. Their boundary was the back porch for play and the front porch for company and for sitting quietly on a Sunday afternoon or summer evenings. The younger girls liked to play "house" under the back porch, large enough for the little ones to stand in. They used cardboard boxes for pretend furniture and a few old pans contributed by Mama. Occasionally when their father was out of town for several weeks, they would set up a play house in the shed, which had been rebuilt and now referred

Corner of State and Thompson Streets

to as the garage. They preferred under the back porch to the garage, however, as the ground floor of the garage was oily (even though Mama placed cardboard on the ground to make a clean floor to play on). On rare occasions or when it rained, Mama allowed them to use the few pieces of adult furniture on the porch to shape a play room there.

Christmas was an exciting time because of the decorated tree and small gifts. There was no extra money to purchase gifts, and years later Kate would recall for her own children that there were many Christmases when there were no gifts except needed items; further, she would have them believe that one Christmas the Pifer girls received only a lump of coal. The girls surely received newly made clothing, yet as adults they did not have memories of many gifts. An orange was the major treat they received. Since citrus fruit was not usually available during the winter, the oranges shipped in to grocery stores during December were a rarity and very expensive. John provided a tree a few days before Christmas because Mama did not follow the German tradition of the parents decorating the tree the night before Christmas while the children slept. She believed the girls should have the fun of helping to decorate and enjoying the tree in advance, a practice followed by her daughters later in their own families. The tree was placed in the front room in the coolest corner away from the heat register so that the pine needles would not dry too quickly and drop, and the family spent Christmas Eve together, perhaps popping, then stringing popcorn to add to the tree.

Despite a shortage of cash in the family, Mama managed to purchase a piano on credit, paying for it "in time payments," even though formalized installment buying was not popularized throughout the country until 1915. Matilda wanted her girls to have lessons, although she

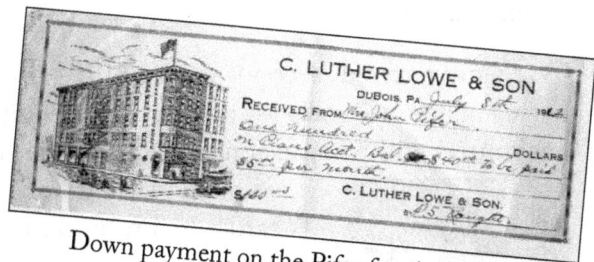

Down payment on the Pifer family piano

was their first teacher, training each one in the fundamentals. It was important to Matilda that her girls be "refined," and being able to play the piano was one indicator of social class.

The girls all learned quickly that "practicing the piano" or simply gathering around the piano to sing relieved them of the cleaning up after supper. Mama expected them to help wash the dishes, but, if they were at the piano she never requested their assistance. Instead, she would listen and quietly enjoy the music provided by "her girls."

The Story of Kate

Elementary School

Only five years old on September 2, 1913 when she entered first grade, Kathryn was a shy child with a strong sense of fairness. She later believed that she had not been ready to go to school at such a young age, and she described her young self as a "scaredy cat" who cried every morning.[8]

Her first grade teacher was Miss Marie Addleman who did not begin to "grade" the children until November. Kathryn was a good student who scored mostly in the upper 80s and 90s. Her lowest grade that first year of school was a 70% in the subject of writing for the month of February and her highest grade was 100% for spelling in November and February. Quiet as she was, however, it is surprising that her deportment grades ranged from 71% to 88%. Apparently her friendship with Kathryn Kephart began very early, for as an adult Kathryn often told stories of how she and her best school friend Kathryn Kephart whispered and giggled a lot throughout their school lives.

The younger Pifer girls and their classmates were among the first to be taught by the newer Palmer method of writing which had recently replaced the more ornate Spencerian. Along with learning to write, the children were occasionally permitted to "color," although in the early days of this century crayons were expensive and frugally doled out in the schoolroom. Few children had crayons at home. Perhaps this is why Kathryn later admonished her own children to take good care of their "colors and coloring books."

Kate entered second grade (1914-1915), continuing her good academic performance as well as greatly improving her grades in deportment. First encountering the confusion she would meet throughout her life, Kate saw the first of many variants on the spelling of her name. Her report card and Promotion Card presented at the end of the year both bore the name Katharyn Pifer. It is also interesting that in every instance, the parent who signed the report cards for the Pifer family was Mama. This is probably a result of John's not being home all the time, but still indicates the matriarchal structure of the family.

Kate always said she was not comfortable being noticed, but in later life recalled one particular incident in seventh grade when a teacher grabbed her by the sleeve of her blouse. The blouse tore away from the shoulder seam,

---

8   Letter from Kate to the author, June 2, 1966.

exposing her entire arm. Both embarrassed and unexpectedly indignant, Kate instinctively pushed or struck the teacher. She was too stunned and angry to cry, and the teacher ordered her to the principal's office. As a result, Kate had to take a note to her mother and return the signed note to the principal the following day. Mama had already heard from Jessie that "Kathryn got in trouble at school today," and when Kate arrived home with her torn clothing Mama was able first to comfort her before asking what had happened.

Music Lessons

As in most families the Pifer girls had varying degrees of interest and success in learning to play the piano, taking lessons when they were young. When they were of high school age, they took the train to the next town (seven miles distance). Once a week, each daughter, in turn, traveled to Clearfield to take violin lessons at the Susquehanna College of Music. Kate dreaded the travel. She would scurry from the train station to the studio, paying her fifteen cents for a half-hour's lesson, then with lowered head, she would hurry back to the relative safety of the train station where she would wait for the seven o'clock train to return to Curwensville. Never once did she deviate from that pattern nor did she walk the one block even to window shop in the town four times the size of her hometown of Curwensville.

Niceties such as playing the piano and/or violin were intensely important to Mama and she was very aware of being the mother of girls whose every move, she believed, would be scrutinized by the general public. The Pifer sisters were expected to behave in a ladylike manner at all times, not wear rouge or lipstick, not be boisterous or call attention to themselves, not to be seen eating in public or talking to boys, and never to be chewing gum. In Mama's opinion, the act of chewing gum was as coarse as one could be, and any action not termed "gracious" was unacceptable in the Pifer household.

Events

In September of 1921, rumors were circulating in Curwensville that a recruitment campaign for membership in the Ku Klux Klan had begun in Clearfield County. It surprised everyone when one warm Sunday evening as the family was sitting on the front porch Mama saw flames in a clearing across Anderson Creek, high on the hill above the opposite bank of the creek about a quarter of a mile distance from the porch. Neighbors began to gather in the street and the girls watched in awe and terror as it became clear that a cross-burning was occurring on the hillside. The girls were sent into the house and not permitted to remain outside to watch from the porch. Despite Mama's admonitions to the contrary, Jessie, Kate, and Jean ran to the attic where they had a clear view of the fire from two small windows facing the hillside, watching in silent fear.

One of the events that many small towns hosted was an annual town musical. Every year professional touring companies went from town to town, much like the rainmaker or music man, managing a production using all "local talent." Following two intense weeks of rehearsals, the production culminated in a grand performance staged two nights, typically Wednesday and Friday. Most of the young people were cast, if only in a group scene, for the more people who were in the review, the more families would purchase tickets. While Jessie Pifer usually had a lead role, Kate and Jean participated in the various ensembles, glad for a reason to have something to do during part of the summer. Although Kate had a pleasant singing voice she did not think so; perhaps this is the result of the extraordinary soprano voice of her sister Jessie, a voice townspeople spoke of even years later when there were few persons left to remember her singing. It also was likely that Kate did not enjoy the spotlight.

The highlight of the summers for the three younger Pifer sisters was the Annual Clearfield County Sunday School Field Day, an event planned to promote friendship and sociability among the Sunday Schools of the County. The event was so popular that one year a record crowd of 15,000 people attended. Sponsored by a committee bearing the same name, the Field Day began operation in 1921 and continued for nearly 20 years when World War II intervened. Each year all programs were broadcast throughout the park, later named Irvin Park, using a public address system. Prominent speakers were brought in for the programs, including the Attorney General of Pennsylvania. Every Sunday School in Clearfield County participated in the program of music and speaking, from 9 a.m. to 9 p.m.[9]

---

9   *Curwensville Sesquicentennial*, 150.

Changes and Modernization

Curwensville underwent a number of changes and a period of growth during the 1920s. In the summer of 1922, two years after his brothers Fred and Francis had purchased land upon which to build the Strand Theatre, Howard J. Thompson purchased the Raftsman Water Company. He made repairs and improvements to the water company which encouraged customers to forego wells for "city water." This, of course, would have an impact on those such as John Pifer whose livelihood was drilling wells. (Yet there was never any comment made by Kate to her daughters of this unusual situation that the son of the man who owned the water company and reservoir would marry the daughter of the well-driller.)

Westinghouse opened the first American broadcasting station in Pittsburgh in 1922, transmitting regular radio programs the following year. By 1924 coast-to-coast radio was available; however, choices were confined to KDKA as it was the strongest—and often the only—station accessible by those in Clearfield County, deep in the central mountains of Pennsylvania. John Pifer purchased a radio even though initially he was skeptical and Matilda was sure she would not be listening to such a thing. By 1927 every third home in the United State had a radio and Matilda and John both found themselves converts.

The original broadcast transmitter of KDKA, Pittsburgh, PA, circa 1920. It was from this transmitter that that KDKA began radio broadcasting in 1922.

The girls didn't spend a great deal of time with the radio at home, after an initial trial period of taking turns wearing the headset. Rather, they were just glad their Papa had finally bought a radio, since they were among the last of their friends to have one in their homes. They did, however, listen to some of the broadcasts with friends at homes where they occasionally congregated. Of course, the only way all of them could hear the music was to place the radio headset in a wash tub so that the sound reverberated enough for more than one person to hear. True, the sound was a bit "tinny," but the young people liked to dance and, when there were orchestras "broadcast live from New York," they were on their feet.

High School

Sixteen-year-old Kate in her junior year of high school was still timid but she had developed several close friendships that had originated in her first year of high school when Rose Bloom (Sandri), Virginia Murray (Bloom), Kathryn Kephart (Smith), Kate, and two others had formed a secret club. They had taken a vow that none of their members would ever reveal what the initials of the TDS Club represented.[10]

In May of 1924, while Jessie was eagerly anticipating graduation, Kate had been told that she had completed the required number of credits to be graduated at the end of her junior year, if she preferred. Such an offer was tempting since her best friend Kathryn Kephart had taken that path. Nonetheless, because she was only sixteen, Kate chose to return to high school the following year and take two classes, French and math.

While intelligent, Kate always said she had lacked the confidence to reach her full potential (although it must be remembered how limited opportunities were in a small town, isolated from many cultural events). Even her wardrobe reflected her conservative style. In a snapshot of Kathryn Kephart and Kate, taken during their junior year, shortly before Kathryn's early graduation, Kate is wearing a dress unadorned, dropping slightly gathered from the shoulders, obviously homemade, while Kathryn Kephart's dress is very full with four wide ruffles circling the skirt. In her own handwriting on the back of the photograph, Kate wrote the names of the two best friends, spelling both names "Kathryn."

The week-end of Kate's seventeenth (and Jean's fifteenth) birthday Jessie helped to ice the birthday cake Mama had made to celebrate the birthdays. Kate and Jean showed their sister the few cards they had received and the even fewer gifts. Their Aunt Jessie had sent birthday postcards to both girls, although only the one to Jean was kept because Jessie had asked to borrow it from Jean as she wanted to copy the verse, and, as typical, the card was not returned to its owner. More important to Kate was the Valentine she received several days later from the young man she later

---

10 Now that none of its members are remaining, it can be told what TDS stood for, and even this might not be exact, for Kate shared this information with her own children only one time in her own very later years. To their collective best recollection, TDS meant "The Daring, Dancing, Darling Six."

If I could find a garden
Where all the
Sweethearts grew
I'd look 'em over--every one,
And then I'd just pick YOU.

HVF

would marry. She kept it among her few mementoes:

> If I could find a garden
>
> Where all the
>
> Sweethearts grew
>
> I'd look 'em over--every one,
>
> And then I'd just pick
>
> YOU.

On Saturdays and some days after school Kate worked at Sheridan's Sweet Shoppe, usually simply referred to as the "Sweet Shoppe," located in the newly constructed Odd Fellows Building, easily identifiable by the brickwork spelling out in four-foot high letters "I O O F." This building, in what was known as the Patton Block, contained apartments, offices, and business places, in addition to its own lodge rooms, social rooms, and kitchens, and was only a short walk from the Pifer home.

High school activities were popular, not always because the activities were appealing but because that is all there was to do. Jean played basketball, Kate served on the yearbook staff, and they both—along with almost all of their classmates—participated in the "Literaries."

51

Literaries and Yearbooks

Literary Societies made up a great part of what would later be called "extra-curricular activities" in high schools. Even though there is earlier evidence of the Lowell Literary Society presenting a program at Curwensville High School on April 24, 1903,[11] according to the 1924 yearbook, "prior to the school year 1923-24, there had been only three literary societies: General John Patton, Colonel Ed. Irvin, and the Junior High."[12] Beginning in the fall of 1923, because of the large school enrollment, five literary societies were formed. Each class had one of its own and the Junior High formed one with 7th and 8th grades combined. Each society met and performed every other week, usually in the large assembly hall, which during the day was known as senior homeroom. The charge for each program was ten cents, the money going into the class treasury to help defray graduation expenses. The programs usually were educational, giving the students an opportunity to recite or read in front of an audience and the parents a chance to see their offspring in a different context.

Jessie had tried to impress upon both Kate and Jean the importance of joining the Literary Society. Dutifully, Kate signed on, later confessing that she was terrified of "reciting" and had joined the organization only because there were so few extra-curricular activities offered. Her senior oratory, "Do It to a Finish," was presented on April 15, 1925; one can only imagine her stage fright, yet her pluck in fulfilling her commitment.

The 1925 *Echo* was only the fourth edition of a high school annual for Curwensville High School. Of its 25 seniors, ten were listed as being the *Echo* Staff and of that number, nine were female. Editor-in-Chief was Rose Bloom; the only male was Murray Clark as the Business Manager; Katherine Pifer was listed as head of the Humor section, a position she neither sought nor desired.

Kate's sister Jessie was, of course, full of advice to Kate on how to produce a yearbook since she herself had spent a few minutes on her assigned pages in the 1924 *Echo.* Kate was sure she had been assigned the post of Humor Editor only because Jessie had been one of the two humor editors the previous year. Kate herself always maintained that she was not one for jokes and that others collected the material used in their class book, as she had no repertoire of "canned" humor.

Jessie also advised Kate to make sure she wrote her own senior "profile" if she wanted it to be accurate. Kate, of course, would never be so bold as to approach the

---

11 *The Echo, 1953,* p. 92, using a reproduction of the 1903 "High School Echo," a four-page newsletter.
12 *The Echo, 1924*, p. 73.

classmates responsible for the senior section and, just as Jessie had predicted, Kate's senior profile was not accurate:

> Kathryn Pifer — Kaddie — "Kaddie is always happy and ready for a good time. If you have ever seen her cross, I'm sure it wasn't for long. To those who do not know her she appears distant and reserved but we know different. Kaddie is a good sport and a friend to us all."

Kate also wondered where her classmates found the nickname they used in this blurb, as it is not the name by which anyone called her. She was also, according to the yearbook:

> Noted for – Blushing [true]
>
> Wants – To be her own boss [Indeed, there was a streak of obstinacy in her]
>
> Needs – A diamond [not according to her!]
>
> Fond of – Bubly [a misprint for "Bubby" Thompson]
>
> Virtue – Capability [a trait that served her well].

The Senior Class appropriately dedicated the yearbook to Mr. William H. Robinson, "Our Benefactor and Friend, who has made it possible for the Curwensville School Children to have a Gymnasium." Mr. Robinson (and his sister) had paid for a gymnasium to be built in the basement of the the new addition to the Locust Street School for sports events and for physical education classes.

The 1925 *Echo* reveals that its senior class did not re-elect the same officers to their posts every year as did many. During their freshman year, Kathryn Kephart had been elected president; Clifford Kephart had led their sophomore and junior years; and as seniors, they were led by Murray Clark.

The Class Prophecy for 1925 was written more to flatter its own writer than its readers, as the prophecy made no attempt on the part of the author to acknowledge possible accomplishments by most of the individuals. For example,

> After months of weary travel, I finally came to Bloomington; and I was pleasantly surprised. I had been told that Theresa Passarelli had settled there but I did not expect to find Rose Bloom, Kathryn Pifer, Louise Kittleberger, Margaret Rankin and Ruth Bilger also. It was a happy reunion we had. Oh,

yes, Theresa is happily married to her school days sweetheart, and all of her children are grown up and of course she still sings. Rose Bloom is a florist, and they do say that her roses bloom all the year round. The other three girls have been more fortunate. They were always so free and independent, if you remember, and they have lived true to their ideas and convictions. I was confidentially assured by the secretary of the "Old Maids House," of that wide awake and prosperous city, that they were the best inmates they had.

By their own admission in the Activities section of the book, the Class of 1925 states that "The social events of the Class have not been as numerous as of some of the previous classes, yet we have all enjoyed what social activities we have had during the years of our work together. . . .

- The only social event during our freshman year was a sleighing party to Clearfield, chaperoned by Miss Walter and Miss Burkett.

- During our sophomore year we again had a sleighing party to Clearfield with Miss Whitaker as chaperone, and a very delightful social in the Moose Hall at which dancing and games were enjoyed by all. This same year we entertained the Class of '23 at a banquet at the Philips Hotel, Philipsburg.

- Our only social activity during our junior year was a banquet tendered for the seniors at the St. James Hotel, DuBois. Monty's Orchestra furnished the music for the dancing.

- Thus far in our senior year we have not had any social activities, but before the year is completed we are sure our class will have enjoyed many activities such as dances, socials, banquets, etc."[13]

Kate realized that her class paled in comparison to the Class of 1924, even admitting to Jessie, "Our class needed you to liven things up!"

The 1925 yearbook's narrative summary of the football season is astonishingly frank to the point of disrespect to the team whose record was a winning season with six wins and four losses. The wins included three shut-outs, including one game in which Curwensville scored 53 points to their opponents scoreless showing; in fact, members of the Curwensville team were loaned to their opponents to complete that game. Therefore, it is surprising that the narrative is so negative. The entire account bears repeating, but the following excerpts provide the flavor of the article:

- "A study of the records of the football team of 1924 shows at the first glance what appears to have been an unsuccessful season. . ."

---

13 Traister, Helen. "Activities," *The Echo 1925*, p. 31.

- "Almost from the beginning the team was handicapped by injuries, misfortune, and all the bad luck that ever falls to the lot of a football team."

- "Toward the end of the season outside influences did much to break the morale of the already weakened team."

- "In a game filled with mistakes and fumbles.—Score: Curwensville 33; Falls Creek–0."

- "In the final game of the season, team morale broke entirely and our ancient enemies from down the river were able to top off the year with a wonderful victory. With the exception of one quarter we were able to do nothing and Clearfield playing the most wonderful football ever seen in these parts managed to mark up some 41 points."

Jessie encouraged both of her younger sisters to become involved in the class play, although that advice was a moot point since nearly every member of the small classes was needed to fill the roles. Therefore, even with her shyness and professed aversion for being on stage, Kate played the role of Miss Dollie DeCliffe, a Vaudeville Queen, in their Senior Class Play.

With or without Jessie's unsolicited guidance, Kate had no trouble reaching graduation, and tried not to be perturbed when the spelling of her name in the Commencement Program was incorrect. As part of the graduation exercises, Kate sang in a quartette with Mary Margaret Adams, Estella Brown, and Ruth Kephart, sister of her lifelong friend Kathryn Kephart.

Her treasured graduation gift was a wrist watch, a gold metal Hamilton from her parents, even more notable since wrist watches were not common, especially for persons of little means. (Watches had, however, become far more acceptable since the early days of the century when they were viewed as ostentatious.) Mama had saved for that graduation gift for more than a year, after purchasing a similar watch for Jessie's graduation the previous year.

Graduation was held in the Strand Theatre on Thursday evening, May 28. Baccalaureate had been held the previous Sunday and the Annual Senior Banquet was celebrated at the conclusion of the Commencement Program. On Friday, May 29, the Annual Alumni Public School Picnic was held at Irvin Park. Jessie, of course, stealing the thunder from the 1925 graduates, made as large an entrance as one could at a picnic, asking all within range, "Where is the section for the young alumni?"

Young Adulthood

Left to right, Kate and Jean

Two weeks later on Sunday June 14, Jessie, Kate, and Jean all attended the town's Flag Day celebration and the dedication of the newly installed war memorial "to veterans of all wars." A memorial tablet, on the stone pedestal on which the monument rests, lists the names of 203 veterans of what was being called the World War. Erected on the Irvin plot of ground at the corner of State and Locust Streets deeded to the borough for the monument, the large bronze figure of a combat infantryman, leaning forward with his left arm outstretched, was paid for through a fund-raising campaign led by the Auxiliary of the American Legion.

Just as he had done the year before for Jessie, Professor Grant Norris wrote a verification and recommendation, dated March 6, 1925, for Katherine Pifer, but even he (or his secretary) had her name wrong, not misspelling Katherine, but by identifying her as "Miss Shields" rather than Miss Pifer, who, he said,

> . . . will be graduated from the Curwensville High School on the 28th day of May, 1925. Miss Shields could have graduated last year, but she preferred to stay in school another year and perfect herself in her academic course; consequently, Miss Shields will be graduated with 18 credits, when only 16 are necessary to graduate. Her marks are comparatively high and she has always maintained the confidence and appreciation of her teachers. Miss Shields is a young lady of promise. Her scholastic attainments, her Christian life, her amiable disposition, and her good moral character, all recommend her to any home and to any community. . . .[14]

Out Into the Working World

The following week, on June 22, Kate went to live with her oldest sister Josephine for the summer in order to attend teacher training courses at the Pennsylvania State College's branch campus in Altoona. Kate chose Penn State's branch campus as she was not one to venture into the unknown or to live on a college campus. She wanted the safety and familiarity of family. Josephine, nearly 30 years of age, was

---

14 Recommendation, collection of the author.

pleased to have her sister live with her since her husband Droz frequently was away on business during the week. Kate usually went home by train on the weekends, likely to see Howard V. Thompson (Bubby) who was working for his father's water company in Curwensville. This was made easy by Mama's suggestion to give Josephine and her husband privacy and time together when he returned on Friday evenings from his job which kept him on the road during the week.

Kate's generation was living in a vortex of change, on the cusp of the greatest time in American history that would change this country like nothing before or since. In her own case she came from a stable family, which, while not at all wealthy, had provided a secure childhood in which she did not have to leave school, as many of her classmates had done, in order to help support their families. She was part of the first generation of middle class Americans, half of whom would complete high school; she had a "circle of social friends" with personal freedom far beyond what previous generations of women had enjoyed; and her family was not pressing to arrange a marriage or to even suggest she should "find a husband." Ahead of her, Kate had the choice to work (teach and remain single) or to marry and have a family. There were more opportunities for the working young than there had been ever before and many young women found teaching an appropriate and safe occupation.

Sports also felt the influx of women into the ranks, as the new sports attire permitted the light calisthenics and croquet to be replaced by more arduous activities such as tennis and swimming. As a result, the young people in towns across America, but especially on both coasts, began to push for tennis courts and swimming pools. Silk stockings, high-heeled shoes, permanent waves, and one-piece bathing suits—all were becoming standard with young women everywhere, leading them to feel at one with all economic classes. An emerging industry in "fashion" was making it easier for classes to resemble one another and even women began to believe in the American dream of equal opportunity for all.

Because Kate had begun school at such an early age, she now found herself a teacher at the age of 17, feeling relieved that she had not been graduated a year earlier, as Professor Norris had suggested. Her first school was the Susquehanna Bridge School, a rural area where there was no nearby train service. Just as Jessie had done her first year of teaching, Kate boarded with a family during the week. The bedrooms were not heated, the lighting was by oil lamps, there was no bathroom, and everyone went to bed very early. This was not a very pleasant situation compared to teaching in a town and living at home, positions typically earned after many years in the country schools.

The Story of Kate

Kate's rural school, like most, was a one-room building; two small buildings were located near the school house, one for coal and the other an outhouse. A tiny porch served as the entrance and on top of the structure was a bell whose rope hung down just inside the door. Inside the door was an offset with a shelf for lunch pails and hooks from which to hang coats. Kate called this "the cloak room" based on her own experience with larger rooms in the town schools for this purpose. In the back corner of the room stood a pot-bellied stove, which did not always radiate enough heat. On very cold days, she would sit by the stove and have the children gather round to keep warm, but they would become scorched on one side and remain frozen on the other.

On each side of the room was a row of windows to admit light; there was no electricity, so on days when it was very dark, reading was not always possible. In addition to no electricity, the one-room school house also had no running water. Four rows of double seats extended from the front to the back of the room and the teacher's desk was at the front, facing the students. A long recitation bench was angled to the right of the teacher's desk; it was here that the classes came to recite. With all eight grades in one building, sometimes grades were combined for their lessons, such as first and second grade reading or third and fourth grade history. The teacher had to rely on older or more advanced students assisting the younger ones, as she could not possibly teach every subject in every grade for the time needed for each subject.

Kate liked her students, and they became fond of the shy and gentle "Miss Pifer." Kate admitted that while often the boys in eighth grade were much taller than she was, they were kind and respectful. One of her favorite school stories is the following:

One day a student was particularly hungry and could not wait for lunch. His seatmate noticed that he was opening his lunch pail from which the boy selected a choice item, an item, in fact, that few students' families could afford—a large, juicy, and very pungent orange. This husky eighth-grader bit into the fruit, obscuring the orange in his large hand. What he had not thought about, however, was that as soon as his teeth pierced through the skin of the orange, the aroma quickly permeated the small one-room school. Trying to deflect attention away from his own guilt, the embarrassed student made a point of stretching his neck, raising his head, and loudly announcing, "I smell **oranges**!"

Miss Pifer did not have the heart to admonish him and it was all she could do to stifle a laugh.

In the summer of 1926 Katherine quietly returned to Altoona to take her courses at Penn State's extension campus; however, there are no available records of the courses she took as she was not one to save these reminders. Most of the time she came home on week-ends, much as she had the previous summer, and continued to see Bubby who wrote to her on a nearly daily basis.

Occasionally Bubby would finish his work early in Bellefonte where his father still had business interests and would take the very long way home through Altoona where he would visit Kate. One day he was able to finish checking the electric lines by noon; he hurried to Altoona where he and Kate spent the rest of the day and evening at Ivyside Amusement Park. There was a large swimming pool at the park, but as Kate didn't care much for swimming and, in fact, didn't care much for the water, she watched Bubby who was a good swimmer. By 4:00 or so they were ready to try some of the other activities at the park and Bubby won a trinket for his Kate at the shooting gallery.

Another memorable "date" was going to the movies at the Capitol Theatre. Bubby never stayed past eleven so that he would get home, he said, before his mother started worrying about him. In truth, it was his father who had set a curfew for his son, even at the age of twenty-two.

That year all county schools opened September 7, the day following Labor Day. Kate, at age eighteen, a second-year veteran of teaching, had received her contract from Lawrence Township on May 27 (1926) for an annual salary of $800 for 7½ months of teaching at the Driftwood School. Her school was only several miles from her home and close enough to a train stop, so she no longer needed to board at a school director's home, even though Mrs. Henry, the director's wife, was most persistent. Kate, always timid, just hoped that Mrs. Henry would not see her hiding behind a tree as she waited for the train. Kate recalled in later years one particular hapless student:

> I remember how this poor boy struggled with his lessons and had difficulty learning. He seldom volunteered because he usually didn't know the answer. One day, I was explaining that the use of "ain't" was sub-standard. I gave examples of sentences in which "isn't" and "aren't" should be used in place of "ain't" as I tried to convince the class the importance of acceptable and appropriate speech. Following the examples, I asked, "Now, who can tell me what we should use in place of "ain't?" The usually reluctant young student raised his hand with great enthusiasm, twirling and shaking his arm. Feeling sure that he could not possibly answer incorrectly, I acknowledged him. He shouted his answer with great pride and assurance, "You should use **h'ain't!**"

Both Jessie and Kate lived at home this year, along with Jean who was a senior in high school. They all helped their mother with the housework, although Mama did many of her chores during the week when the two older girls were teaching and Jean was still in school. On Saturdays Kate and Jean often went shopping together, saving Mama a trip to the grocery store. Saturday was the major shopping day when farmers and others who lived outside the borough typically would come into town. Because stores were open through the evening hours, these became social times in the town, as so it remained for many years.

Nearly every Saturday evening Kate spent with Bubby. He was most eager to marry her, even though at age eighteen she was not ready to marry. She didn't want the routine of housework and loneliness she saw with Josephine's marriage nor the strain she sometimes observed in Ruby. While she had no desire to live the life of the social butterfly that Jessie sought, she did enjoy the company of friends she knew well, such as Kathryn and Mearle Smith. She was content with the status quo.

She sometimes felt, however, that she didn't quite fit the marriage pattern and wondered if there was another direction she might take with her life. She didn't have anyone with whom to discuss these feelings, since everyone she knew—except, of course, Jessie—thought that being married was the end-all and be-all of existence. Years later she held the same opinion and would tell her own daughters, "Don't rush into things. Getting married is no great accomplishment. Married you can always get." Even talking to Jean, with whom Kate was close, about her concerns didn't seem appropriate. Jean envied what she called her older sisters' "freedom," not understanding that freedom had its own price.

Marriage

In the spring of 1927 Katherine finally agreed to marry Bubby and, consequently was no longer eligible to teach, for married women were not permitted to teach in public schools, the rationale being that they now had someone to support them, and to keep them employed would be "keeping jobs from men who had families to support." While her friend Kathryn had married earlier in the year, keeping marital status a secret so that she could live at home and continue to work, Katherine and Bubby decided against secrecy, agreeing that Kate would no longer teach and would work only if she chose to; actually, they didn't really discuss it at length; it was simply understood that Kate would not return to teaching.

Wearing a peach silk pongee, dropped-waist dress for the occasion of her marriage, Kate had no regrets at not having a church wedding as she and Bubby stood in the office of the Justice of Peace in the early evening of June 27, with Kathryn and Mearle Smith serving as witnesses. The newlyweds took a wedding trip to the state capital at Harrisburg and to Gettysburg, with Kate never dreaming that fifty years following her wedding date she would be making her permanent home in the Harrisburg area.

Kate and Bubby set up housekeeping in a second floor apartment in a private home. They later moved to an apartment in the two-block-long retail business part of town where Kate began life as a "young married," going about town, shopping and doing errands. Kate found steady employment in Jimmy's Sweet Shoppe and sometimes took care of the youngest child of her husband's Uncle Francis, himself youngest of the entrepreneurial Thompson brothers. Thus, Kate began a lifelong friendship with Bill Thompson, a fair-haired, handsome child who one day would live in New York City and Charleston, South Carolina as an interior designer for the properties of Richard Jenrette, financier, who "collected" and restored antebellum mansions.

On July 11, 1929 Kate wrote to her sister who was taking courses at Penn State College and rooming, as Jessie liked to note, "in a fraternity":

You certainly have some address! [Jessie was pleased when anyone noticed she was rooming in a fraternity!] *How do you like 80-minute periods? Do you have any use for my text book? Mama said you might wonder why we didn't write but there isn't much to write about. We moved last Wednesday and are nearly fixed up except the windows of which there are 21. I like it much better and so does Bubby. It is real large and we also have a phone now. It is to be connected this week so I do not know our number yet. Neither Helen nor Kate came up to tell Mama anything about their visit with you, but I suppose there wasn't a whole lot to tell. It's nice you have all p.m. off, especially these terribly hot days.*

Mama had letters from Ruby and Josephine last week. Jo doesn't know yet where Droz will be sent so I don't know when we are going to Ohio [to see Ruby's new baby]. *Jo was to come over Saturday evening but they didn't show up. Mama made me a dress yesterday, figured pique. I also straightened up the third floor for her.*

I hope you can eat the cake I sent yesterday [for Jessie's birthday]. *I think the cake was good enough, but I have grave doubts for the icing. Do you get good meals?*

The Story of Kate

Kate Smith and Helen Decker have simply nothing to do. I see them walking around nearly every evening. That girl from DuBois has been down with Helen a couple of times and Marjorie Murray is home with another big diamond.

Aunt Jessie was down the other evening. Jake is running for sheriff.

If anything interesting ever happens I will write and tell you about it.

Lovingly, Kayran[15]

November 12 and 13, 1929 were the dates of the town's annual musical production, "Spanish Moon," under the direction of Mary Pat Robinson, a local woman. The Opera House was filled. Jessie had a featured role. Other familiar names on the program included Kathryn (Pifer) Thompson and other young women.

Kate's Girls

While after three years of marriage Kate had almost resigned herself to being childless, she became pregnant in early 1930. She and Bubby began talking about renting a house, agreeing it would be helpful to be in a larger place before the baby's expected arrival. Kate also spent many Saturdays alone, as the Curwensville Firemen's Club had formed a Drill Team and Bubby was a very active participant.

One of the founding members, he was instrumental in finding interested young men to join the team, and he himself never missed a practice. Kate would not have expected or asked him to miss either a practice or a parade. She knew how important this was to her husband who finally could have a uniform and be part of at least a quasi-military group. She occasionally went with him to nearby parades and shared his excitement when the Curwensville Firemen's Drill Team, in its first year, took several first prizes and performed in exhibition with Barney Ferguson's Fife and Drum Corps at the Fourth of July celebration at Irvin Park.

The following Sunday after the Fourth of July celebration, at her last public appearance prior to the birth of her child, Kate and Bubby went to the Park Hotel Tea Room which had opened earlier that year under the banner, "Chicken Every Sunday, 75¢." Following the meal, Bubby suggested they take a drive. He drove to New Millport, only a few miles from Curwensville, when he said, "Just one more quick stop, Kate, if you're not too tired. I have a surprise for you."

Several blocks into (the) South Side of Curwensville, Bubby turned right on Hill Street and stopped at the second house. "What do you think?" he asked. "Mama said it will be available sometime after the first of the year. Papa owns it so the rent

15   One of the many coined nicknames the Pifers used among themselves.

will be reasonable. You'll have a back yard and be close to the park. Would you mind living on South Side?"

While just a little disappointed at living so far from the center of town, she was pleased to soon have her own home. Early Halloween night Kate's labor pains began and her daughter was born at home, shortly after midnight, November 1, 1930, under the watchful eye of Mrs. Bornhoff who assisted at many births in town. As this was the first female grandchild, Kate gave her child the name of "Matilda" for her own mother and the middle name "Kay," by which she would be known.

Two years later, even with the Depression—or perhaps because of it—Bubby and Kate were offered a larger home for purchase. It was still on South Side, but was a little closer to town and his mother was willing to help underwrite the cost of purchase. This house on Schofield Street was much larger than the young couple's home on Hill Street, with bigger and better rooms. It was far from luxurious, but a nice "step up" and it had potential. Kate particularly liked the roomy kitchen and large walk-in pantry where the sink was located and where there also was a Hoosier-style cabinet. The second floor contained a large main bedroom with two smaller bedrooms and a bath in the rear part of the house. What the Thompsons could not have known in advance is that the very best thing that the move would bring was exceptional neighbors.

On a bitterly cold Friday night, January 25, 1936, with the temperature at zero or below, a kerosene heater exploded in the barbershop of Gilbert Norris. The fire quickly spread through the walls in the adjoining office of the *Curwensville Herald*. At least ten businesses and four homes were lost in the devastation at an estimated total cost of $90,000.[16] Fire was followed by a flood the following spring. This March 17 flood, which was precipitated by a quick spring thaw, reached the covered bridge at Schofield Street, the Irvin Hill Bridge by the Susquehanna House, and the Filbert Street Bridge, flooding all the surrounding lowlands, and, in effect, separating both Irvin Hill and South Side from the central area of the town. Basements were filled with water and the flood waters threatened to reach the first floor of many houses.

Kate and Howard were prepared to evacuate as the meadow, used as a cow pasture, behind their home was flooded and the floodwater encroached into their basement and rose about halfway before the flood abated. Several items not belonging to them were found in their back yard when the waters receded, in particular a sturdy, long wooden bench. There was no way to discover its owner, so the bench remained with the house during the time the Thompsons lived there and was left when they moved ten years later.

The Story of Kate

After such a ruinous winter and spring, by fall the townspeople of Curwensville were ready for something good to happen. And it most definitely did when the Curwensville Golden Tide became the Western Pennsylvania Football Champions of 1936. On December 5 a trainload of fans traveled to Kingston (a town of 21,000, seven times the size of Curwensville). Among the hundreds of passengers were Bubby and Jessie (Katherine, at the time six months pregnant with her second child, decided it was better not to make the tiring trip.) Many who remembered the experience viewed the excursion as the highlight of Curwensville sports history, even though the yearbook account of the game never mentions that Kingston won.

In March of 1937 Kate gave birth to her second child, a daughter she named Judith Evelyn (known by her family as "Judi"), her middle name in honor of their neighbor who yet was to be a most positive influence in the lives of Kate's middle daughters. Eighteen months later Kate's third child, sweet-tempered Jo Ellen, was born. As Howd and she entered the house with the third baby, he said to Kate, "If the babies keep coming, we shall have to find a larger house." Kate laughed and said to her husband, "Just remember that if Mama had stopped at three daughters, I wouldn't be here!" She was beaming as she reflected on her good fortune and healthy family, the only concern in her life the far-off rumblings of war.

Baby Judith, Howd, and Kay

Baby Judith, Kate, and Kay

At the decade drew to a close, Christmas 1939 brought difficulties both in finding, and having the money to purchase, gifts. One comfort to Kate was that toys could be passed down to each child since all three children were girls. She also tried to make a practice of purchasing presents throughout the year when she found something nice, especially items she was sure the children would like. Thus, as a result of her early planning, on Christmas Eve when she and Howd were arranging the gifts under the tree she was quite satisfied at the array.

Each child had her own "section" under the tree so that on Christmas morning it would be clear as to whose gifts were whose. The items were neatly arranged in separate sections, making it possible not to have to wrap every gift, particularly in times when wrapping paper was a luxury. Kate also had begun the custom that each child could look forward to one "special" gift and several other smaller gifts, including necessities such as socks and slippers.

Kay was nine, Judi nearly three, and baby Jo Ellen a little more than a year old—all three at ages in which Christmas would be exciting, both to them and their doting parents. Kay led the procession down the staircase which opened directly into a large hall where the Christmas tree stood, with all its lights shining (Howd having already made a trip two hours earlier to add coal to the furnace and to connect the tree lights). Kate followed, carrying Jo Ellen, and Howd walked down the stairs with Judi.

Jo Ellen was fascinated by the lighted tree and the packages from Aunt Mary Alice (always wrapped beautifully with expensive paper and large bows) as she and Judi began reaching for the new toys. Kay, however, was silent. Noticing this, her mother asked, "What's the matter, Kay?" The oldest daughter looked at her parents, surveyed the gifts, stepped back and drew an imaginary line on the floor. She then replied, "I remember when my presents came out to here." These words would later haunt her family.

During the austerity of wartime Kate, like most housewives, would carefully regulate her baking days and make only those sweets that were highest on her family's priority list. Howd's favorite treat was what the family called "double-decker" fudge, a two-layer arrangement of vanilla and chocolate. The daughters' first choice was their mother's chocolate caramels, made only in the coldest part of the winter. Following the mixing, cooking, and pouring into a metal pan, the pan was taken outside and placed in the snow to hasten the hardening of the candy. The girls would check it periodically (far more often than needed) by pressing a finger into the mixture. When no indentation could be made, the caramel pan was retrieved from the snow in which it had been lodged and returned to the kitchen where Kate would slide the solid candy from its buttered pan onto a sturdy counter. She then used a wooden spoon to break it into pieces. The caramels, meant to be wrapped in waxed paper, seldom lasted long enough to need their wrappings. Some years later, another favorite treat was something new with Kate, brought to the family through a friend. The preparation for this began with raw peanuts, still in their skins, but out of their shells. Purchased loose or packaged, these peanuts required blanching, followed by wrapping them in a tea towel and rolling the towel to loosen the skins. After manually peeling any remaining skin, Kate either roasted the nuts on a shallow tray in the oven or deep-fried, then salted them lightly.

Parties and Annual Adventures

Kate and Howd were members of a small bridge club of eight to twelve members who met once a month, rotating in the homes of its members. Kate's daughters found these grown-up events exciting, even though they were confined to their bedrooms, supposedly fast asleep. In the mornings following these bridge parties, the girls would purloin the peanuts from the mixed nuts, but had no interest at all in the unappealing "bridge mix."

More interesting to the children than the bridge games, however, was a special party once held at one of the fraternal lodges during the early 1940s. The event is long forgotten, but not the costuming of their mother, complete with powdered wig and cardboard buckles fashioned to fit on her shoes most closely resembling the fashion of the late 18th century. The Rebekahs (women's auxiliary of the fraternal organization known as the International Order of Odd Fellows) had drawn lots to decide who would dress as ladies and who would be costumed as men. While fascinated at their mother's transformation, it was nonetheless disconcerting to the children to see her in male garb, regardless how elaborate.

Life was happy for children the summer of 1942 in Curwensville, away from the war and carefree with picnics at Irvin Park, Elliot Park, and Parker Dam. Memorial Day and the Fourth of July were Family Picnic days at Irvin Park. Kate would be up early that morning (having boiled the potatoes and eggs the previous evening) making two large meat loaves, deviled eggs, and potato salad, her specialty for every family picnic. Aunt Jean would prepare baked beans, a relish tray, and a basketful of sandwiches for the children; Aunt Josephine would bake her wonderful cakes (angel food and Lady Baltimore); and Aunt Jessie would furnish the breads and condiments. Mama often made the rolls, depending on how hot the morning was expected to be.

On Memorial Day by eleven oclock, Kate, Jean, and Josephine—with the six children—would be sitting on Mama's porch, just as nearly every other family would be sitting on porches or standing on curbs, watching the parade from South Side along Susquehanna Avenue, up Filbert Street after crossing the Anderson Creek Bridge, turning left on State Street for a block, and then up Thompson Street to Oak Hill Cemetery. Every flag in town was hoisted this Memorial Day and every home and business that could find bunting had it prominently draped. Most spectators fell silent as the Great War (WWI) veterans passed by, followed by the boys in the Class of 1942 who had enlisted in the service and would be leaving later in the week, following graduation.

Irvin Park (Pee Wee's Nest)

This was also the last year—for the duration—for the adults traveling to the Sunset Ballroom in Carroltown, Cambria County to hear the big bands.

On the Fourth of July, weather permitting, the children would be dropped off late morning at Irvin Park to claim a picnic table. They would place a few belongings, often including a basket or box with paper plates and other necessities, knowing the items would not be moved and that they would be assured a table when everyone began to gather in the mid-afternoon.

Six weeks later that summer of '42 Elizabeth Nan was born, the fourth and last child of Kate and Howard. The next day Howd took the three girls to see Kate and the new baby. As he always did when they drove onto the hospital grounds, he pointed to the small, separate building, the Cora Arnold Swoope Maternity Wing, noting that both Judith and Jo Ellen had also been born there. The little girls retained only hazy memories of the details, but distinctly remember seeing their baby sister Nan for the first time.

Just as summers brought picnics, so winters brought made-from-scratch hot cocoa for breakfast and occasionally on Saturdays or holidays, homemade doughnuts. These were deep-fried, and placed on paper bags on top of newspapers to drain, and then, still warm, carefully placed in a brown paper bag with powdered or granulated sugar and gently shaken. One afternoon while Kate was busy with Baby Nan, Judi and Jo Ellen decided to add powdered sugar to otherwise unappealing "store-bought" plain doughnuts their father had brought home. They climbed up on the

Hoosier cabinet and found the yellow box. With complete confidence, the two little girls shook the dry doughnuts in the requisite brown paper bag after which they reached greedily into the paper bag. Biting into the confectionary, their faces immediately revealed their error. It was not powered sugar, but baking soda they had used to coat the doughnuts.

When Judi and Jo Ellen weren't playing house, they might go sliding down the stairs on sofa pillows or sliding straight down the banister sans pillow; this held a danger beyond that of falling off the railing, such as the mishap of breaking a glass ship, one of their mother's prized accessories that had been purchased at Leonardson's in DuBois. Following the breakage, Judi approached her mother with a give-away question, "When is the next time we will be going to DuBois?"

The War Effort

One of the many war initiatives that had permanent influence on the economy included more women entering the work force, taking places of the men who had entered the military. Kate arranged for a baby sitter, Margie Zwolski, to come to the house every day after school to be there for the children so that Kate could work second shift at the parachute factory. Because workers were badly needed and parachutes were essential to the war effort, Kate had agreed to work "for the duration." Earnings were good and growing—at least until President Roosevelt froze wages, salaries, and prices to forestall inflation. Wages were still more than Kate had ever earned and it gave her some independence and the ability to pay for piano lessons and other niceties for her girls, as well as starting her own savings account. What she had not counted on, however, was that by 1944 people were not allowed to leave any jobs related to the war effort. Everyone was working, young and old alike.

Judith singing at a war bond rally

Children took toiletries to school to pack kits for the soldiers and bought war bond stamps, after the war to be known as savings stamps, 10 cents a stamp, with the promise of a higher face value to be repaid to the purchaser "after the war was over." Gathering silkweed and collecting tin cans were other war efforts, although only the boys were allowed to stomp the cans.

Rationing was hard on everyone, but because it technically affected all citizens (discounting the black market), a sense of camaraderie in doing without goods and services prevailed among the citizenry. Anyone over the age of six or seven during the war remembers standing in line for almost any purchase while clenching a ration coupon book.

In the summer of 1943 Kay's self-designed Necco Camp kept Jo Ellen and Judi occupied most of the summer season. Houses on the lower half of the block on Schofield Street had been built on only one side of the street, facing a hill that children referred to as a mountain. It was steep by anyone's description and, while there were houses on top of its sheer cliff, there was no possibility of building anything on its face. There were, however, a few ledges and narrow passages accessible from a path that led to the Sneddons who lived at the edge of the cliff. Blackberries grew in these thickets and it was while on one of many blackberry-picking adventures that Kay conceived of the idea to form a club.

She convened the first club meeting on the side of this hill, but because of its natural terrain limitations, she moved the campsite to the lowlands, cattycornered to the Thompson house, across the dirt road that led to the dump and the tannery. Borrowing paper, writing materials, and an old hectograph from Aunt Jessie, along with a few remnants of chairs from the basement storage area, Kay established Necco Camp (named for the Necco wafers she favored) in an area overgrown with wild shrubbery and sumac. Complete with a camp song and camp rules, the girls spent many happy hours that summer in an area out of the sight of, but not far from, home.

Some of the hiking trips taken by the campers were not so happy, however. Occasionally Kay would lead the troops on an excursion into the center of town by way of a shortcut—walking on one of the two parallel railroad trestles that began on our side of the old covered bridge. We were permitted occasionally—with adult supervision—to walk on the lower trestle but the higher one was off-limits. To tease us, Kay would choose to cross the high trestle, leaving us to walk by ourselves on the lower one. True, there was solid ground under this one rather than the water flowing under the higher one and the ties appeared to be closer together, but walking on railroad ties under any condition

Covered bridge over Anderson Creek

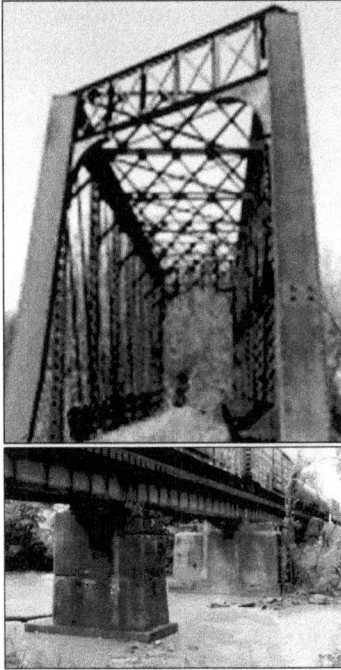

and at any elevation was somewhat risky and upsetting to small children.

Worse than the trestles, however, was the swinging footbridge from the tannery across the Susquehanna River to the base of Irvin Hill. All children were *forbidden* to ever cross the swinging bridge, a suspension bridge built for the tannery workers who lived on Irvin Hill. But, under the order of our big sister, cross it we did, terrified and trying not to watch the contaminated water swirling beneath us.

Happier adventures on Schofield Street included roller skating, jumping rope, and riding bikes. Kay had a two-wheeler that she let us sit on while she pushed us around. Indoor and "on the porch" activities included cutting out paper dolls and coloring in scarce coloring books. Kay had a large collection of paper dolls, all packed neatly in a suit box, each set carefully stored separately with sheets of tissue paper between each layer.

By 1943 Christmas catalogues were restricted in number of pages allotted to them and many listed items were stamped with the words, "Sorry, not available." Thus, even those who had money found that many items could not be purchased. Parents became ever-increasingly creative in finding gifts for their children, as children did not understand that Santa could not produce items tagged "Unavailable." When one of a series of government Limitation and Conservation Orders prohibited the use of traditional toy materials such as steel, tin, rubber, and lead, manufacturers substituted cardboard and wooden toys.

This was also the year the packing box from Montgomery Ward arrived late the evening of December 22 and Kate decided to leave it on the front porch until the next morning, because the children were not yet in bed. Schofield Street was not on a major thoroughfare and she felt sure the large box would be secure until she could bring it into the house the following morning, after Kay and Judi left for school and before Jo Ellen and the baby awoke. The next morning, as the girls exited from the kitchen door, Kate opened the front door. The crate and all its contents were gone, presumably stolen. The mail order company did replace most of the merchandise for a late Christmas and the girls were placated Christmas morning by a handwritten note from Santa.

Post-War

Following the war and the rise of mass production, the number of personal dressmakers decreased. Mrs. Buterbaugh was one of the few who continued to make one-of-a-kind items. Part of the fun in going to her home was that the fabric remaining from a garment was available to make matching hat bands for the ladies and dresses for the children's dolls.

Kay, Judith and Jo Ellen

With a large family of girls, Kate enjoyed seeing them as well dressed as possible, given all the post-war limitations. However, she took pride in our accomplishments whatever they were. For example, at the end of the 1944-45 school year, as Judi was completing second grade in the shared second and third grade classes taught by Mrs. McClosky, it was suggested to Kate that her daughter be skipped the following year to fourth grade. Of course, no one in the school system offered any objective data or comparison of academic ability and standardized test scores upon which to base a decision. Because Kate did not feel knowledgeable enough to make such a decision, she conferred with Jessie who, with her twenty years of teaching experience, advised against skipping a grade, telling Kate that "it might catch up with the child later."

Potpourri of Memories

- ✓ Hanging freshly washed curtains on curtain stretchers and the distinctive "clean" aroma as the curtains dried, but warned to stay away from the sharp pins

- ✓ Carpets hung over the clotheslines/wash lines and "beat" with a rug beater to release the dust

- ✓ Killing chickens by cutting off their heads, dipping the bodies in hot water to make it easier to pluck the feathers to prepare the chickens for cutting, cleaning, and cooking

- ✓ Gathering eggs

- ✓ Powell's and Barr's vegetable stands

71

The Story of Kate

- ✓ Decorating Valentine boxes

- ✓ A single pair of brown roller skates for whomever they fit

- ✓ Rubber swimming slippers, with the same condition

- ✓ Aluminum foil tinsel

- ✓ Christmas cards from Santa

- ✓ Weeding the garden

- ✓ Making caramels in the winter

- ✓ Double-decker fudge

- ✓ Clearfield Dairy ice cream, especially orange sherbet and chocolate chip

- ✓ Miller Dairy chocolate milkshakes

- ✓ Herman's hot dogs

- ✓ Natoli's pizza

- ✓ Roasted peanuts in the shells from Frankhouser's

- ✓ Kerstetter's cream puffs

- ✓ Homemade ice cream in a hand-churned mixer

- ✓ Junket (milk custard) and toasting marshmallows in the fireplace

- ✓ Vanilla sherbet made by the Grange

- ✓ Sitting on the front porch, particularly on Thompson Street and Schofield Street

- ✓ Deep-frying home-made donuts cut out from rolled-out dough with jar lids, large ones for the donut itself and small bottle caps to cut out the donut holes. Then shaking each donut (or two or three) in a paper bag lined with powered (confectioners) or granulated sugar. (See accompanying story)

- ✓ Coined names for people, some personal, some a general term, such as Aunt Ruby's referring to any small child as "Toad"

- ✓ Nan's horse Scot and his blanket (See accompanying story)

- ✓ A double wedding

Our Kate ❧ Our Kaki ❧ Our Mother

- ✓ Collecting horse chestnuts and trying to sell them door-to-door in the neighborhood

- ✓ Counting out clothespins borrowed from Laura Bressler

- ✓ Toni Home Permanents given by Mrs. Sneddon

- ✓ '49 Dodge, Mother's first car when she was first on her own after "the break-up"

- ✓ Voting sites—first ward on upper Thompson Street and second ward on Susquehanna Avenue

- ✓ Saving S&H green stamps

- ✓ Cleaning the theatre aisles

- ✓ Ruby's turban hats

- ✓ "Mrs. Smythe" and "Mrs. DeWayne" playing "missus" dressing up in Mother's clothes no longer worn by her

- ✓ Mother's brightly printed housecoat that I remember as being frightening, or perhaps that she wore this once when hiding behind the attic door and jumping out scaring us (details not complete here)

- ✓ Boxes of clothes from Brody's "on approval" and returning what we didn't choose to purchase

- ✓ Kay's wearing a pink wedding gown and her off-the-shoulder yellow taffeta blouse and plaid taffeta long skirt to the high school prom (all created, of course, by Mrs. Buterbaugh)

- ✓ The gowns of stiff pink netting required for purchase in order to join the Rainbow Girls organization

- ✓ Fritzie Smith teaching eager elementary students how to twirl a baton

- ✓ Patrol boys

- ✓ Pigtails

- ✓ No chewing gum

- ✓ No bare feet

- ✓ No drinking from a soda bottle.

Moving to Town

That summer of '44, when most people's attention was focused on winning the war in the Pacific, Burgess Harry J. Leathers issued a citation to Matilda Kay Thompson for wearing shorts. As Kay was a very slender, not-yet-developed fourteen-year-old and the entire matter was rather silly, Mr. Leathers still was obliged to respond to a complaint and to issue the notice "against a local ordinance governing proper attire for ladies." Nothing more came of the order, but many years later Don Bloom, Jean's son, said that the young men "at the pool hall" got a good laugh out of this incident, saying the Burgess had cited the wrong person, that it was Kate who had the "best legs in town." She also was known all her life as "a head-turner!"

With four children, Kate had little time to worry about working outside the home after the ban was lifted in 1945 on not being allowed to leave factory jobs essential to the war effort. In some ways she missed the independence of having her own earned money, but Howard had provided her with her own spending money, and she was not unhappy. However, much as Kate loved her neighbors and the kind of life that provided for her children, she felt isolated and, following a scare or two with tramps appearing at her back door, as well as the occasional local businessman who would appear at her door on some pretense hoping she would welcome his attention, she began to feel less safe living at the end of Schofield Street.

Further, once Nan outgrew her crib, the house seemed too small. Kate began to enumerate to Howard the advantages of living "in town" (in reality probably less than a mile from their home), including being closer to the stores, piano lessons, and the high school, as well as the theatre he managed and the water company he worked for (both owned by his father). With a growing family involved in many activities, Kate wanted to be within walking distance of the center of town.

One day in December 1945 Howard came home early to tell Kate that the Charles Wall property had been placed on the market. It was a large house on lower Thompson Street, equidistant between Josephine's home and where Kate's parents and Jessie lived. Kate was familiar with the house and jumped at the chance to purchase it with help from Howard's mother, whose sister Grace's home it had been. Selling their Schofield Street house for approximately $4,000 (originally purchased for $3,500), they paid $6,000 for the Wall property with plans to move sometime in March.

Kate spent the winter months preparing to move to the large home on Thompson Street, gathering boxes (still a scarcity) and sorting everything from dishes to dolls. The family moved "to town" in early spring 1946, with many tears shed by the children who did not want to leave their neighbors, the Milligans and the Bresslers. Amid promises to return to visit, the children said their good-byes, feeling somewhat mollified by leaving the lawn swing for the Bresslers' use. There it was to remain for a quarter century, enjoyed by both Laura and John, although it became John's "station."

The Wall house on Thompson Street had been a stunning property in its day and still retained many of its original amenities. It was large, with an immense kitchen and a sizable walk-in pantry, a dining room with full-length glass French doors to the generous foyer, a formal living room, and a sitting room on the first floor. The children loved the double staircase, the one in the foyer being open on one side, featuring curves of highly polished mahogany. The largest bedroom was originally shared by Jo Ellen and Judi, with baby Nan in the smallest room, but this changed after a couple of years to give Judi more privacy, as she tended to be one who needed space of her own. Kate and Howard each had a bedroom, and Kay took the private suite on the third floor complete with its own small bathroom. In true Kay-fashion, she decorated the sloped ceiling of the room with a border of Petty girls.

The 1946 labor strikes, added to the GM strike, resulted in shortages in housing, cars, refrigerators, stockings, sugar, coffee, and meat. Standing in line at the meat counter again became the norm. Occasionally Judi would take a place in line a half hour before school and Kate would arrive with Nan in tow in time for Judi to get to Mrs. Lucy Bloom's fourth grade class at the Locust Street School.

To her dismay, Jo Ellen was enrolled in the third grade class of her aunt, Miss Jessie Pifer, newly assigned to this school. Kate had some reservations about this assignment, but had no idea of the strain this placed on Jo Ellen. Jessie's imperious tone took its toll and Jo Ellen developed a case of shingles, generally remembered as a time of being confined to bed in her mother's bedroom for the duration of the illness.

This was also the year Jo Ellen and Judi became fluent in Pig Latin and, as a result, Jessie and Kate had to devise a short cut version by which to communicate information when the children happened in on a conversation. Sometimes the Pifer sisters spelled out words in their conversations they didn't want the children to understand, but, as the girls became adept spellers, that method also had to be dropped.

Each elementary school teacher was known for various specialties of direct or indirect teaching remembered by all their students: Mrs. Errigo for reading stories, Mrs. McCloskey for smacking hands with a ruler, and Mrs. Bloom for having the students read and make oral book reports on each book read. She also awarded a prize at the end of the year for the most books read that year. Mrs. Muir, in fifth grade, made writing reports her goal. All knew going into fifth grade that they would be "writing, writing, writing," but they did not expect the resulting bump in the inside of the middle finger of the writing hand—the result of holding the pen for all of those reports. That "Muir bump" remains today on the hands of many former students.

And then there was Mrs. Houser who believed—and correctly in some cases— that under her tutelage the students would have their last chance to learn good manners. This was not a formal part of the sixth grade curriculum, but it certainly made an impression on the students. To this day some still re-open a door to close it a second time if on the first closing it was "slammed" shut, following the movement that had become automatic to the sixth grade students.

In the summers many of the family discussions were conducted on the large front porch which held heavy, comfortable wicker furniture with thick cushions left by the previous owners. Although the wicker was viewed as a bit "old-fashioned," it was of perfect proportion for the age and size of the house. The porch itself was large and had decorative banisters and spindles on three sides. These had to be scrubbed with a brush, a most tedious job, and one the girls performed reluctantly. An easier task was the bi-weekly (in season) porch floor scrubbing handled by two people, one to carry the hot water and one to scrub with a broom, the method Mother had learned from her own mother and sisters years earlier.

Until the girls were older and had the strength and ability to balance a bucket without spilling its contents, their mother carried bucket after bucket of hot soapy water from the kitchen sink, through the front hall and to the doorway of the porch where she would carefully pour the water over the ledge of the threshold. The young "scrubber" would swish the broom back and forth on the surface of the wooden porch. Working from the center out to both sides, the scrubber herself would then have to carry (less full) buckets of water once leaving the center of the porch. The buckets of hot water were followed by buckets of cooler water to rinse off the soapy water, and finished with cold water from a hose attached to an outside spigot. The young workers were permitted to be barefoot for this job, one of the rare times this was allowed. A sense of satisfaction at the completed job was the only reward, along with being part of family gatherings that evening on a "nice, clean porch."

Jessie and Mother enjoyed the porch late at night when their laughter could sometimes be heard by the girls through their open bedroom windows. Occasionally in the evenings they would join the ladies on the porch and listen to their conversations. One evening the telephone rang and Judi went into the house to answer the call. A gentleman asked to speak to "Beverly." Kate and Jessie both maintained they had no idea who "Beverly" might be. It was not until years later that they realized that Jessie frequently gave a false name to interesting gentlemen she might meet, including the telephone number of her sister. However, in typical Jessie style, she promptly forgot giving her middle name and the hapless gentleman caller was left in perpetual perplexity.

In their first full winter in the Wall house, Kate at last could enjoy having a furnace with a stoker. This anthracite coal burning furnace that automatically fed itself was a big improvement in the amount of work required to keep the heat going in the house; however, the second and third floors still were heated by a convection system and the bedrooms were rarely warm. The girls continued to dress in the bathroom which had an electric heater, as did the third floor occupied by Kay.

One afternoon in early spring of the following year (1947), as Jo Ellen and Nan were playing in the area of the basement close to the fruit cellar and Judi was using her chemistry set at the oak table, the curtain surrounding the commode in the basement began to go up in flames. Nan and Jo Ellen called for their mother with Nan running up the stairs to get her. Judi ran for the bucket in the laundry sink, quickly filled it with water and doused the fire. By the time Kate came tearing down the stairs, the fire was out, but the odor of singed fabric and the small Bunsen burner found on the floor left no doubt as to what had happened. Kate was too relieved to give more than a cursory scolding to all three girls.

Jo Ellen and Nan enjoyed swimming and the two of them spent most of the summers at the park. Nan, turning six years of age in August 1948, had become a fearless swimmer, strong and sure. Her older sisters saw nothing unusual in this skill in their baby sister until one day when their mother unexpectedly walked into the swimming area. Kate usually established a time to pick up the girls at the park, driving across the traffic bridge, stopping the car and blowing the horn. By the time she had crossed the river, turned around and come back to the parking area of the park, the children had gathered their belongings, climbed the steep bank, and made their way to the car. Coming down the bank one particular day when the children were not in sight where she had parked the car, Kate asked where Nan was. Jo Ellen pointed across the falls to the pier. There Kate saw her youngest child jumping and diving off the diving board into the deep water of the swiftly moving river (At that time the swimming area had no lifeguard).

Nan was sociable and out-going with all the confidence a child could muster, and without a care in the world. Her innocence, which strangers found charming, was at times viewed with alarm by her family. For example, sent on an errand one day to Dot's Restaurant to purchase a loaf of bread for 14¢, Nan handed the waitress the quarter her mother had given her. Having observed what adults do in restaurants, Nan declined the offer of the 11¢ due her with a cavalier "Keep the change," leaving the waitress speechless. More embarrassing to the family, although taken in good spirit by the pastor's wife, was a telephone call Nan made to the Reverend Ezra Parks. When Mrs. Parks answered the phone, Nan ingenuously requested to speak to the pastor by asking, "Is Ezra there?"

That happy summer of '48 also saw the formation of The Pigtail Club, established under the back porch at 319 Thompson Street and replacing for most of the season the "living room" area of the playhouse. Based on a concept made popular by a comic book series, Judi and Jo Ellen obtained orange crates which they planned to transform into chairs, following what they had read in the comic book. Having no saw or hammer, or any idea how to use either, they dragged the crates a block up Thompson Street where they sought assistance from their Grandfather Pifer, returning triumphantly with their orange crate chairs to the clubhouse-under-the-porch.

The Sesquicentennial Celebration in the summer of 1949, while successful in the eyes of those involved, had been costly and the debt cloud hung over the entire community. To defray that debt the townspeople produced a minstrel show the next spring (1950) with a resulting full house for each performance with strong, complimentary reviews in the newspaper. Kate basked in these events as all four of her daughters performed: Judi and Jo Ellen in a vocal duet of "Indian Love Call"

then as a trio with seven-year-old Nan for a vocal rendition of "Three Little Sisters." Kay performed a hula tap to the delight of the audience. The second year's show (1951) earned enough to retire the debt and included Jo Ellen's clear soprano in "Alice Blue Gown," and Judi with her cousin Noel Hamilton in a cabaret musical number "How Could You Believe Me...When You Know I've Been a Liar..."

In December 1953 the Curwensville High School Choir presented for the first time "The Messiah," for which Jo Ellen was a soloist, with Arch Johnstone conducting.

(Even in a small town high school there were many activities to keep young people busy and productive through all of the natural teen-age angst and the added unidentified stress we all went through. Kate, while protective of us girls, was totally supportive in our making the most of the opportunities our small town could provide. We seemed to be popular and were most definitely very involved in activities ranging from music to working at the theatre now managed by our mother.)

After the Break-up (See details in "The Story of Howard")

As a result of the family break-up, Kate's furniture from their house on Thompson Street went into storage in the Water Company Building owned by H. J. Thompson. Kate was offered the position as manager of the Rex Theatre, the job previously held by her husband. Judi, at fifteen, went to live with her Grandfather Thompson in his large home attended by a housekeeper; Jo Ellen moved in with Josephine; and Kate and her youngest, Nan, moved in temporarily with Kay and Albert who were living in the home of Albert's parents while they spent several months in Texas with their daughter. Kay welcomed the help of her mother, especially after the birth of her daughter, Mavis Kim. When the senior Brunettis returned home, Kate and Nan moved in for several months with Kate's parents and Jessie. As the three bedrooms were in use and Kate would not hear to displacing her parents, Kate and Nan carved out space in the attic, much as her mother had years before. As it was nearly spring and not bitter cold, they could manage. By mid-summer they moved into a small apartment in the home of Kate's sister Jean. Jean had offered the space earlier, but the tenant was slow in vacating.

Kate On Her Own

(Author's Reflection: I am sure none of us realized the stress Mother was going through and her total devotion to her daughters. There was never a whisper of her leaving her girls with Howd. We never asked and, while I remember struggling with all that a divorce implied, I am sure I did not see the full hardship this was for our mother. In retrospect, the experience of breaking up the family and "farming out" the three younger daughters had to have been traumatic for all of us, but Mother never flinched. [She always hid her anxious moments from us.] She rarely displayed even natural impatience with her children and there was a sense of normalcy in every action Mother took to provide for us. Today, I can weep for the distress she surely endured at that time and the anguish that would occur years later.)

The Story of Kate

H. J. Thompson had added a large second bedroom in a small apartment, recently vacated by his son Philip and his wife, located at the rear of the Rex Theatre into which we moved, but never fully realized how relieved Mother must have been to find a place to house her three younger daughters under the same roof. We certainly had been resilient and had adjusted well to the several changes in our living conditions the last two years of which being separated and living with relatives, with very few real worries. (I marvel now at all she did while we took it all for granted.)

Once they were resettled, Nan purchased a horse with part of the money from a $1000 bond each of the Thompson sisters had been bequeathed by the estate of their Grandmother Thompson. Judith's inheritance was earmarked for college and Jo Ellen's had been loaned to Kay to add to her own $1000 for the down payment on the house she and Albert had bought. The horse, Count Scot, was Nan's delight but the bane of her sisters, particularly the day she brought the horse blanket home and put it in the small bedroom she shared with Jo Ellen. Nan closed the door and went to bed in the windowless room. Jo Ellen was in the living room, waiting for her mother to return from the theatre. When Kate arrived home she went to check on Nan. When she opened the door, she was almost overcome by the odor of horse, completely unnoticed by the sleeping child.

In the spring of 1955, Kate's mother died and despite the grief all five sisters experienced at the loss of their mother, Kate would not allow a pall of gloom over the graduation activities for her second daughter. She did not ever speak to the girls of the depth of feeling at her loss—either at the time or later, but did her best to keep their lives as normal as possible despite her personal grief. Like most of their generation, the Pifer sisters kept their emotions in check. Their children never saw the Pifer sisters cry, except upon the death of Jean, nor did they ever see them hug each other or openly show affection for their own children. Thinking nothing of this at the time, like most children they viewed whatever they experienced as typical.

With Judi's strong desire for a college education, Kate was again faced with trying to find funds. Very few people knew about scholarships and there was little counseling from the school, so most families were left on their own to resolve any difficulties. Kate gathered all her strength and again faced her former father-in-law, asking him to pay for Judi's college. He turned her down. Mary Alice, Howard's sister, heard of the dilemma and after asking for details from the school superintendent, she offered to pay all expenses, including a spending allowance, for Judi's college education. Relieved and grateful as she was—once again, Kate found herself beholden. Always Kate put her daughters first and every one of them could recite instances when a way was found to acquire what they needed, while Kate herself would do without.

80

In the summer of 1956 Jo Ellen was adapting to city living in Washington, DC where she resided at the Meridian Hill Hotel for Women, took her meals in its cafeteria, and rode the bus to work. At seventeen she was likely the youngest person working for the Federal Bureau of Investigation and because of her age needed working papers. Understandably, she was frightened living alone in the capital, but she also realized there was no other choice. She couldn't easily return home and had to make the best of it. To sustain her courage, she would write notes to herself in shorthand: "I can do it. I can do it." Even on her modest salary, she managed to send money to her mother, a generous practice she continued throughout her mother's lifetime.

A year later Jo Ellen began working for the National Security Agency where she soon moved up the General Services Administration classifications, quickly obtaining top security status. One of the most exciting events of summer 1957 was Jo Ellen's becoming a vocalist for a Washington DC dance band and being selected as a finalist in the Miss Washington, DC competition, part of the Miss America pageant.

On the Move Again

Also in 1957 Howard J. Thompson sold the Rex Theatre and Kate had to vacate the apartment that was part of the building. Kate could not afford to either buy or rent a place and she had nowhere to go, for not only did she lose the apartment, but, with the sale of the theatre, she also lost her job as manager of the theatre. Before long, however, she found a suitable position as front desk manager at the Dimeling Hotel in Clearfield.

Kate discussed her housing dilemma with Josephine who suggested that her younger sister consider moving into the rental side of the property that had been their mother's and whose ownership was now shared by the sisters. As Kate saw no other options, she called her sister Ruby to ask her advice as well as discussing the matter with Jessie and Jean. The four sisters readily agreed that Kate should live in the house. They knew that was what their mother would have wanted and that she had written her Will giving their homestead to Jessie and the rental income of the other half to the other four girls only because Jessie was the only unmarried daughter and didn't have a home of her own. Thus, Kate moved into 410 Thompson Street (jointly owned by the four sisters) in the early spring of 1958, with Jessie (the fifth sister) retaining ownership of 408.

Kate took on the daunting task of making needed repairs to the house, both structural and cosmetic. As the half house had not seen many improvements except when painting or repairs were made to the entire property, there was much to do. Fortunately, the kindly Carl Tagliente, better known as "Tag," volunteered to do most of the work that began with tearing out an inside flue. As the interior floors were not level, a lolly colum was used in the basement to shore up the floor. As a result, the bedroom doors needed to be planed and everything then had to be painted. Tag also put up drywall and the reliable Mose Whitaker did the paper hanging. Perhaps it should be noted that when kind-hearted Mr. Whitaker sent his invoice he included the message, "You don't have to pay this now—or even at all." New carpeting was laid in the living room and master bedroom while Sandran (a new upgraded type of sheet vinyl flooring; some patterns resembled hardwood) was installed in the dining room and congoleum and throw rugs were used in the other bedrooms. There was no laundry area, so Tag fit a washing machine in the landing of the stairs to the basement that was a dirt-floored cellar except for the splash of concrete upon which the furnace sat.

While Kate needed to vacate her apartment and move into her half of the double house before all the work was finished, she was very grateful to have her own home. It became a comfortable, albeit small, house and Kate relished the independence, anticipating that in time she might arrange for sole ownership.

Kate had very little time to prepare for the double wedding of her daughters Jo Ellen and Judith in September 1958. She borrowed a few pieces of "newer" furniture from her sister Jean to enhance the appearance of her modest furnishings and was able to use the Dimeling Hotel ballroom for the reception at no cost for the rental, only the cost of the meals that she arranged to pay for over time. No one was the wiser.

One must wonder, however, if Kate didn't feel a twinge of regret eight years later in 1965 when she saw her former grand house on lower Thompson Street advertised for sale at 80% of the price she and Howard had paid when they had purchased it fourteen years earlier: "Large 5-bedroom frame home. Hardwood floors. Brick garage. New roof. Large, high basement. 1 ¾ bathrooms. Needs repairs. But a good buy at $4,900."

Soon after, Kay left Curwensville with the man who was to become her husband, leaving her young daughter with the man she had divorced. Thirty-five years later, Kate admitted to her three younger daughters, "I was embarrassed by Kay's actions and was glad she was leaving." It was inconceivable to Kate that any mother could go off on an adventure not knowing when she might ever see her child again.

Seeds of Sorrows

Even more unthinkable to Kate was the death in late 1958 of her sister Margaret Jean at age 48. This loss was devastating to Kate, as not only was Jean her sister closest in age—they shared the same birthday of February 11—but was also her best friend. Kate continued to mourn deeply for Jean the rest of her life.

In June, as if to come full circle in a year of stress, Kate was indirectly associated with a lawsuit Howard, Jr. had filed against his father. She had been deposed by the attorneys, and was hoping she did not have to take the witness stand, as being embarrassed by the headlines in the county paper would be more than enough of a reminder of her unfortunate situation.

On the brighter side in 1960, Judith was graduated from Penn State with a B.A. in English Literature and Nan was graduated with honors from high school after a fun-filled four years of being called "the last Thompson star." Kay had sent Judi a graduation gift with a qualifying explanation, "… the necklace is sterling and good," not understanding that an item of quality speaks for itself nor, apparently, did she remember Kate's explaining to her girls that if one had to call attention to quality possessions it only demonstrated that one was not accustomed to having them.

The tone of Christmas 1960 was an unfamiliar one for Kate, as it was the first time in 30 years she was without children living at home. Kate realized with a sudden sadness that an era had passed and that there was no one to whom she could express these feelings of longing. Jessie, childless, could not understand the emptiness of a house once filled with children. Josephine would perhaps comprehend Kate's quiet anguish, as her son had not lived at home since he had left for college in the fall of 1952, but Kate didn't want to upset Josephine further with Noel's wedding only three weeks away.

Adding to the holiday sadness Kate was experiencing was the lingering mourning for her sister Jean. This bereavement still weighed heavily on Kate's heart, even though she kept her grief private, the deep loss ever present. It was not, however, until six years later when Nan and her son (who had been visiting in Curwensville) returned to California that Kate finally expressed her loneliness to her oldest daughter who, in turn, wrote to one of her sisters, "I got a letter from Mother on Friday and she signed it 'Lonesome Kak.' That is the first time she's done that. She said she hated to see Nan and Shayne go."[16]

---

16 Letter to the author, September 13, 1966.

The Story of Kate

One of Kate's unspoken regrets was the change she saw in her oldest child, the wanderlust, not only in exploring a move to New York, then settling in Philadelphia following graduation from high school and more recently relocating to California, but also harboring a desire to "be" someone. While she had made very precise plans to go to New York City, then Philadelphia after graduation and, later, on a far more complicated journey that led her to California, Kay lacked a specific course of action that would take her to a life she so desired. Kate also worried about what she saw as an "edge" to her daughter. In some ways she was coarse and used language with which other family members were uncomfortable and unfamiliar. She was witty, but her clever comments often were sarcastic, having a sharpness to them, sometimes to the point of being hurtful.

Most disturbing to Kate, however, was Kay's attitude of thinking she "deserved" whatever it was she wanted and believed that she was "entitled" just because she had worked for something or had cajoled to get it or simply because she was Kay. She also enjoyed demonstrating her cunning in talking her way out of ever paying full price, stalking the stores until an item was reduced to a price that suited her, or finagling ways to pay less for services, including legal, medical, and dental.[17, 18] Thoughts of these incidents returned time and again to haunt Kate.

For all her shrewdness, wit and style, Kay appeared to feel cheated, as if someone or something had not worked for her or that the world was out of sync for her. Such individuals grow up expecting great things of life, and they are disappointed if they don't achieve them.[19] As Kay herself admitted, "I'm the type that wants everything right now."[20] Worse, they truly believe in the American idea of a natural right to happiness and material success because, as they tell themselves, "I deserve it." This became Kay's credo as she sought recognition, happiness, and, most of all, secure material success at the expense of all else.

Kate spent much of the mid-1960s rebuffing continual offers of marriage from Carl Tagliente, a handsome bachelor some years younger than she. "Tag" was devoted to Kate and wanted her to marry him. Kate's daughters were fond of Tag and would have been pleased to accept their mother's choice. It took many years for them to understand why their mother chose not to marry and to not have to be concerned about supporting herself. A letter written to Judi perhaps best captures Kate's reservations, as she explains Tag's persistence in wanting her to accept a ring:

---

17 Letter to the author, November 12, 1965.
18 Letter from Kay to Kate, circa Thanksgiving, 1966.
19 Lerner, 689.
20 Letter to the author, May 7, 1965.

Our Kate ❧ Our Kaki ❧ Our Mother

Right now he thinks I'm what he wants, but I'm not too sure I'd "wear well," never having spent an entire 24 hours with him. I asked him if he realized what a ring meant and he said, "Yes, I'm ready." [However] He is interested in his family [his five—also unmarried—adult siblings] and I am in mine. … I don't want a ring. I didn't wear the one I had and how would I explain it? I'm "engaged" at my age and don't know when the wedding will be?!! …I don't want another failure and it would be doomed from the start.[21]

Kate continued to struggle with her relationship with Tag. They had continual fallings out over Tag's family, yet he always came back with such pledges as "If you make up your mind and let me come back, I'll do anything for you."[22] But Kate never said "Yes." Thus, Kate and Tag remained close friends, but through the next fifteen years both realized that they were first and foremost committed to their respective families. Carl Tagliente continued his devotion to her, but Kate was right—families came first.

Kate's New Year's Eve in 1963 was spent in the company of Tag and her lifelong friend Kathryn Kephart Smith and John Husack, the gentleman she was seeing (having been widowed a few years earier). Kate wrote, "We hit Cha Ru for about an hour and a half, wanted everyone to see my dress and shoes. I stole the show both places (conceited as it sounds, it's true) and Tag was beside himself![23] Indeed, Kate continued to be a "head turner," even at age 55, with many invitations extended to her, including one from retired Penn State football coach, Rip Engle, which she turned down.[24]

On Friday, June 11, 1965 Kate, Jessie, and Judi attended the second of the three evenings of scheduled performances of Mrs. Eileen Brown's piano students. One of the final soloists was Janet Lynne Bloom, Aunt Jean's daughter. It was a

---

21 Kate's letter to the author, December 12, 1963.
22 Letter from Kate to the author, October 14, 1964.
23 Kate's letter to the author, January 2, 1964.
24 Kate's letter to the author, late February 1966.

bittersweet evening for Kate who had to blink back tears as she observed the same familiar physical features, voice, and gestures in Janet Lynne that she had known in her sister Margaret Jean at the same age. Kate's voice broke as she whispered to Jessie, "Jean would be so proud."

In addition to attending recitals and school events involving her late sister's daughter, Kate helped Jean's husband Chet with Janet Lynne's teen-age rebellion against her father's rules. While by no means "wild," Janet did struggle with what she viewed as her father's old-fashioned ideas and she turned to her aunts—particularly Kate—for advice as well as clothes for special school events. Janet wore the same size as Kate who lent her some of her own best outfits and, occasionally, gowns or coats would be mailed or hand-delivered "on loan" from her cousins in Washington D.C., Hummelstown, or Los Angeles for Janet's use. Kate further relied on her daughters to affirm the advice she gave Janet and through letters Kate shared these experiences:

"Janet's hair piece finally came and she is elated; she was here awhile this morning for me to style it."[25]

Janet Lynne

"Janet is coming over for the dress and my good black coat. I've instructed her thoroughly on how not to sit in my good dress—knees spread apart, etc. In fact, I said, 'Don't sit at all except when compelled to.' Incidentally, she looks choice in it and I couldn't refuse."[26]

"Janet is counting on your help and wants also to try on Nan's floor-length sheath dress (selected especially for Nan by Mr. Mahlon while on a buying trip to New York City for Brody's) for one of the spring affairs. So if you don't mind bringing it up for her to try so she will know whether or not it fits."[27]

"Janet is all set and quite pleased with the gown and accessories. She has white silk shoes and elbow-length gloves. She didn't quite believe me about "white is right" and it took both your and Nan's advice to convince her not to dye the shoes green."[28]

"She wants a white coat like mine so I ordered it from Brody's—foolish perhaps—she has a good rain coat like yours, but Chet agreed."[29]

---

25 Letter from Kate to the author, October 9, 1964.
26 Letter from Kate to the author, February 20, 1965.
27 Letter from Kate to the author, March 25, 1965.
28 Letter from Kate to the author, May 27, 1964.
29 Letter from Kate to the author, May 14, 1965.

"Janet came looking to borrow my leopard coat for a football game. Also my black dress with dotted chiffon sleeves, and my black fur-collared sweater. She asked me about gloves and I told her she might as well buy herself a good pair of black, so Ruby gave her $5.[30]

In August 1966 Ruby and Tom Wayne had made a visit to Curwensville where they stayed with Josephine. On Saturday Ruby and Tom, Jessie and Jack (whom Jessie had recently married), Kate and Josie, along with Kim and Janet Lynne, all spent the day at the Wayne homestead farm near DuBois where they stayed for supper and into the evening. "Janet got a kick out of our 'going on' like we do [reminiscing and retelling favorite family stories with a great deal of laughter] and we didn't get home until midnight."[31]

The following morning over breakfast at Jessie's, Josephine expressed to all of them her worry over the cost ($900) of a new furnace. Kate, always worrying about being beholden, took this opportunity not only to reassure Josie that she had not been overcharged, but to let her three sisters know the amount she had spent in repairs in her half of the double house. She also shared with them an estimate of $600 she had just received on an oil furnace for her half-house that had less square footage than Josephine's home. In addition, Kate had the chance to show bills from taxes and sewerage amounting to $160 a year, a sum more than they would have received if the house were rented.[32] When Ruby noted that Kate had put as much or more in the place as anyone would get out of it, Kate felt confident enough to then go ahead and convert from coal to oil heat.

While Ruby's visits had become increasingly infrequent through the years, her sisters eagerly awaited each one. Ruby had a madcap sense of humor and easily fell into paroxysms of laughter over stories that those outside the family couldn't follow. Kate relayed to her daughters the merriment of such a visit in September 1966, "Ruby was in on Saturday, and we were invited to Josie's for supper. I wore my wig. After dinner I said, 'Do you girls like the way my hair is cut?' Ruby said, 'Yes, but it looks darker.' Janet said, 'It looks smart. Did Nan cut it for you?' With that, I pulled the wig off my head and they screamed and laughed as only Ruby can. She says she is going to get one. They all tried mine and Ruby just couldn't stop laughing when Josie put it on. By then Ruby was in rare form!"[33]

It should be noted that it was quiet, reserved Kate who had emerged as the strongest of the five Pifer sisters, serving as the family's center. Jessie, Kate, and

---

30 Letter from Kate to the author, September 27, 1966.
31 Letter from Kate to the author, August 25, 1965.
32 Letter from Kate to the author, August 25, 1965.
33 Letter from Kate to the author, September 27, 1966.

Josephine continued to plan family events so that Janet Lynne would be assured of the same family gatherings and support that her older cousins had experienced. "I'll be at Chet's for Thanksgiving," Kate wrote, "Janet, Josie, Don and Lorraine. I'm taking cranberry salad, Josie the pie, and Chet is having Fye's restaurant fix the chicken."[34]

While Kate frequently accepted Kay's invitations to visit her, in November 1966 Kay expressed concern over what she termed "Mother's reluctance to come out here," adding that she thought their mother was "acting funny" about visiting in California and Kay expressed worry that her mother might not feel welcome.[35] On the 22nd she again asked her sister, "Did you ever ask Kak[36] why she is acting funny about coming out?"[37] A month later Kay may have answered her own question: "I know she felt uncomfortable when she was here this time, but I don't know why. Maybe we acted different, I don't know. I do know she makes me nervous anymore and I suppose she senses it."[38]

Five weeks following that insight, Kay added, "Nan said she thought I had been mean to Kak when she was here. It's just that she made me nervous at times when she wouldn't come right out and say what she wanted to do. I wanted to take her where she wanted to go but she didn't want me to go out of the way. I didn't want to go to San Francisco at all but I wanted her to see it and I'm sure she enjoyed herself."[39] (Kay never did understand that guests—particularly mothers—do not want to feel beholden, especially mothers like Kate, of modest means, but independent.)

In Kate's own family Nan produced the first grandson with the birth of Shayne Scott on December 9, 1965. Fully expecting a girl based solely on the fact that her grandmother Matilda was one of five sisters, her mother Kate was one of five sisters, Nan herself was one of four sisters, and Kay and Judi each had a daughter, Nan had been completely convinced that her firstborn would be a girl. When the doctor announced that she had given birth to a boy, she told him that there had to be a mistake, "My grandmother had all girls, my mother had all girls, and my sisters both have girls. I am supposed to have a girl. It can't be a boy." But, despite her protestations, the baby was indeed the first boy in the family.

---

34 Letter from Kate to the author, November 22, 1966.
35 Letter from Kay to the author, November 7, 1966.
36 Kak is the name the family began to use after Shayne dubbed his grandmother with the shortened version.
37 Letter from Kay to the author, November 22, 1966.
38 Letter from Kay to the author, December 31, 1966.
39 Letter from Kay to the author, February 6, 1967.

Two years later Judi, much to her surprise at being pregnant after a lapse of nine years following the birth of her daughter Jean, gave birth to a son. She, too, had been expecting a girl. Ross, as he was then called by his family, became a real live doll for his sister who became his unquestioning advocate. The following year, in early January, Jo Ellen had her first child, a girl, whom she named Janelle Corinne. A brother, Eugene Kendall, would follow on April 17, 1970, completing the Lorenz family. These children completed the circle of babies for Kate's family — at least for the next decade and a half.

Kak with Baby Janelle

New Joys

Kate's world soon began to revolve around the grandchildren much as it had around her own four children. Even though she worked fulltime, she managed to arrange her schedule to be with each of her daughters after the birth of their children, thus establishing an immediate bond with her grandchildren that continued throughout her lifetime. Each grandchild found a special niche and relationship with their grandmother, whom they called "Kaki," the nickname bestowed upon her by her first grandchild, Kim, and later shortened to "Kak" by some family members. Early references in Kate's letters reveal her attachment to the grandchildren as she recalled their various visits, writing to each daughter about her own:

> *The dress and slip from Sears for Jean is satisfactory, dress is really fresh and sweet. I sent for a white furry hat for Kim, and it is smart and nice for the money. I came across the Indian character dolls, so decided to give one to Kim and keep one for Jean. I also have given Kim the annual $5 to do her Xmas shopping. It makes me feel better to know she doesn't have to beg Albert for a little money before the 24th.[40]*

> *Shayne is quite entertaining and such a good baby. We have become good friends, although he wasn't so sure the first day.[41]*

> *Jean showed me how she could dance—on her tip toes yet—and, of course, was certain she was entertaining like on television. Her Grammie told me Jean*

40 Letter from Kate, December 12, 1963.
41 Christmas card from Kate to the author, 1965.

had asked for a ballet skirt for Christmas, but she was afraid Jean would catch cold. Naturally, as soon as I got home I headed for the attic. I found a skating skirt and a tap dance costume which I took down pronto. I told Jean, "It isn't a ballet skirt but maybe I can find one."' To which she replied, "I don't care if it isn't a ballet skirt. I just wanted a dancing costume."' So we shall see about dancing lessons.[42]

Shall we plan a party for Jean? How about the skating rink? I'll call and find out how many bratty older kids usually go on a Saturday, making it dangerous for smaller ones. Jess said she would drive so we would have two cars, yours and hers.[43]

I think a bird would be nice for Jean, or how about a basketball set or a dart game to tack on the garage?[44]

Jean called me this afternoon. She asked me what I wanted for Christmas. I must be on her list this year.[45]

Judi frequently visited her mother on the weekends and Kay visited with her several times a year either in California or by coming to Curwensville. However, Kate missed Jo Ellen who did not get home often and she pined for her youngest daughter Nan after she and her husband had moved to California in 1964:

I called Nan last night, just felt like hearing her voice…[46]

Nan sounded a little wistful and said even the rain [in California] is not the same.[47] *Jo Ellen had called Annie [Nan] before she left and said she sounded cheerful. I wish she would write.*[48]

And Kay wrote, *"She [Kate] seems to worry about Nan."*[49]

Nan also was having pangs of loneliness, something she had not expected with her move to California. She had thought about returning to the East and as early as January had written to her sister, "I'm not mentioning it to anyone else yet (especially Kay), but Joel and I don't like it here, not really. We're talking about moving back to Pennsylvania already. This might be a temporary 'homesickness'; I don't quite know

---

42   Letter from Kate to the author, January 20, 1966.
43   Letter from Kate to the author, February 7, 1966.
44   Letter from Kate to the author, late February, 1966.
45   Letter from Kate to the author, November, 1966.
46   Letter to the author, March 18, 1965.
47   Letter to the author, April 4, 1965.
48   Letter to the author, July 20, 1965.
49   Letter to the author, May 7, 1965.

for sure."[50] Six weeks later, in a letter to Jessie, she again mentioned returning home, "Joel and I were already to pack up and return to winter wonderland when I called Mother last month. Now we're going to give California another chance, but I feel as if the only change is that we'll be moving East later rather than sooner."[51]

Kate made a concerted effort to encourage Kim to visit her during the time she lived with her father in Curwensville, and Jessie and Kate both tried to make those visits special. Once as a young teen-ager Kim "ran away from home" and went to her grandmother's house (a distance of only two blocks). Kate called Albert, although there were conflicting stories as to the reason for Kim's leaving home.[52] Regardless, the unsteady situation was upsetting to everyone in both families.

Early in March of 1966 Jessie began to withdraw into herself, much as she had two years earlier. Jack told Kate that her sister was not talking to him, was lying on the davenport for hours, and wouldn't go out even for a ride or to a restaurant. Kate knew she had to tell Josephine before she heard any rumors and with a heavy heart, she walked the three blocks to her sister's. Before she had her coat off, Josie asked, "What's wrong, Kate?" Kate related the sad news that it was possible that Jessie was slipping back into a depression. Josephine looked stricken, but could get only two words out, "Oh, Kate," she sighed, plaintive words that continued to echo in Kate's heart for the rest of her life.

There really was no other choice at the time and Jack made arrangements for Jessie to be re-admitted to Ridgway before her condition worsened. When he returned he told Kate and Josephine what he had done. "This is the hardest decision I have ever had to make," he said, trying to keep his tears at bay. He asked Kate and Josephine to go with him, as he anticipated he might have trouble once they got to Ridgway. Kate later said, "Josie cried more this time than she had two years ago, and I didn't know which sister my own tears were for."[53]

In the spring of 1966 it became apparent that it was time for Kate to replace her Ford Falcon that seemed to be in for repairs more days than she was using it. In late April she found her dream car, but not at all what she had been looking for, as she had no garage. Chet, who had been casing the neighborhood on his milk route, found one for her and she found it easy to rationalize that the walk to the garage would be good exercise and that in winter walking the distance would be no harder than covering the car and cleaning the snow off in the early morning hours.

---

50 Letter to the author, January 13, 1965.
51 Letter from Nan to Jessie, February 25, 1965.
52 Letter from Kate to the author, late February 1966.
53 Letter from Kate to the author, March 27, 1966.

She loved that car, and as she said, "I should never have gotten into it, for I was hooked before I rounded the corner."[54] Her 1966 white Chevy Malibu convertible with red leather interior became her prized possession for the remainder of her days.

As was typical, Kate's four daughters were planning their mother's 1966 Christmas gift as early as September. This year's surprise was to be a new television set, as the one Kate had was ten years old and the picture was no longer clear enough for viewing ease. The only questions seemed to be whether Kate would want black and white or color, and whether it would be better to have their mother select her own set or to purchase it in California where the prices were better. Color televisions were still not universal; in fact, a letter written from a student at Wittenburg College to a friend in February says, "Whatever happens on the 25th when I am home, I must see your color TV. You know I've never seen one—not even in the stores."[55]

In April 1969 Kate embarked on a tour of Europe with Kay. It was a glorious trip, and Kate at age 61 kept pace with her daughter nearly 23 years her junior. Beginning in London, they visited Amsterdam, cities in Germany, the major sites of Italy, and ended in Paris—15 days filled with all the highlights

Queen Elizabeth 2   Photographed on board 1982

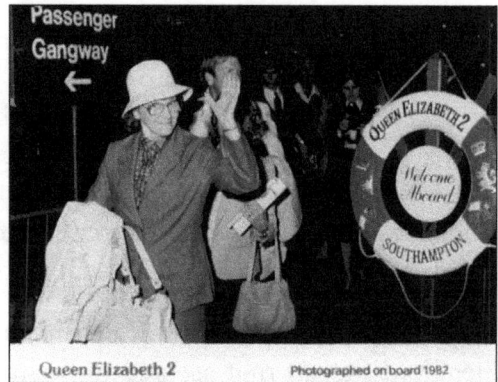

and historic places that made a lasting impression on Kate. She never dwelt on regaling others with the details of this European tour, but she always said it enhanced her understanding of and appreciation for her European heritage. This was to be the first of many trips, including an excursion on the Queen Elizabeth 2, mother and daughter would take together (courtesy of TWA discounts), an opportunity Kate would be the first to admit that she otherwise would not have had.

54 Letter from Kate to the author, May 9, 1966.
55 Letter from Lois Downs to the author, February 12, 1966.

Our Kate ❧ Our Kaki ❧ Our Mother

1970 marked Kate's retirement from the Dimeling Hotel. Not having anyone to advise her, she had laid no claim to the Social Security benefits of her late ex-husband, even though she would have been entitled to a portion of his earned benefits. Instead, she made do with the minimum amount, based on her own limited time of employment (approximately seventeen years) as Rex Theatre manager and then front desk manager at the Dimeling Hotel. At age 62 she was expected to retire and it isn't clear whether or not she made a deliberate choice in the matter. Her daughters, like most young adult children, viewed Kate's retirement as "time for a rest," not fully appreciating how vibrant their mother was. Still very attractive, few would ever have guessed her age.

Even before retirement and on a very limited income (despite Kay's claims to her sisters that their mother "…makes $60 a week and pays no rent and spends little on food and, thus makes out OK"[56]), Kate managed to run her household and provide gifts and treats for both her children and grandchildren. She made herself available to help when any family member needed her and was in attendance following the birth of each grandchild, regardless of the distance or the amount of lost income during those times she had to arrange for someone to "cover" her shift at the Dimeling Hotel desk.

Following her retirement, the grandchildren, usually one at a time, "visited Kaki" for an extended stay every summer. Kate also spent several weeks each summer at Jo Ellen's beach house in Bethany Beach, usually with one or more of the Pennsylvania grandchildren in tow. She could be counted on to find interesting things to do with each child in turn and she readily took part in their many enterprises, from Shayne's worm farm in California to Kendall's sand castles in Ocean City. Such times were idyllic and led to a close bonding between Kate and, in turn, each grandchild. All of them confided in her, knowing their secrets were safe and her support of them boundless.

Shayne Scott and Thomas Ross, being close in age, would occasionally visit their grandmother at the same time and, thus, they share many of the same memories. Even without having had brothers or sons, Kate seemed to know instinctively how to engage both boys in activities and conversations personal to each one's interests and sometimes concerns. And both boys loved riding in their grandmother's white convertible, with the red leather interior. They would sit in it and "pretend" driving while waiting for Kate to take them for a ride. Shayne, being the older, was particularly enamored of the car and when Kate heard Ross talking about his dad buying him a car when he turned sixteen, quickly assured Shayne that when he was sixteen, he could have her Chevelle. Such was heaven!

---

56 Kay's letter to the author, March 17, 1964.

Since those summers together in Curwensville, Shayne and Ross have laughed at their adventures-in-common with Aunt Jessie. They still roll their eyes in recalling how Jessie instructed them to go across the street to greet the neighbors when they exited their homes in the mornings. She was particularly insistent that they visit "Ray" who spent most of his summer—day and night—on his front porch and that they say "Hello" to Joe Errigo who lived in an apartment in the same block. Jessie was also very willing to take the boys to Irvin Park where they would swim and she occasionally treated them to an evening at the movies.

Of course, she constantly "corrected" their manners, and was forever offering to prepare something for them to eat. To this day, all one of them has to say is "Would you like a cheese and relish sandwich?" and they both go into spasms of laughter. And yet they would not for anything trade the memory of their grandmother's gentle pressure to accept whatever offering was made by their great-aunt and of the never-ending admonition from Kak (their preferred name for her) to "Make sure you thank Aunt Jessie."

While Kate was not in the habit of giving unsolicited advice she did not hesitate to pass on to her daughters the advice her own mother had always given Kate and her sisters, "Married you can always get," meaning that simply being married was no great accomplishment. The other was a remark made with both innocence and wisdom by a young Jo Ellen, as she tried to reassure herself following her parents' separation, "You know, you really don't need a dad."

The Seeds Take Root

Shortly after her mother's retirement, Kay began planting seeds for what later would be recognized as a plot, but in the early 1970s was not yet identified as such by her sisters. Kay initiated her plan by telling her mother that she should consider what she would do when she might not be able to take care of herself independently. At the same time, Kay began dropping hints to both her mother and sisters that she herself was considering moving back to Curwensville upon her own retirement, although she never made a clear connection between her two suggestions. Kay did not propose that she would move back home to be near her mother and to take care of her when the time would come for Kate to need assistance. Rather, her approach was low-keyed and offered only as part of general discussions of "what if..." and "when..." with no details, just thoughts for her mother to ponder.

At the same time she was advising her mother to make plans for her future, Kay began recommending to her three sisters that the four of them talk about options for their mother as "she probably gets lonely there in Curwensville with all of us gone." She kept returning to what later became a theme: "We-should-make-some-kind-of-arrangement-for-Mother."

Notwithstanding that Kate was very healthy and that the women in her family were known for their longevity, Kay still wanted a definite plan for her mother's future. The fact that Kate's mother and aunts all had lived into their eighties, as had her father and his siblings, didn't seem to enter much into the discussions Kay continued to hold with her sisters. Rather, it was as if Kay were focused on "getting this settled" even though Kate, in her early sixties, was not yet ready to make any such arrangements, yet alone acknowledge any pending "old age."

Kay's early conversations with her sisters on "plans for Mother" were subtle and, initially, only somewhat uncomfortable for the younger three. It was not often that all four sisters were in the same place at the same time, so most of the talking (or correspondence) occurred one-on-one, Kay and each of her sisters in turn. Typically, each of the three would defer to their oldest sister, and in most conversations on this subject they would just listen and nod, only occasionally asking questions. The younger three didn't want to discuss someone else's business, especially when this someone was their mother. At one time or another, they all had indicated willingness to have their mother move in with them "when the time came," but curiously none of the three discussed this much with each of the others except Kay who badgered them individually.

It soon began to annoy Judi, Jo Ellen, and Nan that Kay kept raising the question of "what to do with Mother." Jo Ellen had long ago offered any help needed as she had been financially subsidizing her mother for years. In addition, Jo Ellen and Judi thought that their mother probably would prefer to live with Nan, but that was only a supposition on their part, not based on any discussion or other tangible substantiation.

Over the next several years discussions were held among Kate's daughters who all agreed it would be an excellent choice to accept Wally's offer to build a cottage on the property of Wally and Judith. Jo Ellen saw the possibilities that she would see Mother more often if she spent part of the year in Hummelstown, as it was almost a six-hour drive from Washington to Curwensville, not easy with children. With the plans for Kate to spend more time in Hummelstown, Judi and Jo Ellen also saw the benefits of their respective children getting to know their cousins better. They began to visit one another's family more frequently and with all being musically talented (mothers and children), it was natural for them to continue their family tradition of performance. They began to rehearse more formally and by 1975 they had formed

T. Ross of T. Ross and Co.

"T. Ross and Company," comprised of Janelle, Kendall, T. Ross, and Jean, occasionally being joined by Jo Ellen, an accomplished vocalist, and with Judi as the accompanist for the troupe. The ensemble performed at various functions in Pennsylvania and Maryland through 1977.

Conversations about plans to build a small home for Kate continued among the sisters, along with possibilities that, in time, both Kate and Jessie might choose to share the cottage. This arrangement to provide a "someday" residence for their mother and aunt seemed to satisfy Kay's behest that something be done—and soon. Each of the daughters contributed.

"Kaki's Cottage," with living room, two bedrooms, kitchenette, bathroom and laundry-storage area, was completed by late 1976 and the following spring Kate would start her pattern of residing there for several weeks each summer. Beginning in the early 1980s, in addition to the summer visits, she would close her own house for the winter and spend December through March in the Hummelstown cottage. There was always the expectation of "someday" Kate "might" make her permanent home there, but no one was pushing—at least not yet, for, just as she looked forward to coming to the cottage, so she was just as eager to return to her own home in Curwensville.

Kate felt a little sheepish that she hadn't told Jessie about the cottage being built for her. She wasn't sure why she hadn't— it just never seemed to be the right time to tell Jessie that her daughters had worked together to provide a home for her use, whenever she wanted to use it. Having

waited to tell Jessie turned out to be even more awkward, as Kate would then also have to explain why she hadn't told Jessie of her plans. Later, in describing this scene to Judi, Kate said, "Even after all these years, I still felt like the baby sister."

The dynamic between the two sisters was typical but complicated, and it did appear to be just a little unfair that one sister would be given the "better" side of the family home and the other four would share ownership of the "rental" side. Other factors of the relationship between Kate and Jessie included the fact that Jack so freely had moved into the family home. Added to these differences in their houses was the natural evolving dependence Jessie and Kate had on each other following the deaths of Jean and Josephine, along with the obvious question in the back of the minds of both of them: "If one of us leaves, on whom will the other depend?"

In November 1979 Nan gave birth to her second child and second son. Again, she had expected a girl—this time for sure!—and had selected the name Jessica Katherine, similar to the name "Jessica Kate" Judi had chosen before her son was born. Nan came east for a visit when Jesse Joel was five months old. After much deliberation and many coast-to-coast telephone discussions, Nan decided that she would not return to California and, at the end of the school year, after selling their home in the high desert, Joel and Shayne packed all their belongings in a moving van and drove East to reunite the family. It had taken her fifteen years, but Nan did make good on her promise to "come home."

The early 1980s were generally tranquil at 408-410 Thompson Street as both Jessie and Kate enjoyed good health, visits from Kate's daughters and their families, and assistance from Don Bloom, who was very faithful in making sure his aunts were not in need. He particularly made a point of stopping to see Jessie since she had no children of her own and he was the only relative of both women still living in Curwensville.

During the first half of the 1980s, four of Kate's seven grandchildren were in late middle and high school and, as they neared the age of sixteen, they each in turn held renewed interest in their grandmother's convertible and a "turn at the wheel." From the time they were small Kate had always been generous with her time in taking them for rides "with the top down," and all of the grandchildren have vivid memories of the red leather interior of the Chevy Chevelle Malibu, no doubt dreaming of themselves someday in the driver's seat.

Jo Ellen's two children had teased their grandmother by calling her "Malibu Mama," but it was Shayne who had been completely captivated by "Kaki's" convertible and who, as a child, would often sit behind the wheel, pretending he was taking his cousins on a great adventure. To Shayne it was more than pretend, because from the time he was six, Kate had promised him that when he turned sixteen (in 1981) she would give him her car. Of course, at the time of the promise she probably had expected that she would no longer be driving. On the contrary, as

Shayne's 16th birthday approached that fall Kate was still very much in need of her car and found herself in a quandary.

However Aunt Jessie saw so many similarities between Shayne and her first and favorite nephew, John Wayne, that by early May, Shayne was behind the wheel of his very own car, a pre-owned Chevrolet Monza Spyder costing only $1,500. All in Kate's family were very pleased, with the exception of Kay who questioned why Shayne should have been so favored.

Kay's response to Jessie's generosity was particularly troubling to Kate because only the year before Kate had handwritten a Will in which she ("generously," as she later told her other three daughters) had bestowed her property at 410 Thompson Street to her firstborn. This decision was based upon Kay's assurances to her mother that she wanted to return to Curwensville upon her retirement. "You know the other girls won't ever want to come back here to live and I do." While it was likely the three younger daughters would not return to their home town, it was Kay's persuasion of wanting to retire in Curwensville that most convinced Kate to will the property to Kay. After having heard Kay's compelling argument for the past decade—that if the other girls all had homes and Kay needed a place to live, then she should have the Thompson Street homestead—Kate agreed to give the house to Kay.

Willing the house to Kay reminded Kate of her own need for a place to live a quarter century earlier and of the willingness of her own sisters to sign over their interests in the property to her. "Who would have thought," she said to Nan a few years later, "that you girls would be faced with the same kind of situation as my sisters were? I am so glad that in both cases all the sisters agreed. It would have been upsetting to me if you girls had quarreled over this. It was so comforting to know you all agreed. I hated to choose one over the other and I am glad everyone understood that Kay seemed to be the only one who was interested in moving back to Curwensville."

True, informal references as to the disposition of the Thompson Street house had occurred after the Hummelstown cottage had been built, but no serious discussions had been held because no immediate decisions needed to be made as far as the younger sisters were concerned. In addition, at that time the three of them were busy with their own increasing family responsibilities.

Jo Ellen's two children, Janelle and Kendall, were very active in school and community activities, along with their music lessons, and she herself was involved in her husband's plans in the development of the Lorenz Building. To be located at Two Bethesda Metro Center, the Lorenz Building was described as "…the architectural finale of downtown Bethesda, it is one of the most important new office buildings in the Washington Metropolitan area."

Nan had a teenager and an infant to attend to as well as settling in a new home. Judith had agreed to resume directing the school musicals in addition to Commencement and Baccalaureate programs and her doctoral program and was involved in the activities of her eighth grade son, as well as watching her daughter enjoy planning her wedding in Clearfield.

And in the spring of 1983 Kay and Bob went to Hawaii. Later that year Kay told Judi that although everyone had thought she and Bob had stopped at Winchester, Virginia to be married on their way to California in 1959, they had not, and that after being together nearly a quarter century, Bob was determined they would be married in Hawaii.

In the fall of that year for the first time, the Thompson sisters had to ask their mother in advance of Christmas if she would like to have a "microwave," as these were very new. Not surprisingly Kate said absolutely not, that she didn't trust them and didn't want to be bothered with one. "But, since you asked," she said, "what I really could use is a new toaster oven." Nan immediately claimed that suggestion, and Judi and Jo Ellen agreed they could think of other things their mother could use.

Betrayal Begins

In early November 1984 Kate made what turned out to be an extended visit to Kay. Upon her arrival at her daughter's home Kate found Kay "on edge," declaring that she was unable to go to work. The following day Kate suggested that she go to the office with Kay, concerned that it might be the long drive on the freeway that was bothering her. The journey to the TWA office building was uneventful but as Kay approached the turn to enter the parking lot, she began crying and said to her mother, "I can't go in." As there was no other place to park and traffic was beginning to back up behind them, Kate suggested that they enter the lot, park the car, and just remain in the car. As they sat, Kay began telling her mother of the nervousness she had been experiencing, of her "crying spells" that sometimes lasted for more than an hour, and of her persistent headaches.

Kate listened with a heavy heart as her daughter began an account of her various medical treatments, ranging from medication and bio-feedback to hypnosis and mental therapy. Kate suggested calling Bob at work, but as his job was an hour the opposite direction from their home, she thought it better to remain in the parking lot for a while, knowing she herself could not navigate the Los Angeles Freeway.

Once Kay had composed herself, mother and daughter returned home. Kate was aware of Kay's history of debilitating headaches and assumed they were "hereditary," as Judith also suffered migraines, although without the emotional breakdowns that periodically seemed to accompany those of her older sister. Concerned for Kay's unstable condition, Kate remained in California for several weeks until Kay located a physician who was able to provide some relief for her through a combination of treatments. This medical plan did not, however, allay Kate's worries.

In the spring of 1985 Kate returned to California because Kay's letters throughout the winter implied that she wasn't well. Shortly after her mother's arrival, Kay told her that after Christmas she had suffered a nervous breakdown and had been on medical leave during much of the winter. (Kate wondered why Kay had not written or called, then dismissed her concerns, rationalizing that Kay probably did not want to worry her.) In tears, Kay told her mother that she was dreading returning to work full time, revealing that if she didn't soon return to her job she would be forced to take early retirement. Kate's worries increased at the bleak picture her daughter was painting of her future.

Even prior to Kay's most recent episodes, but more recently with increased concern, Kate was wrestling with the possible cause of Kay's illness, thinking perhaps it was rooted in Kay's own perception of financial insecurity, as Kate could discern no medical reason in what Kay was telling her. Kay had always acted worried about having enough money to live comfortably and to have a dependable retirement income. She appeared to see everything in terms of money and at times became obsessed with the cost of things, from grocery items to the price of gasoline—whatever she was buying at the time. Even in describing gifts Kay would persistently make comments such as, "It cost a lot" or "I got a bargain."

Only later did Kate begin to suspect that she could have been "set up" by her daughter. When Kate tried to reconstruct the chain of events leading to the incidents that later distressed the family, she began to wonder if this "nervous breakdown" of Kay's had been only a ruse, a piece of a much broader scheme, the beginning of a carefully designed plot. In looking back Kate would surmise that the first step in Kay's master plot against her family had been Kay's establishing in her mother's mind that she (Kay) was frail and needed support. Thus, when Kay would later turn to her mother for help to carry out her plans Kate would be primed to not risk upsetting Kay's possibly "unstable" condition. Kate would later be dismayed to think that she had fallen for such a devious trick and that her general concern for her daughter's emotional health had led her to appease Kay, leading to a consequence Kate could not have imagined.

100

However, for now, the thought that her daughter would betray her own mother's trusting nature was inconceivable to Kate and, thus, allowed Kay to believe that her mother would champion her to the fullest. Once Kay believed that her mother would support anything she did, she was further emboldened in her plans.

It is also likely that Kay was confident that her mother would take her side in the event the "other three," as Kay began to call her younger sisters, questioned any steps of her plan. Kay had reminded her siblings time and again how close a relationship she had with their mother. By advantage of birth order, Kay supposed herself to be favored and supported by her mother, and took much pride in the many vacation trips she had taken with her. Thanks to TWA employee passes and generous discounts, Kay was able to take her mother on many trips—even when Kate was reluctant to go, but her financial contribution to Kate's daily living expenses was non-existent.

None of the four sisters had questioned the monetary or other gifts given by one or the other of them to their mother, just accepting that each gave according to her means. Commenting on "who gave what" was not of concern and it later saddened Judith, Jo Ellen, and Nan to discuss such matters when circumstances changed in the family dynamics. For years Jo Ellen had sent her mother an allowance without mentioning it; in contrast, in more recent years Kay announced to her sisters that she had established a savings account for her mother, jointly held in both their names. She indicated that she was making regular deposits into the account rather than sending money directly to her mother as Jo Ellen did. Nonetheless, Kate never wrote a check against that account, as she never could accept that the money was hers; however, Kay herself used the money from that account.

That summer Kay convinced herself she needed cosmetic surgery. As was her custom with all expenses, she began whining about the cost of the procedure and fretted at her need of extra funds to cover the costs. She had always been masterful at what the family termed the "poor me" syndrome and years earlier had earned from her family the sobriquet of "poor mouth-a-go-go." As a result of Kay's lamenting the necessity for the surgical procedure and her lack of money—as well as her emotional state, Kate suggested that Kay use the money in their "joint" account to pay for what she wanted.

Kay's sisters were aware of, but made no comment on, Kay's elective surgery, mainly because they never questioned one another's choices and all were kept busy with their own lives and families. Young Jesse entered first grade in Hershey where Nan and Joel had recently purchased a home and Nan began working for Penn State's Hershey Medical Center, following two years at Dickinson College in the Office of Development. Around the same time Jo Ellen began working part-time in her husband's business. Ken wanted her to more fully understand the daily operation of his firm, the unsaid reason being that his father had died at an early age (the age Ken was approaching). Judith was still taking doctoral courses, teaching, and directing individualized Commencement programs and the high school musicals.

In the summer of 1986 amid all the changes that were occurring in the family, a curious incident occurred when Kay made a two-day visit to Hummelstown where her mother was spending the summer. Following an afternoon of reminiscing and laughter in Kate's cottage, Judith returned to the main house, excusing herself from the family conversation to begin dinner. A short time later, Kay entered the house and began talking to Judith about how worried she was as to what would happen to her if Bob should die.

The conversation began on a melancholy note, a complete change from the laughter they had shared only a few minutes earlier. Kay spoke of the limited joint income she and Bob would have upon retirement, and that by herself, without his retirement income, she probably could not afford to support herself and would not have enough Social Security income for her living expenses. Then, without warning, Kay began to cry. Judith was at a loss as to how to react. They were not a family to readily express their emotions and Judith remembers later thinking that she had never seen any of her sisters cry as adults.

Through Kay's tears came an odd request, "If something happens to Bob, can I come live with you?" Judith was at first speechless. Kay continued, "With Bob gone, I won't have enough money to support myself and I won't have any place to go." Hearing both sadness and desperation in her sister's voice, Judith answered without hesitation, "Of course." She never questioned the cause of her sister's outburst, believing it had been an aberration or caused by unidentified stress. While she remained uncomfortable with what had happened, she did not share this incident with anyone until years later.

Despite subtle, but increased pressure from Kay to convince their mother to relocate permanently to Hummelstown, the three younger daughters continued in their reluctance to force such a discussion with their mother. They preferred to show consideration for her independence and not to influence any decision she might make. She was in good health, both physically and mentally; in fact, among themselves they would laugh and say that their mother was in better shape than they were. They all listened respectfully any time Kate wanted to talk about "someday," but none of them would even think to try to influence her choice as to where she preferred to spend her later years. All four sisters had previously expressed their satisfaction with their mother's current status to spend part of the year in Hummelstown, and all assumed that "when Mother is ready," she probably would make her permanent home in the cottage built for her use. Only much later, once they recognized that Kay's plan for their mother and Aunt Jessie had been carefully crafted far in advance, would they look back and understand that Kay had been using her sisters to persuade their mother to move to Hummelstown for Kay's own purposes.

It was also during this time that Kate disclosed to Judith, Jo Ellen, and Nan the contents of her holographic Will and her current desire to add a codicil. On October 28, 1986, Kate added this codicil to her Will:

> You all know that Nan has received my bank stock. As of this writing, I may sell my car if Shayne Edmunds's support of college from Aunt Jessie ceases. In reference to what was previously written, I would like to note that in 1980, convertibles were not in production; now that they are, my '66 Chevelle convertible is not worth more than my house in Curwensville.[57]

In early December Kate drove to Hummelstown for what had become an annual three to four month visit. An invitation had been extended to Jessie that someone from the family would make a trip to Curwensville to bring her down for the holiday or make arrangements for her to come by bus as she sometimes preferred.

On the 17th Kate wrote to her sister,

Dear Jana J.[58]

I'll reply promptly like you "done,"[59] got my three Christmas cards off today—Kathryn Kephart Smith [her lifelong friend], JoAnn [Kay's lifelong friend who also years ago had moved from Curwensville to southern California], *and Kay and Bob. It is quiet around here, too. I'll have Jesse on the 24th. Can't believe that is next week!*

You didn't mention coming down, so I gather you "ain't." Judith did say she'd send her car if the bus idea turns you off. Jo Ellen and her family will be leaving on their Christmas cruise on the 22nd; Janelle and Kendall have a fun time or did last year as there were quite a few passengers their ages.

If you haven't already sent the gloves back to Shayne, don't. I'll get them next month.

---

57 Codicil to Katherine Pifer Thompson's Will, June 8, 1988.

58 In typical fashion the sisters used fanciful names for each other, a trend begun when all were still children.

59 Another mark of their intra-family communication style was intentional grammatical errors.

The Story of Kate

We both told him not to spend anything on us; we don't need "nothing."

Nan's home is beginning to look real nice and cozy—guess I told you lots of work and fresh paint and her way with curtains. She made corduroy drapes for Jesse's room and used the ones she had in California in her room. I gave her one of my chairs since I got the Lazyboy!

I got a new prescription from Dr. Kaiser, a new medication he wants me to try. I feel OK most of the time—not any excess energy though. I've been avoiding crowds—back of my throat hurts a little sometimes. Dr. checked but didn't order X-rays. Probably it's my acid reflux. See you sooner or later?

Latoya Leah

Thus, the two remaining Pifer sisters continued their communication regardless of whether one or both were in Curwensville, a point worth noting in light of what Kay later alleged.

The following year Kay finalized the retirement plans for both herself and Bob who was quite willing for Kay to make all of their plans. Kay had always said that she and Bob got along so well because he acknowledged her superior planning skills; thus, there was rarely any disagreement. She definitely was the brain power in that union and later it would be shown that every step in her plan had been calculated, with allowance for change only if it would further benefit her design. Initially, her sisters had no inkling of Kay's schemes and how her machinations would impact their lives. Only later did they discover that Kay's plans were much more detailed, structured, and cunning than they had realized—and only later did they realize that these plans would affect the family in irrevocable ways.

Kay and Bob had for some years been exploring retirement sites for their "second home," with their primary residence planned for Curwensville. They earlier had invested in land in northern California that was to be developed and upon which they had hoped to install a mobile home that would serve as one of the two retirement homes they hoped to maintain. They also had invested in a restaurant specializing in chicken dishes in Laguna Beach. Both ventures failed. As a result Kay and Bob became desperate to recoup their losses, and, of course, to find a location in which they could afford to retire.

The high cost of living in southern California prohibited their remaining there in retirement even if its lifestyle had not left both of them jaded. They also considered the high desert where Nan and Joel had lived, but it was a bit too remote for Kay's liking, even though Bob found it ideal. Palm Springs area was another of their favorite sites, but, again, priced out of their reach. They looked at Florida as well, but didn't like its "retirement community" atmosphere and its "touristy" flavor. As could be noted in Kay's letters and conversations with her family, her anxiety increased with each disappointment.

After several trips to Alabama, Kay and Bob agreed the area along the Gulf would be ideal for their needs as it was close enough to Florida to enjoy the attractions there. It was near water in a gated community within their price range and boasted a lower cost of living than Florida offered. "Alabama, Here I Come" became Kay's theme song as she and Bob finalized the purchase of a mobile home in the summer of 1987. At that point their plan was to live six months in Alabama and six months in Curwensville. From all appearances, Kay had made it very clear to her mother that she and Bob would be making their "headquarters" at 410 Thompson Street.

Somewhat lighter in heart once their decision was finalized, Kay and Bob concentrated on selling their California home as well as most of its contents. In addition, they made many trips to Alabama, closing on their lot purchase and overseeing the installation of their new mobile home as well as selecting new furnishings. Kay loved decorating and relished creating a new look in the Alabama mobile. She regaled Kate with tales of her acquisitions. "We can buy all new for Alabama," she told her mother, "because I won't need to buy much for Curwensville. I'll be using most of the furniture you already have. This thoughtless comment was typical of Kay who excused her insensitivity by saying, "Well, at least I'm honest in saying what I believe." There was no disputing that.

Judith in particular did not like her sister's peremptory comments concerning their mother's possessions and advised her mother to tell Kay what items she wanted taken to Hummelstown. Worse than Kay's proprietary attitude about the house and furnishings, however, were her derogatory comments about the age and condition of the items in her mother's home as well as the house itself. More than once Judith came near to saying, "If it is so bad here, why are you moving back?" What she told her older sister, however, was that it was inappropriate to belittle their mother's property. In addition, Judith told her sister it was hurtful, and insensitive to make derisive comments about anyone's home, especially that of an older person who might not have the resources to purchase new items or who, in their mother's case, had made a comfortable, attractive home with very little income.

While it hurt the younger sisters to hear negative comments when they knew (as did Kay) their mother's limited financial circumstance, Kate for the most part didn't argue with Kay about using the furniture, whatever its condition. As she later said, "What would have been the use? I knew I wouldn't be taking all my furniture since the cottage was furnished and I believed I could choose later what pieces I wanted to bring down to Hummelstown."

What was not clear at that time in 1987 is when Kay and Bob would move to Curwensville permanently. According to Kate, "It was my understanding that Kay and Bob would keep most of their belongings in Alabama and would 'visit' Curwensville on a limited basis until I decided if and when I would make a permanent move to Hummelstown. I was not yet ready to make a final move just because they had decided to come back to town. I was perfectly content with the arrangement to spend part of my time in Curwensville and part of the year in Hummelstown. I was in no hurry to move permanently. Further, I was perfectly willing for Kay and Bob to share my home in Curwensville, figuring that most of the time they would be in Curwensville I would be in Hummelstown."

The entire situation of Kay's early retirement and imminent return to Curwensville had prompted more frequent conversations among all the sisters as to their mother's options. Kay's persistence in trying to influence Kate to permanently move to Hummelstown sooner than expected was the major topic of their discussion. Subsequently, when general conversation did not lead to the quick result she wanted, Kay began an intensive campaign to convince her sisters that the move would be best for everyone, and every conversation Kay held with her sisters was geared toward the persistent theme: "Get Mother to move."

Kay used every tactic she could think of—persuasion, argument, crying, and badgering. She presented herself as desperately needing their mother's home. "It isn't right for Bob and me to be so unsettled after all we've been through. Your fighting me about getting Mother to move is upsetting me. I am trying not to have another nervous breakdown, but this is driving me toward the edge." Her crying was convincing enough that Judith, Jo Ellen, and Nan began to observe their mother closely to see if Kay's anxiety was affecting Kate's health.

The other consideration concerning the decision to "move Mother" was Aunt Jessie. Nan and Judith were particularly uncomfortable uprooting Kate from her sister. While Kate's daughters could not fully understand the intricacies of the eighty-year relationship between the two remaining Pifer sisters, they did hold a sense of discomfort at the thought of their mother and aunt being separated after so many years of living next door to each other, each alone yet in many ways interdependent. Even though Nan didn't think Kate would miss Jessie as much as Jessie would miss her younger sister, both she and Judith worried that their mother would miss her own home. Judith also knew—perhaps even more that Kate did—that a move from one's home and hometown is traumatic for older people.

When Kate hesitated to leave her home as quickly as Kay had expected her to, Kay unnecessarily and unkindly reminded her mother, "You have another house you can go to in Hummelstown. Why do you think we all helped pay for it?" Kate later told Nan she felt her face redden at these words, as none of the other girls had ever spoken so bluntly of the assistance they had provided.

Kate continued to wrestle with the decision to leave her home, knowing there would be no returning, yet questioning herself if maybe she really was being selfish in not leaving if her daughter needed the house. Yet Kate simply wasn't ready to permanently uproot and at that time she wasn't even yet willing to tell the others that she had promised to give the house to Kay.

Kay's next tactical move in this uneven war of wills was to convince her sisters that this unresolved situation was affecting not only her own health but their mother's as well. She approached her sisters, each in turn, championing her case and refuting any points of resistance specific to each sister's concerns. As a result, collectively they agreed to broach the subject with their mother, but more for Kate's sake than for Kay's. They wanted to do what their mother wished for herself, but at the same time they were wondering if the uncertainty of making the decision was harder on her than simply making the break.

"We should let Mother decide what she wants to do," Jo Ellen said at the time. "It seemed so interfering," Nan would later say. And Judith's constant refrain was, "This has been Mother's home for most of her life and we cannot dictate this choice for her. There is no hurry for her to move to Hummelstown." On the other hand, they couldn't imagine that Kate would want to share her home in Curwensville with Kay and Bob and they could only hope that Kay would respect their mother's wishes and not intrude upon her to vacate her home until she was ready.

Finally, when Kay and Bob arrived in Curwensville in the fall, Bob went to live temporarily with his Aunt Ruth in Clearfield. Ruth, a widow, was fond of Bob and welcomed her nephew's company. Kay bunkered down at 410 Thompson Street, from which she spent a good deal of the time on the telephone with the mobile home park in Alabama and with her husband, repeating to Bob nearly every word of the conversation with various entities. The crash on Wall Street on October 19 (1987), at which time the market lost 22.6 percent of its value in the biggest fall on record to that date, added to Kay's fretfulness as she lamented, "Everything we invest in crashes!" This situation likely added to her sense of desperation to cover her losses as soon as possible and by any means.

In addition, Kay had taken on the task of planning her high school reunion for the following spring. All of this was handled by telephone, entailing many extended and loud conversations. Kate, not used to constant company and particularly the long, repetitious telephone conversations, became impatient to the point of annoyance. At the same time, Kay's irritation at her mother's constant presence was becoming more evident to everyone, particularly after the day Kay shouted at her mother to turn off the television which Kate had on low volume only to muffle the incessant telephone conversations. This incident led to sharper exchanges between mother and daughter, along with hurt feelings on both sides.

Throughout the next several weeks, Kay moved into phase two of what later would be exposed as a deliberate plan. Whenever she could create the opportunity, she would suggest to her mother, "You know, it might be a good idea for you to sell this property to me now for a dollar since I'm going to inherit it anyway. It would be easy to do." Offended by Kay's bluntness and indirect reference to her demise, Kate initially resisted. When Kay repeated the suggestion the following day, Kate asked her daughter, "Why should I do that? You sound like you can't wait till I die." Kay replied, "That's not so, and you know it. It just would make better sense to have the house in my name. That way there would be no question of my ownership. Besides, it would save inheritance taxes later." Kate said she would have to think about that. It wasn't that she didn't want her daughter to have the house; it just made everything so final.

Kay persisted. "You're going to Hummelstown to live anyhow, so why not sign it over? That way I'll pay the property taxes and all the expenses and you won't have to worry about it." Kate couldn't argue that point, but said, "It just doesn't feel right to sell it with Jessie next door. If I sell the house she might think I am abandoning her."

"Well, you will be!" said Kay. "But so what? If you are going to move, what difference does it make? Besides, I'll be right here if Jessie needs anything."

Kate wrestled with herself as to whether or not she should discuss this state of affairs with Jessie, but she simply didn't have the courage. She lived to regret this decision, for what Kate didn't know is that her daughter was not only trying to manipulate her, she was also laying groundwork on the other side of the double house, telling Jessie that Kate would soon be moving to Hummelstown, but that she, Kay, would look out for Jessie.

While telling her mother only that she and Bob would probably eventually purchase their own home in Curwensville, in reality Kay was making plans to purchase a mobile home near Irvin Park. When she told her mother that she had found a house she liked along the Susquehanna River, Kate was upset. "What do you mean, you found a place at the park? It was my understanding that you and Bob were going to live here until you were sure you wanted to make Curwensville your permanent home. You have hardly been in town two months; you are buying a house in Alabama, and now you tell me you are buying another one here?" Her voice revealed her disbelief and anger as she added, "You are putting me out of my own house so that you can buy a new one?"

This was not the response Kay had hoped for. "I wish you wouldn't say it that way," she said to her mother. "You promised me the house. What difference does it make if it is now or later? You certainly wouldn't expect that Bob and I would want to live in *this* house? All I need is the deed so I can sell the house. I can't sell the house without the deed. I don't want to live here. I want the money to buy something Bob and I like."

That being said, Kay continued to pressure her mother to move to Hummelstown. "It's for your own good. Why would you want to stay here and end up having to take care of Jessie? You don't even like her. And you'd be closer to most of your grandchildren in Hummelstown. I'll take care of whatever needs Jessie has and I will bring her down for visits with you." Unable to control her sarcasm, she added, "Or, if you are so worried about Jessie, maybe you want her to move into the cottage with you."

The next few weeks were fraught with apprehension and anxiety as Kate continued to prepare most of the meals for the two, and often three, of them with Bob joining them most evenings. As she later related to her other daughters, "I tried to be helpful because Kay was so stressed with her investment losses and the unexpected complications in settling their home in Alabama."

Kay, however, did not see her mother's efforts as being helpful. Rather, she viewed her very presence as a hindrance to her plans. Thus, Kay's interactions with her mother became brusque, clearly indicating her annoyance that Kate would not acquiesce to her demands. The displeasure soon turned into resentment of her mother's very presence in the house. Simply put, the sticking point was that Kate was not ready to give up her home to Kay for any other reason than for Kay and Bob to live there, while at the same time Kay was not about to have her plans thwarted, not now and not later.

Kay's persistence won out as she continued to bully her mother as well as her sisters. Judith, Jo Ellen, and Nan, concerned for their mother's health in this hostile impasse, agreed they would try to persuade their mother to leave her home in Curwensville. That is all it took, and within two weeks Kate reluctantly agreed to deed the house to Kay and remove herself to Hummelstown as soon as it could be arranged.

Holding the unsigned deed in her hand was still not enough for Kay. Once her mother consented to leave, Kay increased her demands for items of furniture and accessories from the house to move to her new place near the park. Adding to the injury, each time Kate balked at these demands for any one of her possessions, Kay lashed out, "Why not? You don't need it." Finally defeated, Kate arrived in Hummelstown the day before Thanksgiving, leaving her remaining possessions to be brought down at a later date.

In early December, with her mother safely out of the way and the glint of triumph in her eyes, Kay purchased the property she had found near Irvin Park along the Susquehanna River. She took the furniture she wanted from her mother's home, along with many accessories, including items Kate specifically had told her she could not have because they were gifts her other daughters had given her. Disregarding her mother's wishes, Kay took all of these articles—furniture and accessories, and placed them in her new mobile home on Trail's End, a prophetic name fitting for its newest residents.

Kay next began her move on Jessie, making comments to the effect that Kate had left Jessie to fend for herself. The remarks were at first subtle, just hints dropped now and then, to raise questions and plant doubts in Jessie's mind, such as "before long Mother's furniture, including the piano, will be moved to Hummelstown." She mentioned the piano in particular because in early December Kay had told Jessie, "I don't think that Mother will take the piano since there isn't space in the cottage for it. Besides, Judi already has a piano. Would you like to have it?" While this offer was made without Kate's knowledge, Jessie took it as truth because of Kay's recent visit to Hummelstown.

At the same time, Kate was reminding Judith that the piano was to come to Hummelstown because it had originally been bought for her and she was the only one of Kate's daughters who was a pianist. Judith, unaware of Kay's promise to Jessie, accepted her mother's desire for her to retain the piano and noted to Nan that for some reason it seemed very important to her mother that she take the piano. Unfortunately, and to Kate's complete surprise, once the piano was moved to Hummelstown it became an issue between her sister and her.

Kay also planted many other negative seeds in Jessie's mind, such as the following:

"You know Mother won't be coming back here to live ever again."

"Did Mother ever tell you why she moved out?"

"Don't be surprised if you don't hear much from her again."

"It was rather selfish of her to take the piano when she knew you wanted it."

"Don't worry. Even though your sister abandoned you, I won't."

By mid-December, a strained relationship had developed between Kay and her mother over Kate's possessions and her feelings of being "pushed out of my own house." After hearing more details from their mother, Nan and Judith also were convinced that Kay had truly forced their mother out of her own home and they regretted even their small part in this move. They further had reason to believe that Kay had at some point bullied their mother into agreeing to allow her to take her choice of the contents of that house. However, the stalemate stood: Kay remained adamant that her mother had told her she could have what she wanted and Kate was just as convinced that she had not.

In late December Kay and Bob came to Hummelstown for a two-day, post-Christmas visit during which several heated discussions were held among Kay, Judith, and Nan. Kay became emotional during most of these arguments, and her actions ranged from defensiveness to lashing out and having crying spells. Several times she became hysterical, making wild accusations against their mother.

Many of these allegations concerned the items belonging to Kate that Kay had taken for her mobile home. At first, Kay insisted that her mother had told her she could have the items she wanted. She then said that the items belonged to her for other reasons, such as their being hers in the first place and that she had only left them in the care of her mother when she first left for California in 1959. Later during the visit she changed her argument, stating the reason for taking the items was that her mother didn't need or want them. In other words, she used whatever defense might work against any specific charge.

Discussions and recriminations continued throughout the entire visit. Near the end of the visit, Kay and Kate had words in private. Kay left the cottage in anger and by the time she had made the short walk to the house, she was crying. As Judith was trying to calm her sister and to find out what was upsetting her, Nan arrived and Kay began crying anew, saying their mother had been mean to her. "After all I've done for her, Mother should not question my decisions. Why is she being so mean and why is everyone ganging up on me on something as stupid as old furniture? I hate her." Stunned, Judith and Nan attempted to explain to their sister that their mother felt that she had been forced out of her own home and robbed of her final possessions. Kay would hear none of it.

The Story of Kate

After Nan left, Judith, in trying to placate her sister, made some comments about an unhappy, but very minor, incident of their childhood that she never otherwise would ever have uttered. At the time she was trying to assure Kay that "everyone has some remembrances about discontentment in their lives," that many people sometime dislike their parents—without hating them, and that Kay was not alone in her feelings that life is not perfect for children at any age. However, Judith would later regret relating this story, when her sister cast it up to her and others out of context.

All of the sisters were to learn over the next several years that Kay had a skill in getting people to say things in confidence that she later twisted to her own advantage in creating a breach between and among family members. With Kay, there was no honoring of confidentiality.

For the next three months, Nan and Judith attempted to serve as peacemakers between Kay and their mother, trying to mend the broken relationship, but to no avail. Judith in particular, even though she could not condone the actions Kay had taken against her mother and aunt, tried to convince her mother that she should try to remember that Kay was still her daughter and that maybe Kay was acting this way because of her own admitted fear of another emotional breakdown. Nonetheless, because the safe return of the items Kay had taken from their mother's house had become almost an obsession with Kate, Judith continued to request—both in telephone conversations and in a letter—that her sister return the items that her mother particularly wanted.

Unfortunately, this only added to Kay's anger toward Kate and fueled her conviction that Nan and Judith were "taking Mother's side" against her. In a last desperate, but futile, attempt to assure that the items would eventually be retrieved from Kay, Kate added a second codicil to her 1980 Will, asking that Kay return the two items that were most important to Kate, items that were to be given to other family members at Kate's death. The codicil indicated that Kay could keep the remainder of Kate's possessions:

> To Kay:
>
> When you sell your mobile home located at Trail's End, Curwensville, PA, it is my wish for Nan to have the rose red chair—it was a gift from Nan and Jo Ellen to me. Also, I want Shayne or Jesse to have the cedar chest [an engagement gift from Kate's husband Bubby in 1926] when Bob decides he no longer needs it. All the other furniture I gave to you to help furnish your home in Curwensville is yours to dispose of as you wish.[60]

---

60 Codicil to Katherine Pifer Thompson's Will, June 8, 1988.

Even this last wish was ignored by Kay, both at that time and later at the occasion of her mother's death.

As the date for Kate's 80th birthday anniversary approached, an invitation was extended to Kay and Bob to join the family in the celebration during the weekend of February 14-15. A partial truce prevailed on Saturday the 14th. Sunday afternoon, however, the arguments resumed. Until that time family arguments had been an unheard of phenomenon in the family, and none of them, save Kay, were comfortable in this mode.

Judith, Jo Ellen, and Nan had hoped to avoid any confrontation on this particular occasion, but their optimism soon diminished. Even before they asked, Kay began defending herself concerning any decisions she had made or actions she had taken since returning to Curwensville and would not admit to even a possibility of misjudgment. She vehemently denied that she had forced their mother to leave her home or that she had taken any of the possessions that hadn't been offered to her.

Rather, as the discussion progressed, she told Nan and Judith (by then Jo Ellen had returned home) that she hated her mother because "She is mean, and Jessie has always been mean in a lot of ways and even Aunt Jean had a mean streak." Her voice rising, she added, "… and you know it. All the Pifer sisters were mean, with the possible exception of Aunt Josephine." Nan and Judith, stunned, made no reply. They could not imagine criticizing these aunts, all of whom had been kind to them and all of whom had taken them in when they needed a place to stay following their parents' separation.

As Kay continued to vent her anger at her sisters and to rationalize her own position in the quarrel with their mother, the atmosphere of discomfort increased during what should have been a celebratory week-end. Finally, she said, "You know, it is really too bad you two can't see things the way they are. You know I'm right. If you can't see the truth of what has happened, then you are all fools." At this point she became hysterical, then slumped into a faint. Bob rushed to her aid, shouting in rage at the others for the harm he said they were causing their sister. Shortly thereafter Kay and Bob left in anger, with Kay in tears and Bob infuriated. His parting words were "You don't know what you are doing. I never want to see any of you again."

In March Nan and Judith, along with their husbands, drove to Curwensville with a U-Haul trailer to transport their mother's remaining possessions from 410 Thompson Street to the cottage in Hummelstown. These belongings included a small kitchen table, a Heywood-Wakefield rattan chair (Kate had purchased this from Kay when she left for California in 1959), several lamps, a gate-leg table, two single straight-back painted chairs (one red, one white), a caned side chair, a whatnot shelf, two additional side chairs, a coffee table, another small side table, the piano that had been purchased in the early 1940s, and Aunt Josephine's prized mahogany bedroom suite Kate earlier had purchased at the sale of her sister's estate.

As they neared completion of the packing, Nan rapped on Jessie's back door. "I'm here! Come on in," Jessie called out. Nan went inside to tell Jessie the others would be over soon to visit before heading back to Hummelstown. Trying to overcome her somewhat uncomfortable feeling, Nan did her best to add a brightness to her voice, "I hope you'll join us at the shore this summer; one of us will come up to get you as usual to visit with Kak and then on to the shore." Jessie did not ask about her sister, so no one knows what might have been going through her mind. Later, Nan said, "If I had known what would happen to Jessie we would have packed her up and brought her back with us."

Two months later things remained strained between Kay and the other members of the family with no real communication having occurred since February. On May 20, 1988 Kate underwent an emergency appendectomy and was hospitalized for five days. Attention immediately was fully focused on Kate's health, as such a procedure was most unusual for a person of her age.

Jo Ellen came to Hummelstown during her mother's recovery but there was no word from Kay. Following even more discussions, the three daughters persuaded Kate to transfer ownership of the Thompson Street house to Kay simply to resolve the issue since owning the house had become an obsession with Kay and everyone was weary of the conflict.

In early June Kay called and asked her mother what she had decided about the deed to the Thompson Street property. Kate told her to mail it to her and she would sign it and have her signature notarized.[61, 62] This was accomplished quickly and ownership of the house was transferred. Unknown to the family, however, was the fact that Kay had been trying to persuade Jessie to buy the house from her once it came into her possession. Later, Kay bragged to her family that she had convinced her aunt to purchase the house. "I told her that it would be in her best interests to own both sides of the house so that she could control who would rent the side Mother had vacated."

---

61 Witnessed by Elmer Nisley and notarized by Mary E. Nisley, Notary Public.

62 The deed is dated June 8, 1988 and recorded July 15.

Jessie on her way to church in 1987

Later evidence shows that Kay had laid out a very plausible scenario for her aunt, convincing her that Kate had left without any personal consideration for Jessie. "OK, so what if I did tell Jessie that Mother left Curwensville without any thought as to Jessie's well-being?" Kay later admitted. "I just told her that she needed someone on her side here in Curwensville and that I would be here for her. I said to her, 'It is to your advantage to buy the property and I am offering it at a very fair price, since we are family. If someone else buys it, who knows what kind of people they might be or if someone buys it to rent, you could have some undesirable neighbors—loud and with a bunch of kids. If you buy the house I'll help you find suitable tenants and will take care of any tenant problems.'

"When Jessie hesitated, I made it very clear to her, 'I need the money from the house and if you won't buy it, then I'll just sell it to anyone who meets my price.' That took care of any argument."

Thus, on July 9, 1988, Jessie's eighty-third birthday and exactly one month and a day from the time Kate had sold the property to Kay for $1, Kay, in turn, sold the house to Jessie for $8,000. A week later, Kay bought a new Ford Bronco for her husband. When the other members of the family heard this, they were outraged, not only that Kay would "sell out" her mother for a car for Bob, but also that she had duped both her mother and her aunt, the first of many such incidents yet to come.

Kate's reports to Judith, Jo Ellen, and Nan concerning Jessie were generally positive. The arrangement for Kay to "look after" Jessie began to be feel more palatable, and the girls were inclined to relax their stance a bit since Kate believed all was well. Initially, Kay did make herself useful to Jessie and she had begun again to communicate with her mother, both by telephone and through letters.

For a period of time it was as though Kay's injury to her mother had never happened. Instead she began to constantly remind her mother (and, indirectly, her sisters) that she was helping Jessie, stopping to check on her, taking her an occasional meal, and running errands—the kinds of things one does for a friend or relative, and the things Nan and Judith were doing as a matter of course for their mother but without reporting every action.

In her letters and telephone calls Kay also mentioned in passing that she was helping Jessie straighten out her taxes. At the time this seemed reasonable, as Kay had once worked part-time for a tax preparer. In addition, Judith had been preparing Kate's tax returns since the mid-fifties when she had learned how to do this in her high school Problems of Democracy class, so helping either Jessie or Kate with taxes was viewed only as routine.

Soon after, Kay told her mother that Jessie's tax records were not in good order, although she used less kind terms in describing Jessie's financial affairs. "Her bank statements are a mess. She doesn't always fill in the amount in the check register, and I don't know how she keeps track of anything. Jessie tells me she checks her statement every month, but I doubt it. And she hasn't paid her taxes for years."

This was not so. Jessie, at best, was careless about details and in 1985, for example, she had sent payments on her taxes but had not returned the form with the payment. She then had written to the Internal Revenue Service in June 1986 inquiring about her tax payments; they responded, and the matter was settled.[63] However, Kay offered to take care of Jessie's financial affairs and during 1988 gained full access to her checkbook, bank statements, savings account information, and bank stock.

Throughout the next year Kay painted for her mother a picture of devotion to Jessie in providing the help her aunt needed. She also made it very clear that when she was not available, their cousin Don Bloom was readily available. Kay enumerated in detail the errands she ran for Jessie, making sure to add how grateful their aunt was for the assistance, and always adding comments such as, "None of you down there need to pretend to worry about Jessie. I'm taking care of everything." Ignoring the personal barb, the information that Jessie was being helped put Kate's mind at some ease.

Despite hearing Kay's account of the care she was providing for Jessie, her family became increasingly uncomfortable with the stories she took such delight in telling of their aunt's eccentricities. Kay appeared to enjoy making fun of Jessie, her clothes, and her living habits. "She seems to think that anything she wears is fine, just because she is Jessie. You should see some of the get-ups she wears. And she doesn't clean out her refrigerator. It is ready to walk. She puts coffee on in the morning and leaves the pot on all day. And she is always insisting that people come sit on the porch with her. People cross the street so they can avoid her." At every opportunity Kay criticized Jessie's housekeeping and lack of organization.

---

63 Letter to Jessie Mohney, June 12, 1986 from the Department of Revenue and five cancelled checks as proof of payment.

"Her house is a mess, with clothes in piles all over the bedrooms, and she often misses her hair appointment with Alliene."

Kate may have described her sister as "clatty," a term used by her own mother to describe someone who was not a good housekeeper—and surely Jessie had never been known for her dedication to housekeeping, but Kay began slipping in such terms as "incompetent." Kay's complaints about having to "take care of" Jessie increased over the next year, without acknowledgement that it was she herself who had created the situation, and, as would be shown, had carefully plotted it.

Kay's grumbling about Jessie's growing dependence upon her led her sisters to further conversation among themselves by phone, letter, and personal visits on the issue of "alternatives to helping Aunt Jessie" and how to determine the best course of action. Kay's only offered solution was to "get rid of the problem" and "put Jessie away." When asked what she meant by "putting Jessie away," her reply was, "There are places for old people. Put her in a home." When her sisters did not agree with her, Kay's retort was always the same, "Well, maybe you'd like to have her live with you!"

Not getting the kind of agreement she was seeking from her sisters, Kay again took matters into her own hands regarding a Will for Jessie. This goal had been on her mind for years and she had been trying to get her sisters to agree with her since the early 1970s. None of them knew if Jessie had a Will and, in retrospect, perhaps they were short-sighted in not directly asking their aunt. On the other hand, neither Kate nor her three younger daughters believed that it was any of their business. Kate's daughters had been brought up to respect others' privacy and to not ask rude questions regarding other people's finances. Only Kay believed she had the right to ask her aunt directly as to her Will, and had been doing that very thing for at least fifteen years.

Kay admitted that she had first asked Jessie about a Will years before on one of her trips home during the fall "to see the leaves changing," an annual pilgrimage she made. Kay and Bob were sitting on Jessie's front porch when Kay steered the conversation to the future and to what would become of the house where Jessie and all her sisters had spent their girlhood. Kay asked Jessie if she had her affairs in order and if she had ever drawn a Will. Initially Jessie ignored her niece's probing questions. Kay persisted, much to Jessie's annoyance. When Kay asked again what was to happen when Jessie was no longer living, Jessie's answer ended the discussion, "I don't want to think about that."

Later that same fall when Kay and Bob had visited Nan and her family in the high desert of California, Kay pointedly asked her sister, "Does Jessie have a Will?" Nan did not want to be drawn into such a discussion and she responded very simply to her sister, "I don't know. Why are you asking me? Why don't you just ask Aunt Jessie herself?" "I have asked her," Kay replied, "and she always says she doesn't want to talk about it." "Well, then, just leave it alone," Nan said.

But Kay would not be deterred. "You know she must have a checking or a savings account; and she owns bank stock, her half of the double house, and her car. She probably got some kind of life insurance from NARCO when Jack died. She has her teacher's pension and Social Security to live on with hardly any expenses. She doesn't buy anything but groceries. I'll bet she has a fairly substantial amount. What will happen to all that when she dies? You know the state will step right in and take everything if she doesn't have a Will. Why should we let that happen? Why shouldn't we get some of her money?"

Kay continued, including the two husbands in her next question, "Can't you just see something happening to Jessie and no one knowing she even had written a Will? Without a Will, the state will take over. We can't let that happen. Is that what you want?"

Nan never forgot the response she made to her sister's question, "It really isn't any of your business." And Kay's reply was seared in Nan's soul, "Then I'll make it my business. I will make sure she has a Will if I have to write it myself."

This earlier promise was now haunting Nan as she listened to her sister in 1990. Confidently triumphant, Kay shared with her sisters the brilliance and cleverness that she had employed to trick Jessie into writing a Will making her the sole beneficiary: "Jessie asked me to make an appointment for her with Cortez Bell[64] for her to have a Will drawn. I called the morning of December 26 (1989) and Mr. Bell was free to see her that afternoon. I picked Jessie up, but on the way to the appointment, Jessie changed her mind. She said she didn't need to talk to a lawyer, and wanted to go home. I turned the car around and took her back home. When we got there Jessie said she wanted me to write the Will for her, that she would tell me what to say. It was lucky I had my tape recorder with me."

In the eyes of many, December 26 seemed to be a very odd date for an attorney's appointment, or, for that matter, to draw a Will. While only speculation, it is likely that Kay had visited Jessie Christmas Day and again preyed on her susceptibility, making a point of telling her that of all her nieces and nephews only Kay came to

---

64 Among Jessie's papers of the mid-to late 1980s was a piece of paper with the name Cortez Bell and his telephone number in Jessie's own distinctive handwriting. She evidently had planned to call him herself. It would be helpful to know if this was for an initial appointment or to make changes in her Will.

visit on Christmas Day. (Kay seemed to have a predilection for conducting such transactions on holidays, a vulnerable time for those, like Jessie, elderly and living alone. The house had been sold to Jessie on her birthday and the Will decision made on Christmas.)

A summary of this taped Will transcript follows:

Kay:

I want the house to go ... to my sister or if she pre-deceases me, to my niece, Matilda Kay.

Jessie:

And now I want my car ... put that down... to go to ... ah, you can put Shayne Edmunds. Now, nothing, zero, next, that's the part I like, is to go to my nephew, Noel Hamilton.

Kay:

All money left... after taxes ...... are paid... I don't know what you want to do with it. Let's see. Let me read this over. The house located at 408 Thompson Street and all contents I want to go to my sister Katherine Pifer Thompson or if she predeceases me to my niece, Kay Thompson Walker. I also want my niece, Kay Thompson, to have my diamond rings. I want the car to go to Shayne Edmunds. All other relatives not mentioned (Laughter by both) ... are omitted intentionally. All money left after taxes and expenses are paid I want ... You're gonna have to put something down. Now, what do you think?

Jessie:

I don't know.

Kay:

Do you want this to be divided among?

Jessie:

I don't know. I haven't made up my mind yet.

Kay:

Well, you have to do it. Do you want me to do this, be the executor?

Jessie:

Yeah.

Kay:

(Indistinguishable) That's all you have to do. I think that's good. I don't know what to tell you here.

Jessie:

I don't know. Why don't you just say (or something like that) I want all money left after taxes

Kay:

and expenses are paid. O.K. If you have any money left over, I want, ah, Kay Thompson Walker,

Jessie:

Kay Thompson Walker.

Kay:

O.K.

Kay:

If that's what you want, that's all you have to say.

Jessie:

I hope so. I don't feel much like doing it.

Kay:

Well, it's just good to do. You know.

Jessie:

I know it is.

Kay:

You'll feel better about it.

Jessie:

Yeah.

Kay:

No one likes to think of themselves as mortal, but, well, everybody has to put something down, or the state will take everything, Jess. You don't want that.

Jessie:

No - - -

Kay:

Oh, no, of course you don't.

Jessie:

I sure don't.

Postscript added by Kay:

Jessie's wishes for her Will were relayed to me on December 26, 1989. I wrote down what she wanted, and dictated it back to her as she wrote it. I would like to point out that she did not want to leave her one remaining sister, Katherine, anything, for various reasons unknown to me, but I stated to her at the time I thought that Grandma Pifer would want her to at least leave the house and its contents to her. [This discussion doesn't appear to be on the tape. Evidently, there was discussion prior to the taping.] She agreed to this. I also asked her if she wanted to leave her diamonds to Shayne or Jesse Joel, but she said, "No, they would just give it to some girl." She definitely did not want Noel Hamilton to have anything of hers and did not want to leave anything to anyone else that she could think of, except she wanted Shayne to have the car. I tried to go along with what she wanted and not influence her in any way. That is why I tape-recorded it so it could be heard by anyone. Jessie and I went down to the Curwensville Bank. Gary Jewett read the Will and he witnessed the Will; also Marie witnessed it in the presence of Jessie signing it; it was then notarized.

Two days later, on December 28, 1989, Jessie's Curwensville State Bank checking account was changed from a single owner to joint ownership of Jessie and Kay. The amount in the checking account was $28,624.51. In addition, Jessie's 360 shares of bank stock were changed from single ownership to joint ownership.

And this was only the beginning....

Kate's Burden

In this last decade of the 20th Century and the ninth decade of life for the two surviving Pifer sisters, in what should have been a decade of dignity, instead became one of confusion, turmoil, and despair—and all of it unwarranted. Early in 1990 Kate was established in her cottage in Hummelstown while Jessie remained at 408 Thompson Street with renters living on the other side of the duplex at 410 Thompson Street.

What Kate herself didn't and couldn't possibly understand is the extent to which Kay went out of her way to talk to people in Curwensville, gathering allies for her final coup and carrying tales about how bad her Aunt Jessie was and how all other family members had washed their hands of the situation. Kay courted people at the bank, at the utilities offices, the drug store, the grocery store, and with Jessie's friends at the Presbyterian Church and the DAR, relating to anyone who would listen that her aunt was becoming demented and that she alone was left to care for her because, as she made sure to emphasize to all who would listen, "No one else (specifically Kate, Judi, Jo Ellen, and Nan) ever visits her."

During this winter of 1990, late in the season, Jessie began mentioning to her nephew Don that she believed Kay had been taking advantage of her, that Kay was "a thief who was stealing money." Don simply did not believe that Kay would steal from her aunt and, thus, he ignored Jessie's complaints. He did, however, report these accusations to Kay who brushed them off with, "Jessie must be even worse than I had thought. She is sounding like a crazy person."

During that spring Judi made three trips to Curwensville (then a six-hour round trip), the third being on June 10 when Kate accompanied her, expecting to visit Jessie. They went to Kay's home after which they planned to visit Jessie. Following a meeting with classmates, Judith stopped to pick up her mother only to find her visibly upset. She did not linger in escorting her mother to the car. Kate said, "It was hard seeing my things in that house, the things that I had asked Kay so many times to return to me."

Judi began driving in the direction of Jessie's home when her mother said, "Kay doesn't think I should see Jessie. She told me, 'You don't want to see her. It would upset you.'" Judi questioned her mother, "Are you sure you don't want to go?" "Yes," replied Kate. "Kay was so adamant in telling me 'You don't need to see her like this' that I'm too upset with everything. Let's just go home." Concerned with her mother's emotional state, Judi considered that maybe her mother really wasn't ready to see either Jessie or the house in which she had lived so many years.

Hard as it may be to believe, Kay used this instance of her mother's not visiting Jessie (that Kay herself had manipulated) against both her mother and sister when a week later she telephoned her mother to tell her that a neighbor of Jessie's had told her that it was all around town that "Jessie's sister was in town and didn't even stop to visit her." Kay told her mother that she was surprised at this information, and Judi and Kate were left trying to imagine who would have seen Kate, who would have known Kate had not been to see Jessie, and, more so, who in town would have cared what Kate did or did not do? Only three people knew that Kate was in Curwensville that day: Judi, her daughter Jeanie, and Kay, and only one of them had the motive and opportunity to poison the thoughts of the townspeople.

Kate and Judi later realized how naïve they had been and how easily they had been duped. As Kate said to Nan, "We just weren't accustomed to devious plots. It didn't occur to any of us that it was Kay herself who had told the neighbor of my visit to Curwensville. What she didn't tell the neighbor, however, is that it was Kay herself who told me my visiting Jessie would upset her. She wanted to discredit me and make it seem that no one except Kay cared about Jessie!"

More intense conversation took place between and among Kay, Kate, Judi, Nan, and sometimes Jo Ellen concerning the kinds of personal assistance that might be available for Jessie, if, indeed, she needed help. During these discussions it was agreed among them (although reluctantly by all except Kay) that "the rainy day" Jessie had so prudently planned for had, indeed, arrived and that they would try to honor her wishes. The one given in all of the dialogue among Kate and her girls was that Jessie wanted to remain in her own home.

Kate's daughters talked about nursing homes in the Hummelstown area, nursing homes in the Clearfield or Curwensville area, or providing arrangements for Jessie to remain in her own home with assistance. During one of Kay's visits Wally made a generous offer to install a mobile home for Jessie's use beside Kate's cottage. Following Kay's departure, Judi said to Nan, "I think we should notify Cortez Bell (Jessie's attorney)." That she did not call him came back to haunt her.

Kay, disgruntled that her sisters didn't agree with her, but seemingly resigned to their joint decision, returned to Curwensville and was to make arrangements for someone to assist Jessie. What was of a more pressing issue for Kay personally, however, was to meet with her attorney on November 5 to draw up an order of power of attorney. Kay's attorney never met with Jessie nor did ever he speak with her by telephone. All communication regarding Jessie was with Kay alone. Kay herself took the power of attorney document to Jessie to sign on July 6, 1990,[65] three days before Jessie's 85th birthday. On July 10th Kay presented the order to the Curwensville State Bank in preparation for transferring Jessie's assets to herself.

Kay then returned to Alabama, having arranged for Jessie's mail to be forwarded to her there. Thus the cards and packages that other family members sent to Jessie instead went to Kay who, in turn, told Jessie that no one else cared about her.

Between July and September of that year, Kay, as Power of Attorney, directly transferred virtually all of Jessie's assets to herself.

Kay further boasted to family members that the $10,000 she paid herself from Jessie's money was for "taking care" of Jessie. Kate reminded her daughter of the many years she herself had taken care of Jessie—during her nervous breakdowns, Jack's illness and death, Jessie's several illnesses, including a two-week period of various tests at the Hershey Medical Center when Jessie stayed with her in the cottage—and had never expected to be compensated, nor would she have accepted payment from Jessie. Thus, Kate asked her daughter, "How could you pay yourself for looking after Jessie when you had promised you would do so as a condition of

---

65 POA legal document, July 6, 1990.

my leaving Curwensville? How could you accept payment when I never did?" Kay's curt response was cutting, "Why would you? You don't need anything."

Also in October Kay asked her attorney to prepare a deed for the 408–410 Thompson Street property to be transferred to Kate from Kay, who had just transferred to herself all of Jessies's assets, which included ownership of 408–410 Thompson Street. The deed was signed on October 25, 1990,[66] but not recorded until November 6. The immediate net gain for Kay was the $8,000 (or more) Jessie paid her for the house on the first sale and the assurance that it would again be hers upon the death of Kate. Later, Kay's attorney admitted there was essentially intent to defraud (by his own client) regarding the inheritance tax. (See document "The Pifer Homestead.")

What Kay's three sisters did not know was that she had been making plans to deposit Jessie into the Curwensville Nursing Home. Fully confident that her plans would hold, she wrote to her mother on November 12, 1990, casually describing all she had done as if it were one of her many travel excursions. Even years later, the letter stands on its coldness and when Kate received this letter she stuck it in a drawer. She didn't know what to do. It was all too much for her to absorb or sort out.

The best Kate could do (Judith, Jo Ellen, and Nan did not know about the letter Kay had written to their mother) was to tell Kay she must discuss this information with Judi and that they needed to come to an understanding and agreement on whether or not Jessie should have home assistance or be placed in a nursing home. Kate wanted what was best for her sister, but as she didn't quite trust Kay's judgment and felt she herself couldn't make the determination for Jessie's care, she faced a dilemma.

There was also a lingering apprehension from an earlier conversation with Kay when she asked her daughter, "Well, what would you do with me if I were the one in Jessie's situation? I don't have the kind of savings and retirement that Jessie does." Kay's reply frightened her, "That's what County Homes are for."

(Within a year Jessie was placed in a nursing home by Kay, through machinations skillfully executed. In retrospect, even considering all we had tried to do to keep Jessie safe, we still wonder how this all happened.)

When her mother asked Kay how she could admit Jessie to a nursing home without cause, Kay replied, "The hearing gave Jessie the choice of Warren or Curwensville Nursing Home." This information, as it turned out, simply was not true. When Kate told Kay that Judi was upset because she knew nothing of this

---

66 Deed for 408-410 Thompson Street.

placement until after the fact, Kay replied, "That's the way I wanted it. Judi would not have agreed and I didn't want to deal with that." She continued to her mother, "If Judi and Nan are going to do anything about the Jessie situation, I want to know." Kate finished the conversation by saying to Judi, "I am not sure I want to know what you are going to do about this. Maybe it's better I don't know so that if Kay asks me if you're doing anything I can say I don't know."

(But despite our best—and many—efforts, nothing could be done without bringing a lawsuit. We were disheartened. Again, there are far too many details, turns, and twists to include the essential information in this profile of Katherine. Please see the latter chapters of *Jebbie: Vamp to Victim—the truth about Miss Pifer* for the details of trying to rescue Jessie and the ensuing lawsuits. Even more detail can be found in the records I have in my computer, in the file Jessie 1, Chapter 14: "In My End is My Beginning.")

To say relationships remained strained cannot begin to describe the stress this placed on Kate. Kay continued to send mixed messages regarding her feelings toward and relationship with her mother. Kay would speak to her sisters against their mother, then call her mother and hold a conversation as if no breach between them had occurred. Other times she would call her mother very late at night, crying and telling her she had a gun by her bed and then making remarks such as, "I have nothing to live for." She might follow that midnight call with a gift, such as a box of candy with a note describing its merits, then would end the note with statements such as, "It's too bad we can't enjoy our twilight years in peace. I never thought my family would betray me. Life is so short."[67]

To the latter, Kate responded, "If you feel you are in your twilight years, then I am surely on borrowed time. Of course we should all be living in peace and if you really want to make amends, let the healing begin with you. We will listen."[68] To that offer there was no response.

Following a Power of Attorney hearing in January 1992, Joe Errigo, classmate and lifelong friend, called Kate to say he was sorry he initially had believed Kay and to ask Kate to convey his apologies to Judi. "I will make this right, Kate," he assured her, "and will tell people in Curwensville the truth of what happened now that I know the real story. You can continue to hold your head high." When Joe told her that the Attorneys Ammerman had said criminal charges should be pressed against Kay, Kate answered, "No; I think we have had enough."

---

67   Letter from Kay to Kate, circa 1991-1992, undated.
68   Ibid.

The Story of Kate

Early the next year (1993), the stress of the family turmoil took its toll on Kate. She developed what was diagnosed as clinical depression. In fact, she told her daughters that she thought that was happening. They had noticed only that she was quieter than usual, but believed that was to be expected after all the family had been through. With treatment the depression lasted only a few weeks, but it did give the family reason to reflect on the effects the Jessie situation was having.

In the fall of 1993 following Jessie's death in June, Kay telephoned her mother on the anniversary of her husband Bob's death—despite the fact that Kay and Kate at this point were opponents in pending litigation on Jessie's Will—and kept her on the phone for three hours. During this conversation, Kate told Kay, "I want you to stop this disgraceful suit." Jo Ellen also tried to convince Kay to drop the Will contest, but Kay's response was that Jessie's money was hers. "I earned it," she claimed.

In January 1994 Kate continued to try to resolve the dispute with Kay, but she could not reason with her. This strained situation and Kay's persistence in the quarrel was very difficult for Kate. She wrote to her daughter, "I am making a last plea to you, to make peace with me, your mother. I simply do not understand your actions against me through your efforts to challenge Jessie's Will leaving her remaining estate to me. I was truly saddened for you when Bob succumbed to his illness. I was hurt when you chose not to tell me of his passing, but let me read it in the paper. It also hurt when you chose not to send me birthday or Mother's Day cards. …

"We all know how you took advantage of Jessie. Did you think we could walk away while you arranged to steal money from Jessie and in addition make yourself her beneficiary? You have all but destroyed your relationship with me and each sister, in turn, because of this deceit. You have become so hardened that you have lost all sense of decency and you are emotionally abusing me to the point that I am ill. …You must stop this aggression against me. If you don't, you will have to live with the fact that you made my few remaining years sad and painful." But Kay did not stop.

A month later, Kate again wrote to her oldest daughter, "What has happened to you? What have I done to be treated so shabbily? Some day when you have recovered and returned to reality, you will regret your vicious vendetta against your family and that regret will be hard to live with. You exceeded by far your power of attorney which was obtained by trickery. I wish you well and hope you find peace with yourself. I will never understand your actions, and now with great sorrow and many tears I say, "Goodbye."[69]

---

69 Letter from Kate to Kay, February 19, 1994.

Three weeks later, Kate's attorney wrote to Kay's attorney asking that Kay's persistent and distressing telephone calls to her mother be stopped.[70] Disturbed that Kay was continuing to call their mother, especially late at night, Judi wrote to Kay, "Why in the world would you ask Mother how she thought you performed when you were on the witness stand testifying against her?"[71] Judith found it bizarre that Kay would testify against her own mother in court and then telephone her asking, in essence, "How do you think I did?"

In July, Kay's attorney continued to insist the late night calls of Kay to her mother were friendly.[72] However, Kate did not welcome the calls and Jo Ellen, Nan, and Judith viewed these late night intrusions as inappropriate and alarming, particularly those that included a harangue as to the choice of burial site for their mother. Kay even admitted that her attorneys had advised her not to call her mother, but she did anyway, because "I do what I want to do."[73] Kate had her telephone number changed.

In January 1996, following a courtroom hearing, Mother stopped to speak to Kay, saying to her, "Aren't you ashamed?" Kay, who had been sitting, stood up to face her mother. "I haven't done anything," she replied. Following another brief exchange of accusations, Kay asked, "How are you?" Kate responded, "What do you think?" At this point Nan linked her arm in her mother's trying to lead her away, but Kate wasn't finished with what she later said would be the last words she would ever exchange with her daughter.

In brief, Kay had betrayed her own mother, her Aunt Jessie, and her three sisters, ruining the last days of Kate and Jessie whom she should have honored rather than destroyed. As typically happens in such cases, Jessie's savings that were intended for her "rainy day" were instead lost to litigation costs.

Kate's last years, while she was in good health, were nonetheless difficult. She wrote a number of notes on scraps of paper about Kay throughout the long saga of Jessie. Because recording these thoughts were important to her, they are being included here. As expected, the handwriting was difficult to read as it was written in anger and frustration, as well as difficult-to-accept truth:

✓ A vicious liar

✓ A sociopath

---

70 Draft of letter from Attorney Frank Zulli to Attorney Frank Clark, May 28, 1994.

71 Letter from the author to Kay, May 31, 1994.

72 Letter from Attorney Clark to Attorney Zulli, July 5, 1994.

73 Conversations between Kay and Kate as Kate relayed to Frank Zulli, July 12, 1994.

- ✓ A thief/manipulator and an embezzler
- ✓ It gives me no pleasure to say these true words. I could say more damaging things . . .
- ✓ Ammermans suggested to prosecute (Kay) and ashamed as we were and are, we couldn't. Sometimes we wish we had. Thievery and abuse of elderly.

In January 1998 we planned a reception in honor of Mother's ninetieth birthday on February 11 of that year. We mailed Save the Date invitations and were ready to send reminders at the end of January. In a mild protest, Mother told Nan that she didn't want to "be ninety" and eleven days shy of what would have been her ninetieth birthday, Mother slipped away from us. It was the saddest day of our lives with much second guessing and even more regret.

 OUR KATE

OUR KAKI

OUR MOTHER

from *My Kate*

Elizabeth Barrett Browning

She was as pretty as any woman I know
And all your best made of sunshine and snow
Drop to shade, melt to nought in the long-trodden ways,
While she's still remembered on warm and cold days.

– My Kate

It was her thinking of others made you think of her.
. . . her presence caused admiration abound,
as through the town
All eyes were on her as she walked around.

–My Kate

If you praised her as charming, some asked what you meant,
But the charm of her presence was felt when she went –
The weak and the gentle, the loud and the rude,
She took as she found them, and did them all good;
It always was so with her - see what you had
She has made our life better, through good and through bad.

– My Kate

The Legacy

Emily Dickinson

If I can stop one heart from breaking,

I shall not live in vain;

If I can ease one life the aching,

Or cool one pain,

Or help one fainting robin

Unto his nest again,

I shall not live in vain.

Grandmother

Linda Lee Elrod

Even though there are times when we can't be together, I always feel close to you.

It must be because I think of you often, and thoughts of you always make me feel good.

I may remember something you've said, or good advice you've given me.

Or maybe just some little joke we've shared, and it makes me realize just how very much you mean to me.

You add so much to my life that no one else could.

So. no matter how often we see each other, or how often we talk,

I want you to know that you always hold a very important place in my heart . . .

and I love you.

129

Our Kaki: Tributes from the Grandchildren

From the grandchildren –

Jeanie Rochelle Ball Jacobs:

When I think back of all the memories of Kaki, it's hard to believe she's gone. But she has left her spirit to live on in my heart. One of my fondest memories is her goulash. No one could make it quite like she could. I remember the countless times she took me on the long bus ride from Clearfield to Hummelstown and back so I could spend time with all my family. Even when I didn't feel good about myself, she had a way of making me feel better. I've always known her as Kaki, but I had to ask her once if she knew she was my grandmother, *just in case!* I remember being outside one day just watching the electric meter go around and around. I never heard her call my name. She was so upset with me, and scared, not because I didn't answer, but because she was so afraid that someone had abducted me.

She loved her sweets. She was like a kid in a candy store when I brought her candy and homemade goodies. She also loved her chicken nuggets from McDonald's.

Following is a poem that to me sums up what Kaki is:

What is a Grandmother?

A heart that can hear every unspoken need,
Wisdom to know when to quietly lead;
Hands that reach out, always helping and sharing,
A grandmother is caring.

Eyes that reflect every joy that you find.
Arms to encircle but never to bind.
A talent for making the most out of living.
A grandmother is giving.

A voice that can soothe or inspire or delight,
A smile that keeps shining when things don't go right.
An angel God sent us from Heaven above -
Kaki was caring and giving and love.

Shayne Scott Edmunds:

Where to start? The influence of ideas and character Kak contributed to all my days past and present are the things about her I value the most. My trip back East to visit when I was 8 years old, staying with Kak and Aunt Jessie, will always be one of my favorite memories of childhood. Many years later, Kak helped me take a trip back to California. Whenever there was a need, Kak was there with an answer or an idea or just some of the green stuff. Sometimes the things that are unplanned come back as wonderful memories, like the time I spent as a housemate with Kak a few years ago. Kak and I would share meals and talk about things like bicycling and my job as a waiter at the Hotel Hershey. I recently thought how sad it is that my brother Jesse will not have the opportunity to know Kak as he grows older. You have a different appreciation for people as you mature yourself. Kak had a way of making everyone feel like her favorite. I want to thank my Aunt Judi for providing Kak a nice place to live and because she was there, we all had more time with her.

I remember so many things. When I was younger, Kak would come to visit in Lucerne Valley, California. She used to sit in the sunroom and read. I have a funny story that Kak and I would still laugh about years later. The son of my dad's friend Jon Turner was visiting his father in the high desert. His name was Chris, and he wasn't the brightest bulb. Anyway, Chris was at our house playing and we decided to go into the house for some reason, entering through the sunroom and stopping to say "Hi" to Kak. Chris said to me, "Is that your old granny?" Kak and I paused for a moment and then we both laughed. We would still joke around from time to time about her being my "old granny."

I have fond memories of visiting Kak and Jessie in Curwensville as a teenager. Ross and I would hang out in Clearfield and watch all the "cruisers" roll around the block in their muscle cars. Ross would always complain about Aunt Jessie trying to hold his hand as they crossed a street (I had to throw that one in there). It just felt like a different world visiting in Curwensville, sleeping in Aunt Jessie's attic and walking over the moss-covered bricks in Kak's backyard. Hearing Kak call "yoo-hoo" from upstairs when I was looking for her. I remember pulling the convertible from the narrow garage and going shopping at Ames. I remember Aunt Jessie, Kak and I sitting on the porch where I was always forced to say "hi" to Ray across the street (mostly at Aunt Jessie's urging.)

132   Kak was a wonderful grandmother and a friend.

Thomas Ross Ball:

I remember my grandmother "Kaki" for

Childhood
... allowing me to put the top down on her convertible,

... picking me up from school and piano lessons,

... playing with empty refrigerator boxes at Aunt Jo Ellen's beach house, using them as forts,

... giving us money so we could go to Tastee-Freeze,

... telling me to "go and hide" when Wally was upset with me,

... taking all of us grandchildren to The Dam,

... watching Janelle, Ken, and me as we prepared for a musical performance.

High School
... always asking if I needed anything "extra,"

... crawling under her kitchen sink to help rid her house of mice (How she hated them!),

... special "snacks" she would make for me.

College and Adulthood
... saying how "good" I sounded while practicing in "The Studio," even though I disagreed with her assessment. She was my #2 fan, second only to my mother.

... The smiles and appreciation she had when I brought a small plant or flower to her for Mother's Day or Easter, commenting on how they were "... just lovely."

... Taking care of "poor, old Kip" in his last years, especially when she used an awful smelling "spray" to cover Kip's natural scent.

... the special updates that I gave her while visiting.

Our Kaki was a little over a week shy of her 90th birthday, yet still she left us all too soon.

Janelle Corinne Lorenz Wright:

Memories of Kaki by her granddaughter, Janelle

As children, Kendall and I complained about the agony of having to wait for my father to set up his "Super 8" Kodak home movie camera. My father taped anything and everything. As we matured, we realized that those home movies are among our family's most cherished possessions. One home movie was in the spring of 1973 when I was four years old. My father asked me what I was going to put in my suitcase when I went to the beach that summer. I flatly ignored my father's question to exclaim, "Kaki is coming to the beach!!!!"

I remember that each trip to the beach, Kaki would proclaim, "We're off!" Trips to Delaware from Bethesda (approximately 3 ½ hrs.) were quite fun once we reached the country roads. The object of the game and a source of amusement for Kendall and me was to find the most beautiful (usually Victorian) house for Kaki and the most run down, ugly, fire-ravaged barns for each other. Oh, weren't we awful?

Kendall and I also used to round up all of the toys that we decided we could live without and sell them to Kaki for a nickel, a dime, or a quarter. I still don't know what she ever did with those broken match box cars and plastic cereal box toys. Hmm....

Kaki was not only fun and games though. I do remember how carefully I ate after her lesson that "little bites look better, taste better, and last longer." I think I will use this one on my own children some day.

It is a complete mystery to Kendall, my mother, and me how in the world we gave Kaki the Lorenz family nickname of "Grandma Tippy Toes." On that note, Kaki was the only person whom I permitted to use a nickname for me. I was often referred to as "sister" and sometimes "Nellie." To add to my mother's description of Kaki as the *grande dame*, I began addressing my letter to Kaki, "Dear Baroness:"

Kaki never forgot a birthday or Christmas. I can't remember any of her Christmas or birthday gifts specifically; however, I am also quite sure that her gifts were not the toy of the moment that we saw on TV. They were special gifts chosen especially for us . . . toys that we did not know of . . . toys which became our favorites. I do remember that one birthday when I was old enough, she gave me an ivory heart pendant.

Sometimes, Kaki would bring us gifts from her travels. One time she brought me plastic and ceramic airline food dishes. She told me that she told the (nice) stewardess all about me and what a special and well-behaved young lady I was. According to her story, the stewardess insisted that Kaki take the plates and cup to me to play with. Those plastic plates were better than any porcelain tea set I ever received.

My final memory of Kaki is the night of my wedding. I really did not shed a tear the entire night, except the first moment that Aunt Nan brought Kaki into the church. I went up to greet her immediately, and Kaki said with exhaustion and relief on her face, "I made it." It took me several moments to regain my composure. Of course, I won't forget her whispering (not so softly I might add) to my mother during the wedding service, "Look at Jay look at her!" She did seem to delight in it. She told me later that night that I was the most beautiful bride that she had ever seen. Without missing a beat, I responded, "More beautiful than my mother?"

I am glad that I always told Kaki how much I loved and cherished her. I think that she really did know that all of us did love her so.

Kendall's First Grade "Favorite Person" Essay:

My Favorite Person

My Favorite Person is my grandmother
She likes me alot and she is
nice. She has get up and go.
She likes to travel. When my mother
goes out she is a baby siter.
She loves me.

Kendall Lorenz

E. Kendall Lorenz, Jr.

April 17, 1970 — January 3, 2013

From the very beginning there was a smile, first tentative, then wide and full of wonder, reflecting a delight in the world, with scrapes and scratches, running to his mother's arms. His mother worried, as all mothers do, through illnesses and bicycle mishaps, while he, smiling through all, continued his quest, first through the neighborhood on a bicycle, and later, over the waves on a surfboard.

Kendall loved the seashore and, as a child, spent all of his summers there with his family. As Leonard Cohen wrote, "There are some men who should have mountains to bear their names to time, as grave markers are not high enough." Kendall should have such a monument, a sea, the curl of a wave, as high as a mountain where one can be master of his own fate. I should like to name one of these elusive waves for him so it can forever herald his name.

Kendall was a free spirit, with the sunny shoreline and the big waves his domain. With that he had the courage in his life to walk to the beat of a different drummer, one we could not hear, but to the sirens' song that Kendall would answer. In heeding the call of the sirens, he, like Hercules, struggled against them, mostly in silence and always with dignity, later leaving us to mourn. Family endured through it all, with each taking a turn in his time of need. If love could have cured, he would still be with us.

In our time of sorrow, we remember the many joys of life he gave us so freely. His childhood nickname was "Deedle," first given to him by his sister Janelle who wanted to talk to him, but at 15 months, could not quite pronounce her brother's name.

Kendall's older cousin Jean, remembers "Deedle," or "Deedie," as a very happy and bright-eyed toddler with whom she spent countless hours at Bethany Beach when our family joined the Lorenzes. Cousin Jean wrote,

"I recall many stories of Ken's youth as told to me by our beloved grandmother, whom we called 'Kaki.' As Kendall grew to be a striking young man who captured the attention of many, he retained the gentleness and soft spokenness of his mother. My fondest memory of Kendall was seeing true delight and joy on young Teddy's face at our latest family reunion when his Uncle Kendall arrived. It was very clear that the mutual love between nephew and uncle was a very special bond that will never be broken."

Kendall's cousin Shayne, adds, "I always appreciated Kendall for his genuine warmth and the great smile. Conversation was always easy even though years would pass between our talks. You need not spend much time around Kendall to know he was on your side. My wife Grace fondly remembers Kendall making her feel like one of the gang the day of Tom's wedding. I think it may have been only the second time they met, but Kendall made her feel like an old friend while everyone bustled about getting ready for that day. He was the one you hoped would be seated at the same table as you at the wedding reception.

"Growing up in California I don't share all of the early beach memories of my East Coast cousins. I do, however, remember the stories of Kendall sharing his beach time with my brother Jesse and being a great friend and surfing mentor to him.

"I'm going to share Kendall's appreciation of cheetahs with my daughter Iris (at age seven a cheetah and big cat expert in her own right), and have her help with our donation to the Cheetah Fund."

The favorite recollection of Kendall's cousin Tom is of pastimes at the beach with a collection of large boxes—refrigerator boxes in size, as a child viewed them—with which Kendall, Janelle, and he built forts, camps, and one ill-fated boat that never left the shoreline.

And Cousin Jess, the youngest of the pack, idolized Kendall, following him everywhere he went, from the kitchen to the deck and from the boardwalk to the shoreline. Kendall was kind to young Jess, more than tolerating a little boy ten years his junior. Later, however, a minor restriction was imposed, when Kendall reached adolescence and had to sometimes leave his shadow Jess to go to the beach "where the girls were," but kindly reminding Jess that he would return to play.

The mothers and aunts of the clan, sisters Judith, Jo Ellen and Nan, close in age as are Shayne, Tom, Janelle, and Kendall, remember the many trips between Maryland and Pennsylvania, and that the children spent time with their grandmother and her sister who found many ways to entertain the brood. A favorite was the car rides in our mother's Chevrolet convertible, with Shayne in the driver's seat, the cousins filling the car, and the car itself securely in the driveway in a locked park position.

Trips to Irvin Park where they swam in the Susquehanna River just as their mothers had done a generation earlier, and excursions to the movies in the neighboring town were highlights of those weeks. To this day the boys fall into paroxysms of laughter recalling Aunt Jessie's packing cheese relish sandwiches for them; these were accepted politely, but taken next door to their grandmother who quietly covered for them.

The young never think of separation nor did the cousins ever consider which of them might be the first to leave this place. In seeing these cousins who have remained friends, I am reminded of these lines,

If I be the first of us to die,
Let grief not blacken long your sky.

Be bold yet modest in your grieving.
There is a change but not a leaving.

The moments shared, the mysteries explored,
The steady layering of friendship stored,

The things that made us laugh or weep or sing,
The joy of sunlit snow or first unfurling of the spring,
The wordless language of a glance each understood.

What they were, they are now.
What they had, they have now—
A conjoined, imperishable bond.

Now, when each pauses,
Reaching for the other's hand,
And finding none
Be still. Close your eyes. Breathe.

Listen for his footfall in your heart.
He walks within each of you.

As an adult Kendall was supportive of his family, tender and caring, always willing to help. This he learned early from his father Ken whom he observed as making friends wherever he went, as did Kendall. The son also learned generosity from the example his loving father lived.

Kendall's flashing smile brought a lift to all who knew him, his clients often viewing him as the bright spot in their day. A gentleman to the core, he had a genial affability marked by compassion. For Kendall, life was not an accumulation of material things; rather, he sought its spiritual connection. Fittingly, then, he leaves to us a legacy of friendship and love of all of God's family.

If John Masefield had surfed rather than sailed, his famous poem would have changed only slightly. I'll ask the listener to think surf board, rather than ship as we hear these words:

I must go down to the seas again, to the lonely sea and the sky,

And all I ask is a tall ship and a star to steer her by,

And the wheel's kick and the wind's song and the white sail's shaking,

And a grey mist on the sea's face, and a grey dawn breaking.

I must go down to the seas again, for the call of the running tide

Is a wild call and a clear call that may not be denied;

And all I ask is a windy day with the white clouds flying,

And the flung spray and the blown spume, and the sea-gulls crying.

I must go down to the seas again, to the vagrant gypsy life,

To the gull's way and the whale's way, where the wind's like a whetted knife;

And all I ask is a merry yarn from a laughing fellow-rover,

And quiet sleep and a sweet dream when the long trick's over.

Kendall now soars with the eagles and the seagulls, although something precious and irreplaceable has gone from our lives. May we be comforted knowing that "in his arms he'll take and shield thee; thou wilt find a solace there."

Good night, sweet prince, may flights of angels sing thee to thy rest.

Judith J. Witmer

References in order of use:

Leonard Cohen, "There Are Some Men"

Nicholas Evans, "Walk Within You"

John Masefield, "I Must Go Down to the Seas Again"

Joseph Scriven, "What a Friend We Have in Jesus"

Shakespeare's "Hamlet"

John and Matilda Pifer

Smith Sisters: Jessie, Lennie, **Matilda**, Rose and Ella

John Pifer
with his twin sister
Katherine Pifer

Matilda Adeline Smith Pifer

Mother of Katherine Shields Pifer

Grandmother of Matilda Kay, Judith Evelyn, Jo Ellen and Elizabeth Nan Thompson

Matilda and John Pifer

John Pifer with his brother Joseph

Pifer Sisters

Baby Jean, Jessie and Catherine

Josephine   Ruby

Jean, Catherine, Jessie, Ruby and Josephine

Jean, Kate and Jessie

Kate, Jessie, Josie and Jean

Jessie and Kate at Jo Ellen's Beach House

Kate and Jessie
in the '30s

Thompson Sisters

1953

Kay with Toddler Judith

Easter Sundays

Swimming at Pee Wee's Nest

On the Ferry to Atlantic City

Late '50s

Jo Ellen, Kate, Judith, and Nan

Early '60s

Judith, Jo Ellen and Nan

'70s

Kay, Jo Ellen, Kate, Nan, and Judith

Early '80s

Judith, Kay, Kate, Nan, and Jo Ellen

Late '80s

Jo Ellen, Judith, Kay, and Nan at Harpoon Hannah's

'90s

Kay, Judith, Nan, Jo Ellen and Kate – Hotel Hershey

Bethany Beach
Palm Springs
World's Fair
Arizona
QE 2
Europe
Hawaii
California

California

Holographic Will of Katherine P. Thompson

Sometime during this time (1986) Kate disclosed to Judith, Jo Ellen, and Nan the contents of her holographic Will and her current desire to add a codicil. By terms of her Will, Kay was to inherit the 410 Thompson Street property:

November 11, 1980

To Kay regarding my dwelling [home] located at 410 Thompson Street, Curwensville, PA. Kay has told me she would like to retire [live here], the deed is clear and is among my papers. Judith is to have the refusal of any pieces of furniture she has given me and the mahogany bedroom suite, she being the only one who would have it refinished as it is surely in need of it and is very expensive to have done, so, this to me seems fair. Judith knows I've helped some in making the guest house pleasant for myself and others and I've given her several items of some value. Jo Ellen will never need anything I could leave to her and being of a kind and giving nature, she will understand and be content with my decisions. I will try to get this rewritten and witnessed soon, but these are my wishes at this time.

My car ['66 Chevelle convertible] I've already promised to Shayne Edmunds…at the time [years ago] I didn't know it [the car] would really be worth more than the house I now live in. Judith should have the jardinière. The signed check may enable you, Judith, to obtain whatever money is in my checking account [never more than several hundred] [This last sentence did not appear when this holographic Will was typed and re-signed with a codicil in 1986.]

I may be writing more at a later date but for now this should be considered as my last will, I being sound in body and mind.

Katherine P. Thompson

On October 28, 1986, Kate added this codicil to her Will:

You all know that Nan has received my bank stock and has used it to help purchase the home she and her family now live in.[1] As of this writing, I may sell my car if Shayne Edmunds's support of college from Aunt Jessie ceases. In reference to what was previously written, I would like to note that in 1980, convertibles were not in production; now that they are, my '66 Chevelle convertible is not worth more than my house in Curwensville.

---

1 At Kay's behest Nan sold her the stock for $5,000

The Pifer Homestead

History of 408-410 Thompson Street

- Early 1900s: double house (408-410 Thompson Street) purchased by Matida Pifer.

- Early 1950s: 408 is willed to Jessie; 410 is willed to the other four Pifer daughters.

- Late 1950s: Kate needs a place to live and gains ownership of 410 through her three sisters signing off on their rights to it.

- 1980: Kate's Will provides 410 to Kay

- 1987: Kate moves to Hummelstown at Kay's behest.

- June 1988: Kate sells 410 to Kay for $1.

- July 1988: Kay sells 410 to Jessie for $8,000 and buys Bob a Ford Bronco.

- 1990: By virtue of her Power of Attorney for Jessie signed July 6, 1990, which transfers all of Jessie's assets, including ownership of 408–410 Thompson Street, to Kay herself, Kay gives ownership of 408–410 Thompson Street to Kate*, knowing the property will be hers (Kay's) again at her mother's death.

* This action by Kay was to hide assets for tax purposes.

Selling the Wall Property: Thompson Street

Excerpts from Letters Written by Kate to Judith

January 27, 1959

Joe Dague called me today. Said Glenn Thomson told him he didn't believe H.V. would object to selling the house and for me to come in Monday p.m. so maybe I'll get somewhere. Also Mr. Hoffman called me and said for us to set a price and let him know, so believe I'd better say $5,000 and come down if I have to.

February 12, 1959

Hoffman is putting an offer in writing to Dague, then Dague talks to Glenn who talks to H.V. to get an agreement this coming week. If no agreement, then force is next which is money wasted. Hoffman is anxious as he wants to cut across the lot to the next lot to put water line in.

Mid-February

Will be hearing about the house soon. Mr. Hoffman makes an offer probably of $4,000, then Glenn sees or talks to his client (H.V.) to see if he will accept or not (a time limit is set for his reply), then action whether or no; "no" means (it) costs each of us money. Mr. Hoffman has called Dague 2 times last week so he really wants it to move along. You see Dague has to have a definite sale and figure to offer for a amicable settlement, the opposite of amicable is, I forget, but is means force. So I believe I'll take my money and run; I wrote all this to someone, maybe it was Kay; hope I haven't repeated it to you.

April 26, 1959

Not much here to write about except I'm anxious for the first week of May—public sentiment is for H.V. – he must be quite sure of winning the case as he has obtained a loan and is paying me off this week. I must sign a paper which will release him from future support for myself and daughters (When did I get any?). He is probably afraid I'll try to get some of his $26,000 to which I am not entitled as I have already checked with 2 lawyers on that score. If I wait I might be able to get more but believe I will take the bird in the hand and pay off all bills.

> $1,200. – bank
>
> $ 75. – furnace
>
> $ 30. – washer
>
> $ 95. – paper hanger [Mr. Whitaker]
>
> $1,400. – down payment on car??

May 1959

Mr. Dague just called to tell me to be in his office at 9:15 tomorrow. I forgot—I'll owe him a fee. I said to him—be sure there are no trick clauses. Don't see how there could be. H. V. thinks he can sell the house for more than $4,000, but doesn't want me in on it—hence, the signature. I believe I'm lucky to get anything.

[Author's Note: Mr. Frank Hoffman, owner of the Sanitary Dairy, which abutted the Wall property at the rear, had indicated that he wanted the property in order to have an easement for a waterline. However, as it turned out, he was interested in expanding the dairy, and shortly after purchasing the property he razed the house and the garage in order to do just that.]

Favorite Family Recipes

Main Dishes

Kak's Kraut (copied from Kate's handwritten recipe)

- Pork roast or chops and Silver Floss sauerkraut.

- Bake meat until almost done at 350 degrees (35-40 minutes per pound).

- Place kraut in a separate pan and bring to a boil. Discard this water.

- Add fresh water—about ½ cup, depending upon the amount of drippings to be added (see below); pieces of apple; and 2-3 teaspoons of sugar (either brown or granulated white).

- Take meat from roasting pan.

- Cut or break it into smaller pieces and place the pieces on/in the kraut.

- Cook slowly for 45 minutes, adding some drippings from the meat pan for flavor.

Chili

- Begin with 1 can of tomatoes (large) and 1 can of Hunt's tomato sauce.

- Break up the pieces of tomato slowly and carefully by hand before heating.

- Add ½ teaspoon (or more to taste)of chili powder.

- Brown onions in cooking oil then add ground chuck. Brown the meat as well.

- Add the meat and onions to the mixture of tomatoes adding pieces of celery and celery leaves. (Remove the leaves later if they are large pieces.)

- Cook slowly one or more hours (longer time for larger amounts than the above ingredients).

- During the final 15-30 minutes, add one can of (rinsed) kidney beans.

Italian Goulash

Ingredients:

- 1 package of elbow macaroni
- Approx. 1 lb. ground beef
- Block of Sharp Cheddar Cheese (to be shredded) or buy 1 to 2 packages pre-shredded Sharp Cheddar Cheese
- 1 large can of tomatoes (whole tomatoes)
- Tomato sauce (Nan uses a large can of tomato sauce as the noodles tend to absorb the sauce.)
- Approximately half an onion (according to taste)
- Bacon - 1 lb. package

(Note: Additional cheese and crushed tomatoes can be added if desired.)

Process:

- Cook macaroni according to instructions on the package.
- Meanwhile cook bacon until extra crisp in fry pan (saving some uncooked bacon for placing on top of casserole before baking).
- Remove crispy bacon and save to make crumbled bacon bits.
- Brown ground beef with chopped onion in the bacon drippings.
- Shred cheddar cheese unless using the pre-shredded package.
- In a large mixing bowl, add tomatoes (carefully mash whole tomatoes so they are in pieces) and tomato sauce to the macaroni.
- Add the drained ground beef and onion.
- Add the sharp cheddar cheese.
- Add crumbled bacon.
- Mix altogether.
- Place in a greased casserole dish.
- Place saved strips of bacon over the casserole.
- Bake at 350 degrees for 30 to 40 minutes.

Potato Soup *(copied from Kate's handwritten recipe)*

- Dice celery and onion; grate carrot.

- Simmer with diced potato (several or more medium sized) in water to cover.

- When potatoes are soft, press with fork or spoon on the side of the pan to crush the potatoes.

- Add large piece of butter and 2 cups of milk.

- Add 1 can of celery soup, 1 can of potato soup, celery and onion salt.

- Add additional milk if the soup is too thick.

Sides

Green Molded Salad

- Prepare lime jello per instructions on the box.

- When jello is nearly set (not as firm as for regular jello), blend in a medium sized-container of cottage cheese in a large mixing bowl.

- Drain a can of crushed pineapple into a separate bowl and then mix in the drained pineapple to the cottage cheese mixture.

- Fold half of a regular-sized container of Cool Whip (it should be slightly thawed) into the mixture.

- Pour into a glass or ceramic pan and top with mandarin orange sections and halved walnuts.

- Chill before serving to allow the salad to "set."

Baked Corn

- 1 can crushed corn
- 1 can evaporated milk
- 1 heaping tablespoon of flour
- 1 tablespoon of granulated sugar
- 1 teaspoon of salt
- 2 eggs, separated

- Mix the corn, milk, flour, sugar, and salt in a mixing bowl.
- Beat the yellow of the 2 eggs and fold into the mixture.
- Beat the egg whites and fold in.
- Bake at 300 degrees for one hour.

Candy Recipes

Millionaire Fudge #1

Mix the following ingredients in a heavy 2-quart pan:

- 2 ¼ cups of granulated sugar
- ¼ cup of butter (softened works better)
- ¾ cup of evaporated milk
- Stir the mixture over medium heat until the sugar dissolves.
- Boil for five minutes, stirring constantly.
- Remove from heat.

Add:

- 5 oz. (miniature) marshmallows
- 1 cup of chocolate chips
- ½ cup of chopped walnuts

Stir until chocolate is dissolved. Pour into a buttered pan. Cool in refrigerator.

Millionaire Fudge #2 (first introduced around 1950)

- 2 large Hershey bars
- 2 packages of semi-sweet chocolate bits
- 1 pint of marshmallow cream
- 2 cups of chopped nuts

Mix the following ingredients in a heavy 2-quart pan. Bring to a slow boil then continue boiling for 7 minutes.

- 1 large can of evaporated milk
- 4 ½ cups of granulated sugar
- 1 teaspoon of butter

Pour this mixture over the above ingredients and thoroughly mix with a folding motion until the chocolate is dissolved. Pour into a buttered pan. Cool in refrigerator.

Old Fashioned Double-Decker Fudge

Chocolate fudge layer:

- Combine **3 cups of granulated sugar** and **4 heaping tablespoons of cocoa**; add **3 tablespoons light corn syrup** and **1 cup of evaporated milk.**

- Cook in heavy saucepan over medium heat until a small drop forms a soft ball in cold water (235 to 240 degrees F on a candy thermometer).

- Remove from heat and allow to cool to lukewarm (110 degrees) without stirring.

- Add **6 tablespoons of butter, 1 ½ teaspoons vanilla extract.**

- Beat by hand until fudge begins to thicken and lose its gloss. Add ½ cup walnuts if desired. Quickly pour into a lightly buttered glass baking dish (preferably oblong).

White fudge layer:

(same as chocolate fudge layer except **omit** the 4 heaping tablespoons of cocoa.)

- Combine **3 cups of granulated sugar, 3 tablespoons light corn syrup and 1 cup of evaporated milk.**

- Cook in heavy saucepan over medium heat until a small drop forms a soft ball in cold water (235 to 240 degrees F on a candy thermometer).

- Remove from heat and allow to cool to lukewarm (110 degrees) without stirring.

Add **6 tablespoons of butter, 1 ½ teaspoons vanilla extract.**

- Beat by hand until fudge begins to thicken and lose its gloss. Add ½ cup walnuts if desired.

- Quickly pour over "set" chocolate fudge. Cut into squares when cooled.

Penuche

- ♦ 1 ½ cups granulated sugar
- ♦ 1 cup of brown sugar
- ♦ 2 tablespoons of light corn syrup
- ♦ ⅓ cup of milk
- ♦ 2 tablespoons of butter or margarine
- ♦ 1 teaspoon of vanilla
- ♦ ½ cup of walnut or pecan pieces

Butter sides of heavy 2 quart saucepan. In it combine sugars, syrup, milk, and butter. Heat over medium heat, stirring constantly, until sugars dissolve and mixture comes to boiling. Cook to soft ball stage (238 degrees), stirring only if necessary.

Immediately remove from heat and cool to lukewarm (110 degrees). Do not stir. Add butter and vanilla and lightly stir it through. Beat vigorously until candy becomes very thick and starts to lose its gloss. Quickly stir in nuts and spread in buttered shallow pan. Score while warm; cut when firm.

Candy Easter Eggs

- ♦ 3 cups of sugar (remove 3 tablespoons and reserve)
- ♦ 1 cup of water
- ♦ 1 cup of white syrup
- ♦ 2 egg whites
- ♦ 2 large Hershey Bars (melted) for coating
- ♦ Boil ingredients until the mixture "crackles" and makes a firm ball in cold water. Beat two egg whites until stiff, then slowly add the reserved 3 tablespoons of sugar.
- ♦ Pour cooked syrup *slowly* into the egg whites, then beat constantly until the mixture is stiff enough to mold into egg shapes.
- ♦ Grease hands well and dip the eggs, coating them, into melted chocolate. (This can also be done with a slotted spoon.) Place on wax paper to cool.

Sea Foam Candy

- ◆   1 ¾ cups of light brown sugar
- ◆   ¾ cups of granulated sugar
- ◆   ¼ cup of light corn syrup
- ◆   ½ cup of water
- ◆   ¼ teaspoon of salt
- ◆   2 egg whites
- ◆   ¼ teaspoon of vanilla
- ◆   ½ cup of broken pecans (optional)
- ◆   Butter the sides of a heavy, 2-quart saucepan. In it combine sugars, corn syrup, salt, and ½ cup of water. Cook, stirring constantly, until sugars dissolve and the mixture comes to a boil. Cook to hard ball stage (260 degrees) without stirring. Remove immediately from heat.
- ◆   Immediately beat egg whites until stiff peaks form. Pour hot syrup in a thin stream over the beaten egg whites, beating constantly at a high speed on an electric mixer. Add vanilla.
- ◆   Continue beating until mixture forms soft peaks and begins to lose its gloss, about 10 minutes. Stir in nuts. Let stand about two minutes; drop by rounded teaspoons onto wax paper.

Divinity

- ◆   2 ½ cups of granulated sugar
- ◆   ½ cup of light corn syrup
- ◆   ½ cup of water
- ◆   ¼ teaspoon of salt
- ◆   2 egg whites
- ◆   1 teaspoon of vanilla
- ◆   In a 2-quart saucepan combine sugar, corn syrup, salt and water.
- ◆   Cook to hard ball stage (260 degrees), stirring only until sugar dissolves. Meanwhile, beat egg whites to stiff peaks. Gradually pour syrup over egg whites, beating at high speed on electric mixer. Add vanilla and beat until candy holds its shape – 4 to 5 minutes.
- ◆   Quickly drop from a teaspoon onto waxed paper. Makes about 40 pieces.

Bubby

Table of Contents

The Story of Howard

The Thompsons

Elizabeth Bailey Spencer

Elizabeth Bailey Spencer and Howard Jefferson Thompson
Wedding Day Photo

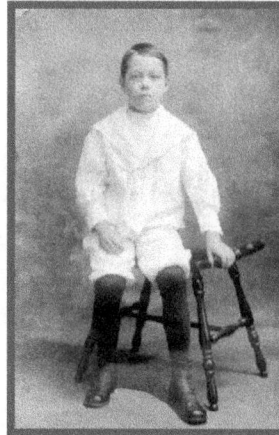

Howard Vincent Thompson

Mary Alice Thompson

H. J. Thompson on the beach
with son Philip Thompson

Howard Vincent Thompson
1922

Unknown, Mary Alice Thompson, Unknown, Katherine Pifer
Thompson, Elizabeth Spencer Thompson, Majorie Wall with
Philip Thompson to the front

Genealogy of Howard Vincent Thompson

Paternal Ancestors: Thompson

Beginning with Peter Thompson

Peter Thompson[1] (b. 1760) came to this country from Ireland and settled in that part of Bedford County which became Huntingdon County. Peter came to Pennsylvania prior to the Revolutionary War and it is believed that he served in the Fifth Pennsylvania Regiment in the Revolution.

Ignatius Thompson (1784-1861), son of Peter Thompson, and his family loaded their possessions on an ox cart and with a yoke of oxen made their journey through the wilderness to their new home, having had to cut their way through the woods in many instances. His wife, Mary, was a sister of Moses Norris who was the progenitor of the Norris families in the Curwensville area. Ignatius Thompson served as County Commissioner in 1832–34. Their family consisted of three sons and five daughters all who reached adulthood. Ignatius was a Catholic communicant whereas his wife was a Methodist. Their children are as follows:

> Nancy Ann, b. 1809, married Joseph Straw
>
> Mary, b. 1811, married Ross Reed
>
> John D., b. 1813; d. 1886; married Sara Hartsock in 1837
>
> James, b. 1815; d. 1887; married Catherine Hepburn in 1843
>
> Elizabeth, b. 1820, married Elisha Ardery
>
> Esther, n.d., married R.D. Cummings
>
> A fifth daughter never married
>
> Josiah, b. 1825; d. 1900; married Ann Eliza Wilson. They had 11 children.

James Thompson, second son of Ignatius, was born October 12, 1815. He helped his father clear their farm. He married Catherine Hepburn (born 1824), daughter of Wm. Hepburn, a native of Scotland, in 1843. (She had two brothers, John and Samuel C.)

James Thompson and Catherine Hepburn moved to Curwensville in 1848 where he engaged in the foundry business until his death in 1887. He was a Democrat and a Methodist. Catherine, born in 1824, lived to 101, dying in

---

1 Bolded names are direct line to Howard Vincent Thompson and the Thompson Sisters.

1925. She was known throughout the community as Aunt Katie. James and John D. Thompson built a foundry in 1850 on Thompson Street. Plows were their specialty. (John D. Thompson served as an Associate Judge, Justice of the Peace for ten years, and was one of the first commissioners of Clearfield County, serving in that capacity for three years.[2])

James and Catherine had the following ten children; three sons and seven daughters:

Francis Ignatius	June 1 or 2, 1846
William H.	February 14, 1848
Samantha	November 12, 1850
Mary	March 12, 1853
Josephine Blanche	June 1, 1855
Henrietta	November 7, 1856
Leonora	November 15, 1858
Frances	May 12, 1861
Nannie	November 17, 1862
Jack	April 9, 1865

Francis Ignatius, eldest son of James Thompson, assisted his father in the foundry. He also engaged in the lumber business to a large extent and served as Postmaster from 1887-1891. He was one of the leading Democrats during his life and served as Constable of Curwensville Borough for many years. He married Mary E. Bell (born 1850), daughter of David R. Bell of Greenwood Township. She died in 1892, aged 42 years. Francis Ignatius died in 1909, aged 63 years. Francis Ignatius and Mary Bell had four sons and two daughters:

Walter, twice married, no children

Howard Jefferson (born January 12, 1878; died January 3, 1968).
He married Elizabeth Bailey Spencer Thompson
(born September 14, 1880; died October 10, 1951)

Maude A., born June 1884; married Clinton Davidson

Fred, born 1887; married Belle R. Forcey

Francis I., Jr. born 1891; married Roxie M. Hess

A daughter who died in infancy

---

2   *The Guide to Historic Homes.*

All four sons (Walter, Howard, Fred and Francis) were said to be mechanically inclined. The three younger sons established the original Electric Plant in Curwensville and assisted with the Clearfield Plant, later branching out into new territory. They later sold their interests to the Penn Public Corporation and went into other businesses.

Howard Jefferson Thompson bought the water company in Curwensville in 1922; he had owned the electric company in Bellefonte before moving back to Curwensville and then purchased the one in Curwensville. Among many other businesses and enterprises, he was one of the founders of the Curwensville State Bank and its first president, serving in the office for ten years. He then founded Mid State Theatres. He also twice ran for State Senator.

Maternal Ancestors: Spencer

Joseph M. Spencer, son of Joseph Spencer, Sr., a leading member of the Quaker sect, of kindly disposition,[3] charitable, and an ideal citizen in every respect,[4] operated his father's grist mill in Bridgeport. He married Lydia Griest (whose father had a business) and were the parents of the following children:

> Lavinia (b. 1852; d. 1871)
> Vincent Uriah (b. May 14, 1854; d. January 12, 1950)
> Roland (b. 1856; d. 1928)
> Almina (b. January 12, 1859; lived past the age of 100)
> Amos (dates unknown)

Vincent Uriah Spencer lived in Bridgeport, which was at that time a busy commercial community of several hundred residents. Vincent worked on his father's farm which was one of the first homes in Bridgeport. When not working in his father's grist mill, he joined the work of hauling timber out of the woods to Anderson Creek. His brothers had a sawmill at Bridgeport and Vincent once rode one of the rafts as far as Jersey Shore. Also, during his lifetime he made three overland trips to the West Coast.

Vincent U. Spencer attended a college in Poughkeepsie, New York, and at the age of 19 began a career of more than 20 years of teaching. Like many other

---

3 Lavnia in her Diary mentions her father several times; a kindly man who tried to find remedies for her illness, including writing to a physician in another state. He also took her place teaching in her school when she was ill.

4 P. 275, *Genealogies*, Straw, 1931.

Vincent Uriah Spencer

persons of that era, he attended summer sessions of the Curwensville Academy, a type of Normal School where one took courses intended to prepare one to teach. His years of teaching included service in schools at Grampian, Chestnut Ridge, Locust Ridge, Bridgeport, and Pike Township. He later served as a school director in Pike Township and Curwensville Borough.

He then followed the mercantile business for a number of years, later becoming interested in developing and installing electrical units in the towns and villages in Centre and other counties.

The decline of Bridgeport as a commercial community with its woolen mills and other small industries began with the Johnstown Flood of 1889, when Anderson Creek went on a rampage and caused devastating damage to many homes and other buildings in the lowlands. (Beginning in 1937 Vincent Spencer made his home with his daughter and son-in-law, Mr. and Mrs. Howard J. Thompson.)

One of Vincent's two sisters, Almina Spencer, married Joseph J. Downing on May 10, 1883 and lived in Xenia, Ohio. A news clipping in 1959 announced:

Former Resident of Curwensville to be 100 on Monday

Almina Spencer Downing celebrated her 100th birthday in Xenia, Ohio in 1959. Born in Bridgeport on January 12, 1859, she was known by her family as "Minie." She is the sister of the late Vincent Uriah Spencer, who died on his sister's birthday on January 12, 1950 at age 95 years, six months. Mrs. Downing is also the great-aunt of Howard Vincent Thompson of Curwensville.

Vincent's brother Roland (mentioned in Lavinia's diary) died in 1928 at the age of 72. [Judith was given the diary of Lavinia, who died of consumption at age 20.]

Vincent married Mary Alice Bailey and they are the parents of two daughters:

Grace C. Spencer Wall (b. July 17, 1879)

Elizabeth Bailey Spencer (b. September 14, 1880)

Maternal Ancestors: Baileys

The Baileys were of English descent and immigrated to the Colonies before the Revolutionary War. They were Quakers and were likely influenced in coming to this country by William Penn who founded the colony of Pennsylvania. The first Bailey of record is **Daniel Bailey** (b. 1731) who married Ann Wakefield (b. 1731). They are the parents of **Caleb** (b. 1759).

The sire of the branch of this family is **Caleb Bailey, Sr.** who arrived in Pike Township before 1806 and purchased a large ract of land on the ridge above Curwensville and began to clear a farm. He married Elizabeth Harry (b. 1764) and their children are as follows:

Eliza (b 1787)	Charlotte (b. 1800)
Reuben (b. 1788)	Elizabeth (b. 1802)
Margaret (b 1791)	Titus Henry (b. 1804)
Ann (b. 1793)	Nathan (b. 1806)
Daniel, b. 1795	Jesse Kersey (b. 1808)
Caleb, Jr., b. 1797	

Daniel Bailey married Jane Passmore (b. 1797), daughter of Abram Passmore. He later purchased land in the Pleasant Grove district in Pike Township. The land was covered with a stand of pine timber. Later purchases expanded his land to four hundred acres. Their children include the following:

Maria (Mariah) (b. July 12, 1816)	Newton (b. February 7, 1827)
Isaac (b. March 17, 1818)	George (b. November 20, 1828)
Abraham (b. November 17, 1819)	Calvin, b. July 26, 1831
Mary Elizabeth (b. 1820)	Levi (b. June 6, 1833)
Joseph (b. March 5, 1823)	Harrison (b. July 17, 1835)
Ann (b. April 8, 1825)	Lewis (b. January 28, 1838)
Ruth (b. February 7, 1827)	Newton, b. April 16, 1841

Joseph Bailey, son of Daniel, married Elizabeth Boal of Centre County. They resided in Pike Township, near his father's homestead engaging in lumbering and farming. He also owned several hundred acres of land, including what is known as the Bailey Stone Quarry tract. H. J. Thompson later bought the Bailey land and the quarry. Their children include the following:

George (b. 1846)	James Dorsey (b. June, 1860)
Mary Alice (b. April 16, 1854)	Annie G. (b. January 27, 1863)
Martha Jane (b. June 13, 1858)	Charles (b. December 17, 1868)

(Mary) Alice Bailey (b. April 16, 1854), daughter of Joseph and Elizabeth, married Vincent U. Spencer (b. May 14, 1854; d. Jan. 12, 1950), son of Joseph and Lydia Spencer. Vincent was a former well known citizen of Pike Township, who was a leading member of the Quaker sect, of kindly disposition, charitable spirit and an ideal citizen in every respect.

Vincent U. Spencer followed the mercantile business for a number of years, later becoming interested in developing and installing electrical units in the towns and villages in Centre and other counties. (He also served as a school director and his signature appears on the diploma of Ruby Pifer.)

Vincent Spencer and Alice Bailey had two daughters:

Grace C. (b. July 17, 1879)

Elizabeth (b. September 14, 1880)

Grace C. Spencer married Charles M. Wall, son of Miles Wall of Curwensville. Charles was a member of the North American Refractories Company and is numbered among the substantial business men of this generation. Their family included the following:

Charles Cecil (b. June 21, 1903) married Marguerite Thorp of Philadelphia, 1929. (Cecil, the name by which he was known, was the Resident Director of Mount Vernon for 40 years. He authored *George Washington, Citizen-Soldier*. As children Kay and our cousin Bill Jackson visited there regularly.)[5]

Marjorie Alice (b. June 4, 1905)

Kenneth Spencer (b. February 12, 1908) married Mauvis Fury of Bellefonte, 1930

Russell Arthur (b. May 16, 1910)

Richard Vincent (b. September 26, 1912)

5   Charles Cecil Wall (June 21, 1903–May 1, 1995) was an American self-taught historian and preservationist, who spent 40 years as resident director of George Washington's estate at Mount Vernon on the banks of the Potomac River, where he endeavored to keep the home and its surroundings in much the same state that it existed when the First President resided there.

Elizabeth Bailey Spencer married Howard J. Thompson, son of Francis Ignatius Thompson and Mary Bell. Their family included the following:

> Howard Vincent (b. April 10, 1904; d. January 14, 1964)
> Mary Alice (b. November 21, 1905; d. April 19, 1998)
> Philip Bell (b. October 20, 1919; d. January 21, 2001)

Howard V. married Katherine Shields Pifer (although he always spelled her name with a "C"), daughter of John and Matilda Smith Pifer, on June 27, 1927.

> Matilda Kay, born November 1, 1930
> > Mavis Kim Brunetti, born September 2, 1952
>
> Judith Evelyn – March 9, 1937
> > Jean Rochelle Ball, born March 7, 1959
> > > Jordan Ashlee Jacobs, born April 17, 1986
> > > Jillian Rochelle Jacobs, born October 29, 1992
> >
> > Thomas Ross Ball, born April 23, 1968
> > > Emily Madison, born July 11, 2002
> > > Olivia Emerson, born June 25, 2005
>
> Jo Ellen, born November 6, 1938
> > Janelle Corinne Lorenz, born January 2, 1969
> > > Corinne Catherine, born May 29, 2001
> > > Theodore Piers, born September 30, 2002
> >
> > Kendall Eugene Lorenz, born April 17, 1970
>
> Elizabeth Nan, born August 19, 1942
> > Shayne Scott Edmunds, born December 9, 1965
> > > Aero Graham, born April 18, 2004
> > > Iris Isadora, born September 2, 2005
> >
> > Jesse Joel Edmunds, born November 6, 1979

Mary Alice married William Jackson and was widowed in WWII; married later to Bradford B. Crunk.

> William S. Jackson, born September 1934

Philip Bell married Eva Hart
> > Patricia
> > Mark Allen

There He Lies—A Remembrance

(written at the time his death was imminent)

As a youth he showed keenness of mind; he was a good student with much potential for mathematics. It is said that he was "good college material." However, his father, whose own mother had died when he was fourteen, was a self-made man who had had to struggle against poverty and who likely believed that his son should spend his time working in the business. The father sent the young man to a business school but became angry with him for coming home on week-ends except to work.

As a youngster and as a young man, he was well-known locally as a tennis champ. He loved the game—it was his one recreation and he played the game enthusiastically and to win. He strived for recognition, but his pleasure was cut short again by a disapproving father who thought playing tennis was a waste of time, even after his son had won several championships.

He married the girl across the street, a girl he loved, and his reason for wanting to come home so often from business school. Against his father's wishes the young man married his sweetheart.

He continued working for his father; in fact, he handled two jobs. During the day he worked as manager of the water company crew and in the evenings he managed the local movie theatre, also owned by his father and mother.

His hobby as an adult was the local Volunteer Fire Department. He attended all of the conventions, often as an official delegate. It was as a result of attending a convention that he lost the position with his father's water company. He had taken the water company truck to the convention; at the close of the three-day event he came home on the fire truck, having forgotten he had come in the company truck, which had been parked since his arrival.

For this, his father fired him from the company and disowned him, even though the truck was retrieved and returned undamaged. He then became manager of the Rex Theatre because of his mother, who, very likely, technically owned this particular theatre or, at least, was part owner of all of the family-owned theatres. His mother knew that her husband was much too severe with their son, while she always supported her son.

Howard served a number of years as the borough tax collector and near the end of his life was the owner and manager of Mid State Theatres and Laurel Theatres. By all indications he loved his children and always provided for them what he could when they were children. Highlights of the week were the weekly grocery shopping trip to the neighboring town and the Sunday afternoon family drives.

With four daughters and a large house to take care of, his wife was not too sympathetic towards his time spent at the Firemen's Hall. They began to drift apart when he started drinking and spending so much time away from home.

He was arrested several times on drunken driving charges; his wife, with the financial aid of his mother, always managed to get him out of these and other minor scrapes.

Like many men of his generation, he was too young for the First World War and too old to serve in the Second World War. As a substitute for enlisting, however, he took great pride in belonging to the Pennsylvania State Guard. He looked forward to the weekly drills and summer camp.

He was an active member of the Firemen's Drill Team which was well-known throughout the area and which won several state championships. When the drill team was dissolved, something went out of the spirit of this man.

Another event which left him heart-broken was the death of his mother. She had been his strength and comfort throughout his life. For many months during her illness and after her death he was inconsolable.

With this loss his drinking increased and with it his faith in himself. He became belligerent at home and less dependable on the job. Finally his wife and children left him, moving out of the family home.

Howard then lost his position as theatre manager. His father helped his wife financially in obtaining her divorce from him. This may appear to be a kindness on the part of Howard's father to Howard's wife and children, but Howard himself must have viewed it as just another slap in the face and another foothold taken away by his own father.

Although all lived in the same town, the children, at this point one married and three in school, seldom saw their father. He remarried and the gap was widened even further.

Howard continued in a pattern of drinking, although during the short time he held a bookkeeping job he had tapered off. He soon fell into ill health.

The past several years of his life Howard and his sister, Mary Alice, were engaged in a legal battle with their father concerning stock left to them by their mother. Their father had swindled them out of their rightful shares in the companies owned by him and Elizabeth, the mother of Howard and Mary Alice. The children (Howard and Mary Alice[1]) won their court case, then quarreled between themselves. Finally, the holdings were divided and Howard became the owner of several local theatres.

Even with this settlement, he was faced with his failures—failure with his father even though he had won two lawsuits against him; failure because he lost his family, including his wife, his daughters, and his sister; and, worst in his mind, failure in that he had lost his best friend with the death of his mother.

At this point[2], any victory over his father is hollow. Howard has been managing the theatres less than a year. His health finally has succumbed to the abuses to which he has subjected himself.

A sad, almost wasted life. At the early stages this was a life with potential, but one that was browbeaten and discouraged at every turn by an unloving, unforgiving father.

So now this life waits for the release of death. The two things he best loved are reflected in his last wish—that he be buried in his Fireman's dress uniform and that he be laid to rest beside his mother.

There he lies, waiting to find in death what he could not find in life: peace of self and soul.

---

1   Philip, their much younger brother, somewhat dependent upon his father, was not a part of this litigation.
2   January 1964.

Howard: A Life Narrative

In the Beginning

The story of Howard Vincent Thompson has its nearest roots in the life of his father, Howard Jefferson Thompson, and this man's direct forebears. Thus, we begin this narrative with an overview of Ignatius Thompson, paternal grandfather of Howard Vincent.

In 1890 the nascent Anderson Creek Electric Company had just been purchased by F. I. (Ignatius) "Nace" Thompson whose brother Jack operated the business. Soon after purchase, the owners were given permission to erect poles from which to string "electric lines." In 1892, in the midst of establishing his business, Nace lost his wife and the mother of his children, two under the age of 12. Walter and Howard were teenagers, young to take on the mantle of a business, but it was here that Nace's sons, Walter, Howard J.—and later Fred, and Francis (known as "Tucker")—learned the electric business—and a difficult life lesson.

The Anderson Creek Electric Company was poised for the world to come and, with the invention of the incandescent lamp providing a promising market, Nace sold the direct current plant to Wm. F. Patton who built a new alternating current plant. In turn the company was again sold and became known as the Curwensville Electric Light Company.[1]

Ignatius and his sons were well positioned in readiness for the new century, and Walter moved to Massachusetts where he managed a tanning company. Howard, Fred, and Francis went into other businesses in the area, including water, electricity, and movie theatres. Howard J. had earlier established the first electric and water companies in Bellefonte, moving in 1921 to Clearfield and later to Curwensville where he owned an electric company. Howard J. also entered the coal business and became the president of Cassidy Coal Company during the 1920s, purchased the Curwensville Water Company in 1922, and in 1924 founded the Curwensville State Bank and served as its first president, leading it through the Depression in the 1930s, re-opening after President Roosevelt had closed all banks. He also ran twice for a seat in the State Senate. Fred and Francis, like their older brothers, were electricians and never lacked for work; both then invested in the burgeoning movie industry.

---

1   *150th Anniversary*, p. 147.

Elizabeth Bailey Spencer

While Howard J. Thompson and his brothers were establishing various businesses, the Class of 1900 of Curwensville High School was more concerned with graduation than they were with science and inventions. They barely noticed that they were the largest class to be graduated to date with 12 members who included Alice Bilger, Sophie Bilger, John M. Carlisle, Goul Carrier, F. Vincent Kester, Day Kirk (whose brothers Bird and Harry and sister Alice had preceded him as alumni), Ella McClure, Wayne Robinson, Elizabeth Rue, Clyde Way, William Wright (who was to marry his classmate Sophie), and Elizabeth Bailey Spencer.

Elizabeth Spencer's father and grandfather both were businessmen and, as a result, Howard and Elizabeth attended the same social events. Both families approved of the match and a wedding of some social note occurred on June 17, 1903, when Elizabeth Bailey Spencer (daughter of Vincent Uriah Spencer and his wife, the former Alice Bailey) married Howard J. Thompson. As an engagement gift, Elizabeth's sister gave her a book, "Bridal Greetings," that contained not only the wedding service and pages on which to write the names of the bridal party and guests, but also held in its 148 gilt-tipped pages much advice for the newlyweds, ranging from the dangers of quarreling to how to handle domestic servants. It is in this book that the newspaper account of their wedding was found.

In the florid style of the day, the wedding announcement of Elizabeth and Howard reads thus:

"A very pretty home wedding took place at 7 o'clock[2] Wednesday morning, at the home of Mr. and Mrs. V. U. Spencer, Walnut Street, when their daughter, Elizabeth Bailey, was united in marriage to Howard Jefferson Thompson, of Clearfield.

The beautiful ring service of the Methodist Church was performed by the Rev. B. H. Mosser, in the parlor where the bride and groom stood under an arch made of fern and laurel. The bride was attended by her bridesmaid, Miss Alice Bilger, and the groom by his best man [and neighbor of the Spencers], R. K. Way. The bride wore a beautiful gown of chiffonette trimmed with silk medallions. The bridesmaid's gown was also of chiffonette. The groom and best man wore conventional black.

After a wedding trip to Philadelphia, Atlantic City, New York, and Washington, Mr. and Mrs. Thompson will make their home in Clearfield. The groom is superintendent of the Central Penn's Light and Power Co. He is an

---

2   This is not a typo, but as it appears in the news clipping.

energetic, thorough, up-to-date businessman and all who know him are his friends as his disposition demands it. He is unassuming and unpretentious and a general favorite among the old as well as the young people of Curwensville and Clearfield.

The bride is one of Curwensville's fairest young ladies, having lived here nearly all her life, and is endowed with many traits of heart and mind which have endeared her to many friends who have nothing but best wishes for a long and happy life. The bride received a large number of valuable presents of cut glass, China, silverware, and other useful articles, tokens of the esteem in which she is held by her many friends."[3]

The following year on April 10, 1904, Elizabeth gave birth to her first child, a son, Howard Vincent Thompson, named for both his father and maternal grandfather. Fewer than two years later, November 21, 1905, a daughter, Mary Alice (named in memory of Howard J.'s mother Mary [Bell] and in honor of Elizabeth's mother Alice [Bailey]), was born.

Childhood and Youth

The year 1903 saw the beginning of industries that would change life forever in every town in the civilized world. Prior to this date, the American automobile was viewed only as an imported toy, a plaything of the rich, even though in Paris, original home of the motor car, cars were driving horses off the Champs-Elysées. The major promoter of the burgeoning interest of Americans in automobiles was Henry Ford, who, with capital of $100,000, had established the Ford Motor Company by building a factory. Nonetheless, cars were not to be mass produced for many years. The first Model "T" Ford did not roll off the assembly line until 1908, but at $850 this automobile had no direct impact (except to draw a crowd and have a photograph taken) on the lives of most of those who lived in Curwensville.[4] By the end of the following year, however, two or three of the wealthier businessmen in the area were among the nearly 20,000 in the country who had ordered these automobiles. One of the first local automobile dealers in the region was an agency for the Overland Car which did a much brisker business by the early 1920s when the price of the Model T, then produced by a more efficient assembly line, dropped to $310.[5] Meanwhile, Mr. and Mrs. Howard J. Thompson, then living in Bellefonte, on September 24, 1920 "came home with a new Franklin."[6]

3   *The Curwensville Herald,* June 22, 1903.
4   Rickard, *Clearfield,* p. 86.
5   "Picture This," *Temple Review,* Winter 2002, p. 48.
6   Diary of Howard V. Thompson, September 24, 1920.

The Story of Howard

Also by 1920 there were three children in the Thompson household, Howard, Jr, his younger sister Mary Alice, and the family surprise, a baby boy fourteen years younger than his brother. The big brother, who worked far more hours a week than any sixteen-year-old of parents who could afford a Franklin should work, doted on his baby brother and mentions him frequently in the diary he kept:

- February 8, Sunday. Philip in high chair part of the time.
- March 23. Went to school. Took 4 pictures of the baby at noon.
- April 7. Baby got his 1st pair of shoes and stockings today.
- April 14. Getting some pictures of the baby at noon.
- Sunday, April 18. P. S. came up to my house to see Baby in evening.
- April 21. Went to school. Baby six months old yesterday.
- Sunday, May 9. Kept baby in evening.
- September 16. Mama & Papa & the baby came home tonight.
- September 21. Mama went away this evening for Middleburg with Philip. Sister went to pictures. I went to bed early.
- October 19. Republicans[7] had 3 speakers this morn. Bought Philip a comb for birthday.
- October 20. Got paid $4.20 total. Philip's Birthday.

Bubby (the nickname bestowed upon him by his sister when as a toddler she had difficulty pronouncing "Brother") had worked nearly every day for his father. His 1920 diary is filled with references to "collecting money" (payments to the electric company), reading meters (both before and after school as well as evenings and week-ends). He frequently missed school to work in his father's businesses, often traveling to nearby towns and villages and walking home, specifically from Unionville, which by calculations in the early 21st century is 8½ miles, from his home in Bellefonte. He kept records of his earnings (25 cents per hour) as well as all of the sports scores of Bellefonte High School and nearby Penn State College. His work also included installing meters and trimming street arcs. His interests give a glimpse of the life of a high school sophomore and junior with expected

---

7   A student group, forerunners of the mock presidential campaigns.

notations of walking his girlfriend home from church services Sunday evening, his family activities, along with comments such as the following:

- April 3, one week shy of his 16th birthday. Got my first suit of long trousers today. Got hat also.
- April 4, Easter Sunday. Had my new suit on. I like it.
- November 3. Papers say [Warren G.] Harding won.
- November 4. Big parade tomorrow nite for Harding.
- November 15. Wore long pants to school for first time.
- November 20. Bought a new suit on sale.
- November 21. Gave sister a dollar bill for birthday present.

It was also during this time that college football attained glory and stadiums began to dominate the campuses. Any college that fielded a football team could find itself with the beginnings of a sports industry because the "open" (out-of-doors with less monitoring of spectators) game of football attracted larger crowds than any other sports offerings. Once college administrators began to realize the potential of college football for added revenue and for recruiting students, they began to enhance their programs by erecting large stadiums with parking lots to accommodate the spectators and their cars.

Many high schools also began forming football teams in the early part of the century, and football became a national athletic sport in nearly all colleges and high schools. Curwensville High School fielded its first team in 1912, but as there was no yearbook annual until 1922, sports records are not readily available for this small town. However, the fact that a playing field was maintained in Curwensville, with its population of only 3,200, is evidence of community interest. This kind of support is reflective of many other American small towns whose citizenry came out in full force for the football games.

An entry in Howard's 1920 Diary cited above reveals the perils of football and the difficulty sometimes in fielding a complete team of eleven players. The diarist tells of a crucial player whose injury determined the entire season of Bellefonte High School in Pennsylvania: "The football season closed after three games because Edward Miller had his leg broken in practice."

Family Businesses

Howard J. (H. J.) Thompson, who already owned the water company and electric company in Bellefonte and had recently purchased the local water company, moved his family to Clearfield in 1921. After his son, Howard, Jr., was graduated from Clearfield High School in the spring of 1922, H.J. moved the family to a brick duplex in Curwensville where they took residence on Thompson Street across from the Pifer family. Mrs. Thompson, the former Elizabeth Spencer, was pleased to return to the hometown of her childhood and where she had been graduated with the Class of 1900.

Curwensville underwent a number of changes and a period of growth during the 1920s. In the summer of 1922, two years after his brothers Fred and Francis had purchased land upon which to build the Strand Theatre, H.J. purchased the Raftsman Water Company (Later in 1924 he would establish the Mid State Theatres, Inc., a chain of as many as 23 theatres in the mid-state area). He made repairs and improvements to the water company which encouraged customers to forego wells for "city water." Further expansion and modernization of the town continued in 1923 with the opening of Bonsall & Holton Chevrolet and Grande's public billiard room. Some townspeople thought Curwensville needed neither automobiles nor billiards; nonetheless, both establishments thrived and provided desired services to a growing population.

Friendship with Jessie Pifer

In the fall of 1922 Howard Junior was scheduled to attend Williamsport Business School, his sister Mary Alice was enrolled in the junior class of Curwensville High School, and baby brother Philip was home with his mother. Jessie Pifer, whose family lived in the house across from the Thompson's red-brick duplex, welcomed Mary Alice into her circle of friends, sensing from Mary Alice's fine clothing and Mr. Thompson's being a successful businessman that Mama would approve of their friendship. This provided Jessie with more credibility in leading her mother to believe she had found a set of friends with "quality." She was counting on this also to give her the latitude to have more freedom.

Golf and tennis, which at the turn of the century had been regarded by the public as effete games of the idle rich, became popular in the 1920s. Curwensville had been surprisingly quick to respond to the building of public tennis courts, and the young people found playing tennis an acceptable form of recreation—as well as a convenient way to spend time with friends and to make new friends.

Kate and Mary Alice (Howd's sister) strike a pose at the local tennis court with Howard and Howard's younger brother, Philip.

Because it was a relatively safe activity and one that attracted the youth in groups, parents generally were willing to agree to their growing children's requests to "go to the tennis courts." While Jessie was more interested in observing than playing (or pretended to be interested since there was no money for frivolities such as tennis racquets and cans of tennis balls), she joined her friends at the tennis court, laughing while she convincingly explained that she wasn't very good at hitting a tennis ball. The fellows scoffed at this excuse because in backyard badminton Jessie was considered a formidable competitor. She would never, however, admit that the family could not afford the equipment needed for tennis. Better, she thought, to simply say, "I'd rather just watch," and smile fetchingly.

Occasionally Howard V. Thompson would coax Jessie into borrowing a tennis racquet and playing tennis with him. While not romantically interested in Bubby, she was flattered to be asked, since he was an acknowledged stellar player who was to win (1) the Clearfield Tennis Association trophy in both 1923 and 1924 and (2) recognition in the county paper,

> "Howard Thompson Jr. continues to lead the Curwensville Tennis Association standings with nine victories and no defeats. The only other unbeaten netter is Leonard Kantar with a 5-0 record."[8]

Oddly, Bubby's father had discouraged his interest in sports or any other activity and had forbade him to play tennis. This situation piqued Jessie's interest.

Jessie found Howd—as she liked to call him—somewhat fascinating when she first had met him in the summer of 1922 because (1) he was new in town, (2) his younger sister would be entering the junior class in the fall and would be a classmate of Jessie's, and (3) his own father seemed to be so disapproving of

---

8   *Clearfield Progress,* circa 1924.

him. Jessie was curious as to whether Bubby had a bad reputation. She knew he had just been graduated from Clearfield High School and was working for his father's electric and water companies. While he told Jessie he would be going to Williamsport Business School that fall, he did not seem to be particularly pleased.

He later confided that he had desperately wanted to attend Pennsylvania State College. Many of his friends were commuting from Bellefonte (where he had grown up and attended school until 1921) and he had counted on joining them. For some reason, his father would not send him to a four-year college, a decision he never would understand since he had been a strong enough academic student, had worked for his father after school and summers since the age of 10, and had never been in any trouble. His father, however, was adamant. Howard Junior, as his mother called him, would attend Williamsport, a two-year school, where he was to board during the week and come home week-ends to work for his father.

Jessie's new friend Mary Alice, officially a junior, had earned enough credits to join the graduating class of 1923, but decided to remain at home for a year and take two additional courses with the class of which she had been a member. Jessie, Mary Alice, and Marjorie Wall (who was Jessie's long-standing pal as well as Mary Alice's cousin) became fast friends. All living on Thompson Street, it was easy for Jessie to ask permission to visit friends whose front porches could be kept in sight of Mama, even though Mama was reluctant to have Jessie—even at age 18 –cross the main street and travel a full block to reach the Wall residence (a large house many years later to become the residence of Howard Junior [Marjorie's cousin] and his wife [Jessie's sister]). And when Papa was home, he often told Jessie she could go only to Mary Alice's home, almost directly across from the Pifer house. Bubby would sometimes join his sister's friends, providing an opportunity for Jessie to know him better.

From time to time he would tell Jessie about Williamsport Business School. He excelled in his studies, but continued to pine for his lost friends who were attending Pennsylvania State College. Once in a while, when Mary Alice and Marjorie decided to walk the block to Marjorie's home, Jessie chose to remain behind to talk with Bubby, knowing that he would not talk about himself when his sister was present. Jessie did not find him appealing personally as a beau, but she did enjoy conversation with someone who, in her limited experience in life, embodied sophistication.

"I always wanted to be a Boy Scout," he began one evening when there were just the two of them. "Papa would never allow me to join. I used to cry alone in my room, especially on the days there were scouting activities and all of my friends were having fun learning things about camping." Jessie just listened, intrigued that someone whose family obviously was financially well-off would not be allowed to join the Boy Scouts. She understood that in families like hers there might not be money enough for scouting, but why would Mr. Thompson deny his son something he so strongly wanted to be a part of?

"I really don't know why Papa wouldn't allow," Bubby continued quietly, "except he thought I should be working. I have worked for Papa's businesses for as long as I can remember."

"Was it the cost, do you think?" Jessie asked, feeling sure that it was not. "No," said Bubby. "He just did not believe it was important. He wanted me to work. Maybe it's because he lost his mother and he had to work. I just don't know."

His eyes began to tear. Jessie placed her hand on his arms that he had crossed on his knees and he began to cry. "I even bought a Boy Scout uniform," he said as he composed himself. "I would wear it sometimes when Papa was out of town on business and there would be no danger of his seeing me. How I loved that uniform and what I would not have given to be a true Boy Scout."

Jessie said she was sorry and asked, "Were you on the football team or basketball or baseball teams at Bellefonte or Clearfield (recollecting that his sister Mary Alice had played high school basketball)?" Before she had finished her sentence she knew what the answer would be, but the words were out before she had a chance to think.

"No," said Bubby, even more softly than before. "And he doesn't like me playing tennis either. He thinks it is a waste of time."

"But you are so very good," Jessie exclaimed. "Does he know you won the county tennis tournaments?"

"He probably read about it in the paper, but, no, he hasn't said anything to me about it."

Marriage to Katherine Shields Pifer

Nothing romantic came of the friendship between Jessie and Bubby, as Jessie was interested in any number of young men and Bubby found another attraction in the Pifer household. In the pocket diary he meticulously kept are these words, written with his prized possession, a fountain pen[9] made of a Bakelite marbleized material, a gift from Papa Spencer, his maternal grandfather, Christmas 1919:

> "Catherine[10] S. Pifer, 411 Thompson Street, Curwensville, PA,
> Saturday, June 30, 1923."[11]

This marked his first "date"[12] with Jessie's younger sister Kate, and began a courtship and later a marriage that was to last for nearly thirty years.

Howard Jefferson Thompson didn't like his son coming home week-ends unless he came home only to work; he saw no reason that his son should waste time with a young woman even when Katherine was teaching during the school year and attending classes in the summers.

In stark contrast to the campus lifestyle enjoyed by her sister Jessie at Clarion Normal School, Katherine quietly returned to Altoona in the summer of 1926 to take her courses at Penn State's extension campus. Unfortunately, there are no available records of the courses she took as she was not one to save these reminders of days that were not as much fun for her as they were for the more social Jessie. Kate, the name most of her friends and family used, most of the time came home on the train on week-ends (to allow her sister Josephine with whom she was staying to enjoy the company of her husband [who traveled on business during the week]), much as she had the previous summer and she continued to see Bubby who wrote to her on a nearly daily basis.

Occasionally Bubby would finish his work early in Clearfield or stay in Williamsport from where he would take the very long way home through Altoona where he would visit Kate. One day he was able to finish checking the electric lines by noon; he hurried to Altoona where he and Kate spent the rest of the day and evening at Ivyside Amusement Park. There was a large swimming pool at the

---

9   Fountain pens were first introduced in 1908 and Bubby longed for one from the day, fascinated with the process, he had first watched his father fill his then-new pen with ink shortly after fountain pens had become popular. Bubby kept the pen until 1945 when he gave it to his second daughter, one also intrigued with writing instruments.

10   The spelling he always used for her name.

11   End page of 1920 Diary, Howard V. Thompson.

12   A term gaining popularity in the 1920s.

park, but as Kate didn't care much for swimming and, in fact, didn't care much for the water, she watched Bubby who was a good swimmer. By 4:00 or so they were ready to try some of the other activities at the park and Bubby won a trinket for his Kate at the shooting gallery.

Another memorable "date" was going to the movies at the Capitol Theatre. Bubby never stayed past eleven so that he would get home, he said, before his mother started worrying about him. In truth, it was his father who had set a curfew for his son, even at the age of twenty-two.

Wearing a peach silk pongee, dropped-waist dress for the occasion of her marriage, Kate had no regrets at not having a church wedding as she and Bubby stood in the office of the Justice of the Peace on an early evening in June 1927, with Kathryn and Mearle Smith serving as witnesses. The newlyweds took a wedding trip to the state capital at Harrisburg and to Gettysburg, with Kate never dreaming that a quarter of a century later she would be making several trips with Josephine to Gettysburg College, and fifty years following her wedding date she would be making her permanent home in the Harrisburg area.

Kate and Bubby set up housekeeping in a second floor apartment in a private home. They later moved to an apartment in the block-long retail business part of town where Kate began life as a "young married," going about town, shopping and doing errands. Kate found steady employment in Jimmy's Sweet Shoppe and also baby-sat the youngest child of her husband's Uncle Francis, the youngest of the entrepreneurial Thompson brothers. Thus, Kate began a lifelong friendship with Bill Thompson, a fair-haired, beautiful child who one day would live in New York City and Charleston as a well-known interior designer of period rooms, particularly those in the mansions owned by Richard Jenrette, a well-known financier and Bill's life partner.

Firemen's Drill Team[13]

In 1929 when the Rescue Hose and Ladder Company reformed its once splendid drill team, Howard found an interest that spoke to his heart. Participating in a drill team was reminiscent of both the Boy Scouts and the military and that likely was a strong pull.

The first Drill Team had been formed in 1892 and by 1898 was described in the *Lebanon Evening Report* newspaper as, "A noticeable feature is their uniform size.

---

13 Written 2009 by Tom & Sue Moore.

Their evolutions were intricate, and hard to beat, in single and double fine echelon, pivot, and extended order. The company of 28 men was loudly applauded. They were attired in dark green uniforms, silver buttons, white gloves, laced trimmings and peaked regulation caps." It operated until 1915 then went inactive until 1929 when a new team was formed.

This new Drill Team became one of the most widely acclaimed precision marching units in Pennsylvania and took many honors, including a state championship in 1942. The 1947-1950s teams were viewed as the best in the state. "In 1956 there was still a drill team which marched at the Clearfield County Fair but by May, 1957, since there was a failure to have a drill team, H. V. Thompson made a resolution to officially withdraw the drill team." There were several attempts to reorganize, the most recent in 1964, but there was not enough interest in a drill team to continue. Two uniforms, a red and a blue, are on rotating display in the social hall of the Fire Company.

As might be expected Kate spent many Saturdays alone, although she would not have expected or asked Howd to miss either a practice or a parade. She knew how important this was to her husband who finally could wear a uniform and be part of at least a quasi-military group. She occasionally went with him to nearby parades and particularly shared his excitement when the Curwensville Firemen's Drill Team, in its first year, took several first prizes and performed in exhibition with Barney Ferguson's Fife and Drum Corps at the Fourth of July celebration at Irvin Park.

In 1935 H. J. Thompson purchased the fire-destroyed Strand Theatre that had belonged to his brothers Fred and Francis. H. J. remodeled and renamed it the Rex Theatre.

After a ruinous winter and spring in 1936 (the year of the second historic Johnstown Flood), by fall the townspeople of Curwensville were ready for something good to happen. And it most definitely did in the form of everyone's favorite sport—high school football. The Curwensville Golden Tide, under Coach Regis A. McKnight, became the Western Pennsylvania Football Champions of 1936, defeating arch-rival Clearfield 58-0.[14] This squad of only 30 players (from a high school population of 300 and a town of 3,100) had won eleven games that fall. Excitement reigned throughout the immediate area, and traveling to Kingston, Pennsylvania for the state championship was the main topic of conversation in the town for the two weeks between winning the Western PA Championship and playing for the state championship. This event brought the town together in a frenzy of support for the players and the town itself. On December 5 a trainload of fans traveled to Kingston (a town of 21,000, seven times the size of Curwensville). Among the hundreds of passengers were Bubby, Jessie, and most of their friends. (Kate, at the time six months pregnant with her second child, decided it was better not to make the tiring trip.) Many who remembered the experience—the first time some had ever been that far from home—viewed the excursion as the highlight of Curwensville sports history. Not so curiously, perhaps, the yearbook account of the game never mentions that Kingston won.

---

14   This became part of a collection of the home goal post pieces begun by Howard, Jr. in the mid-30s.

The Story of Howard

Daughters

By 1938 Kate couldn't help but compare herself to her own mother who also had not expected to start a "second family" with the birth of Jessie a number of years after her two older daughters had been born. With a third child expected, Kate had surpassed her married sisters who had one, two, and two children respectively. And Kate was the only one with girls, all the more reason to think she was cut in the pattern of her own mother and her mother's mother. However, nearing age thirty-one Kate wasn't sure she would look forward to two more children. Howd loved all his girls and never once expressed a desire for a son, any more than Papa had to Mama when daughter after daughter arrived in the household.

As Howd and she entered the house with the third baby, he said to Kate, "If the babies keep coming, we shall have to find a larger house." Kate laughed and said to her husband, "Just remember that if Mama had stopped at three daughters, I wouldn't be here!" She was beaming as she reflected on her good fortune and healthy family, the only concern in her life the far-off rumblings of war.

On the morning of August 19, 1942 the fourth daughter in the family was born, making the family number just a little above the national average of 3.76 children per household.[15] Named Elizabeth Nan (Elizabeth for Howd's mother at his request), this child would use the name "Nan" just as Kay, named Matilda Kay for her maternal grandmother, was always known as "Kay." While Jo Ellen and

Judith and Jo Ellen with babysitter Ann Zwolski

Judith claim only hazy memories of the details, they distinctly remember seeing their baby sister before she was brought home from the hospital. She had been delivered, as had Judith and Jo Ellen, by Dr. H. A. Blair who, for the third time, told Kate, "You have the prettiest baby in the hospital."

---

15 http://hypertextbook.com/facts/2006/StaceyJohnson.shtml. Retrieved November 5, 2009.

190

WWII and the 1940s State Guard

In addition to the national Office of Civil Defense program, State Guard units (organized by most states prior to the war after the President had federalized the National Guard) were geared up to provide any assistance should there be an enemy attack. Members of the State Guard unit included draft-age men with deferments and men too young or too old (up to 65 years of age) for the draft. Among those many state guard volunteers from the community was Howard V. Thompson, at last fulfilling his lifelong desire to be part of a military unit. These groups met weekly to train and to plan for boosting civilian morale. To help keep the attention of the townspeople focused on the war effort, the guard sponsored dances held once a month in the armory located in the small town of Hyde City, four miles from Curwensville.

In summer 1944 Howard's Pennsylvania State Guard unit was sent to Indiantown Gap (a military facility not far from the state capital) for two weeks training. Jessie suggested to Kate that they visit him during the weekend his unit would be stationed there. Kate reluctantly consented to go after Jessie convinced her that such a short trip would be a welcome break and, as she said, "I need to use up my gas coupons." Margie Zwolski, Kate's reliable baby-sitter, agreed to stay with the children, so in July the two women headed southeast to the state capital. They arrived late Friday afternoon and took a room at the Harrisburger Hotel, close to the Capitol Building and twelve miles from the military training base.

Howard had hoped to have a pass for Friday night to join "the girls" in Harrisburg. However, they found a message waiting for them at their hotel that he would not be allowed off base until noon on Saturday. Jessie said, "Well, we'll just have to make the best of it," as she began to page through the hotel listing of restaurants. Following advice of the desk clerk, the sisters headed to the Warner. (Twenty-five years later, Kate recalled that evening, ". . . the Warner where Jess and I had such a good time."[16]) By dessert, Jessie had made friends with a group of young people at the next table who, in turn, introduced them to a table of Army officers from the Army War College in nearby Carlisle.

The following morning Jessie and Kate did some shopping, with a special stop at Troup's Music, the largest music emporium either of them had ever seen. At one o'clock they headed to the bus station to meet Howard and a friend he had brought to make a foursome. The sisters had made a bet with themselves that Bubby would ask them to drive to Gettysburg, 45 miles south, and when he framed the sentence, "Jess, why don't we all . . ." they broke out in a paroxysm

---

16   Letter from Kate to the author, November 23, 1966.

of laughter. When the men offered to take them to dinner at the Gettysburg Hotel, they accepted their fate and headed to the Civil War battlefield, with Howard reminding the others that he and Kate had honeymooned in Gettysburg seventeen years earlier.

Through the many hardships on the home front, those living in Curwensville were mainly affected by rising costs for the coal most families still used to heat their homes. Many whose heating systems had pipes only to the first floor, counting on a dispersal system through a ceiling vent to heat the second floor, vowed they would install new systems following the war. Howd and Kate, whose house had a diffusion system such as this, talked about moving to a larger home with a better heating system. Kate longed for a stoker that would automatically feed the coal to the furnace.

A House "In Town"

One day in December 1945 Howard came home early to tell his wife that the Charles Wall property had been placed on the market. It was a large house on lower Thompson Street, equidistant between the home of Kate's sister Josephine and the house in which Kate's parents and Jessie lived. Kate was familiar with the house and jumped at the chance to purchase it with help from Howard's mother, whose sister Grace's home it had been. Selling their Schofield Street house for approximately $4,000 (originally purchased for $3,500), Howard and Kate paid $6,000 for the Wall property with plans to move sometime in March.

This house the family moved to on the euphoniously named Thompson Street (likely so named when in 1850 James and John D. Thompson built their foundry in that location) had been a stunning property and still retained many of its original amenities. It was large, with an immense kitchen (Kate always added, "with seven doors") and a sizable walk-in pantry, a dining room with paned French doors to the generous foyer, a formal living room, and a sitting room on the first floor. The double staircase provided hours of entertainment, especially for children with creative imaginations. The front stairway was made of mahogany and was considered the "good" stairway with railings that received frequent dustings and polishing. The "back stairway" was enclosed and could be entered from the kitchen or the sitting room. The two stairways met on a shared landing where they took separate turns leading to the four bedrooms and a bathroom. Jo Ellen and Judith originally shared the largest bedroom, with Nan in the smallest room. This changed after a couple of years to give Judith more privacy, Mother realizing how important it was to her to have a room of her own.

The large dining room became Howard's office when he became Curwensville Borough's Tax Collector. He was diligent in this and we all got used to the occasional traffic when tax payers came to the house rather than the Borough Building where he had regular office hours. I don't recall if the dining room suite traveled with us from Schofield Street; the room certainly would have been large enough for—and probably did hold—the dining set as well as the office desk and several chairs. A child size roll-top desk was also housed there.

Kate and Howard each had a bedroom, and sixteen-year-old Kay was given the private suite on the third floor complete with its own small bathroom. She decorated the sloped ceiling of the room with a border of Vargas and Petty girl pin-ups, which the younger children found scandalous, although they didn't have the vocabulary or full understanding to voice the source of their discomfort.

Importantly, a capacious porch graced the front of the house with large, comfortable wicker furniture left by the Wall family, Howard's cousins from whom the property had been purchased. This became Kate's favorite place during the hot summers as, with its broad awnings, the porch was relatively cooler than the interior of the house and we all gathered there, with the children more likely to be sitting on the wide steps. No one had air-conditioning.

Scenes from Childhood—Judith's Personal Account

Porches and Playhouses

Beginning in the summer of 1942, the favorite pastime for Jo Ellen and me was "playing house" under the "back porch" of the house on Schofield Street. (The house actually had two side porches and we identified the one that opened into an interior anteroom as the front porch and the one that gave entrance to the kitchen as the back porch.) We would drag out dolls, doll clothes, the one doll bed we shared, and anything else we could use for furniture. We would make pretend food by adding water to sand or soil, taking an egg from the Frigidaire (which we thought was the term for any refrigerator) to try to bind the mixture so it would not split when it dried. Irises, both purple and the old-fashioned yellow, white, and brown variegated variety, grew in clumps in various areas in the yard and provided other ingredients and spots of color to our "cooking."

Even at ages four and five we could barely stand up under the back porch and we coveted the area under the much higher front porch. Hollyhocks and climbing flowers covered the trellis on this higher porch, making it even more appealing. That space, however, was declared off limits by our dad because he needed to use it for storage of the porch swing and odd sizes and shapes of lumber scraps. Once or twice he hesitated during his response to our plea, but there really was no other place for the items since the property did not contain a suitable garage.

During the winter or when it rained too heavily in the summer to go outside, we claimed underneath the dining room table as our playhouse where we could pretend that sofa pillows were doll beds that I topped with a satin quilted doll-size coverlet Evelyn Milligan had made for me. The dining table was large, and its placement allowed for us to play for hours and days on end, secluded in a corner of the room, without disturbing the household routine or impinging on other needed household space.

May 1945 was exciting to us not because of the impending victory in WWII, but because of a large chicken coop, constructed of brand new, scent-filled wood which was part of the lumber order our father had placed a year earlier at Sandri's Lumber Yard. The 8 by 12 foot finished chicken coop looked to us very much like a playhouse and that is just what our dad allowed us to use it for the entire summer. No more playing under the porches. Here was a real playhouse with room in which even an adult could stand. Mother said all the girls could share the space, but with Nan not yet three and Kay nearly fifteen, in actuality, the playhouse was completely owned by Jo Ellen and me. Bliss it was.

194

Scenes from Childhood

In March of 1946 when we moved to Thompson Street "in town" we discovered that the front area of the floor under the back porch was concreted halfway back (much better than the ground we had been used to in earlier "under-the-porch" playhouses). Further, it made an almost perfect playhouse because we could stand up in it. Why we didn't establish our playhouse area in the very large basement I don't recall. Perhaps under the porch just felt more personal One of our treasures was an old army cot—perfect we thought with the idea in mind of sleeping under the porch.

What I really had my eye on, however, was the brick two-car garage with its side door accessed from the yard. That space held an interior sink with running water as well as wonderful paned windows and cupboards. It was a perfect playhouse on days the car wasn't housed there which, unfortunately, was seldom.

The commodious basement level of the big house did, however, provide a large play area around a large, heavy oak table. It was ideal for such activities as working with clay ("real" potter's clay Jessie had ordered from the teachers' catalog of authentic artists' supplies) and chemistry "experiments," with chemicals in a marvelous red-wooden-cased "Junior Chemistry Set," a long-coveted gift the first Christmas in this house.

We also discovered a delightful hide-away in the storage area off the small third-floor bedroom suite. More than a crawl space, the inner part of the area that followed the perimeter of the house was large enough for a child to walk through it, although the house roof sloped to the edge, so that we had perhaps a four-five foot width of usable space and as far forward as we dared venture. An electric light illuminated enough area for us to use as a playhouse when it wasn't too hot or too cold, which was frequent since the area was not well insulated. We dragged pillows and cushions and whatever else we could fit in and had dreams of making the space more habitable, but didn't have the skill to make this area much more elaborate than multiple sleeping areas for the dolls and a pretend sofa of porch furniture cushions for us. While not as appropriate for a playhouse as it might have been, again we loved its seclusion.

We even began to set up a playhouse in one of the dressing rooms in the theatre. There was one room in particular that was accessible from the wings of the stage by way of a short set of stairs. While we carried in some doll furniture and contrived additional playhouse accoutrements, it didn't take us long to realize that it was a long trek from the Thompson Street house to the theatre when we already had space at home under the back porch and in the attic.

Both outdoor on-the-porch and indoor activities included cutting out paper dolls and coloring in coloring books, both scarce items during the war years. Jo Ellen and I usually shared a coloring book and had to negotiate which double page to color, Jo Ellen on the right and I, being predominately left handed, on the left. Typically one or the other of the facing pages was appealing, but rarely were both. (Was it my imagination or were the pictures on the right side of the open coloring book really more attractive? Since only ten percent of the population is left-handed, the part of me that analyzes marketing thinks so.)

Remembered favorites were a *Snow White* coloring book and *Gone With the Wind* paper dolls. Kay had a large collection of paper dolls, all stored neatly in a suit box, each set carefully packed separately with sheets of tissue paper between each layer. We younger sisters were thrilled when an invitation was extended to join her in playing with that coveted collection.

Another of our pastimes was "putting on shows," using the commodious kitchen as the theatre and the large pantry as the dressing room. Adult neighbors and friends humored us by attending the performances. Neighborhood children were pleased to serve as the audience and on occasion were also invited to perform.

Later, when we moved to the Wall property "in town" we took over the garage a time or two for shows as we loved its self-contained structure with its large space and window-paned side entry door. Nan remembers being excluded from one of the "acts" and running into the house to tell Mother of our unfair treatment of her.

Family Trips and Sunday Drives

We enjoyed the time with both parents and took everything for granted. During the summers we occasionally went "to the shore." At the time we didn't know any other shore than Atlantic City, so "the shore" was just a synonym for the beach and the boardwalk in New Jersey. And, of course, there were those dark, dank, dreadful cabins. I hated going to the shore.

We rarely rode the rides on the Steel Pier, being told to wait until the local Clearfield County Fair as the rides were less expensive there. We did, however, on several occasions sit in the "grandstand" at the end of the pier to watch the diving horse, which seemed quite daring for the rider, to say nothing of the safety of the horse. Most of us in the family didn't care for salt water taffy so little money was spent there. One year the highlight of "the shore" was taking the ferry across the water to Ocean City. The one photograph that remains of our shore vacations likely was taken by our dad. I was as disinterested in being there (not liking to be on or in any body of water) as my facial expression and posture indicate. I wanted to be home.

Another favorite destination of our dad was Niagara Falls. I was terrified by the falls, and suffered from a fear of heights, but we all made the best of it. Truly, we were not as grateful as we should have been despite our father's efforts to take us "on a vacation." Our Great Aunt Maude Davidson lived not far from the falls so it was a convenient visit all around. She was always so welcoming, even though I am sure it had to be an inconvenience for her to have three to five guests (Mother and Nan did not always go with us). Aunt Maude had to take on many responsibilities at the young age of eight after the death of their mother at age 42. (In retrospect it may be understandable that Howard Jefferson Thompson was so stoic, so harsh, and so unforgiving of the son who spent most of his life trying to please his father—and without success.)

My tendency to become car sick also likely contributed to my own reluctance to vacations by automobile, but I wish I had shown a little more enthusiasm for the efforts my dad made on our behalf. Occasionally we traveled within the region to visit state parks and some amusement areas such as Bland Park and Hecla Park. At a young age we learned, when asked where we wanted to visit a nearby park, to select Parker Dam or Black Moshannon Dam where there was swimming available. As I recall, when the entire family traveled together, our dad drove, mother sat in the front seat (unless the distance were such that I might be favored because of my car sickness) and Nan, Jo Ellen, and I sat in the back seat. No one ever mentioned that the space was crowded; when the weather was warm enough, we cranked open the windows as there was no air conditioning in our car.

Sunday afternoon family drives were frequent. We were not always aware of the destination, as more often than not, it was just "something to do"; perhaps it was just our dad taking us to give Mother a break. However, I do recall him either coaxing or wanting her to go along on some occasions. If we were lucky—and happening more often than not—we would stop at the Clearfield Dairy for an ice cream cone. To this day I long for their orange sherbet or the best chocolate chip ice cream ever.

Halloween

Halloween 1945 was filled with costumes suggestive of military victory, including various combinations of Uncle Sam and Japanese uniforms. As a third grader, I

197

had the courage to "go Halloweening" (the term "trick or treat" not being famliar to us) with a group of fourth graders who decided to knock on the door of Miss Thurston, the fourth/fifth grade teacher whom all students feared. Her reputation was one of sternness and, despite her slender build, she was, indeed, formidable. To have the temerity to visit a teacher one did not yet "have" was considered very risky by the neighborhood children. However, we did just that, and to our great surprise, Miss Thurston was able to guess the identity of every one of us.

The Halloween Party at school that year was the highlight of the season as children went home at noon and returned in costume. This required careful planning as our mother and another mother who lived on the other side of South Side decided they would "switch children" in that Jo Ellen and I went home at noon, changed into our costumes, and lay down in the back seat of the car. Mother drove us to the Boyce home where there were three daughters in grades 3, 4, and 5. She picked up Betty and Vera, the two younger ones, and took them with her to Schofield Street. All of the girls thought this an exceptional plan, as we were sure our friends, during the "guessing identity" activity of the afternoon would be sure to guess that the Boyce girls, arriving on foot from the direction of Schofield Street, were the Thompson sisters and vice versa. It was a great surprise to our classmates and a memorable day for those directly participating in the ruse.

Halloween parades were an annual staple, except when interrupted by the war, with most of the elementary school classrooms participating. The fall of 1946 again saw many of the school groups in crepe paper, with the Locust Street fourth grade in dresses made of crepe paper ruffles. Each girl in the class could chose a color and Mrs. Bloom would work out the pattern for the greatest effect as the group passed the judges. The night of the parade I led the class in my variegated, multi-colored pastel, densely ruffled dress created especially by Mrs. Buterbaugh. The other girls each had a color selected from this and the effect was appealing to the eye. The class won first prize.

Christmas

Christmas was special, although, like most children we took everything for granted, not realizing how hard our parents worked to distribute the gifts as equally as possible.

For Christmas 1942 our mother, no doubt like many others with more than one child, made an inventory of what toys might be recast that Christmas. She decided to paint some of Kay's toys—a small doll carriage and a wardrobe, and to have new doll clothes made for one of the dolls I no longer played with. Mother then used these items as gifts for Jo Ellen, feeling confident that her four-year-old would not recognize the old toys in new wrappings.

Whether Jo Ellen did or did not notice the refurbished toys was irrelevant, as both Kay and I clearly did and we complained about what we felt was unfair, not at all understanding our mother's plight.

By November 1943 another bleak holiday season loomed as nearly every American family had one of its members "away in the war." Christmas catalogues were restricted in number of pages allotted to them and many listed items were stamped with the words, "Sorry, not available." Thus, even those who had money found that many items could not be purchased. Parents became ever-increasingly creative in finding gifts for the children, as little ones struggled to understand that Santa could not produce items tagged "Unavailable." When one of a series of government Limitation and Conservation Orders prohibited the use of traditional toy materials such as steel, tin, rubber and lead, manufacturers substituted cardboard and wooden toys.

Even in the midst of the terribleness of war, however, parents wanted children to look forward to Christmas. In 1944 the holiday fell on Monday which we found to be an interminably long time from Friday's early dismissal from school. Like most families, we had our traditions, one of which was that the week-end before Christmas Daddy would take us to select a Christmas tree. There were a few years when only Jo Ellen and I would be with our dad, likely the period before Nan was old enough and Kay—twelve years older than Nan the youngest—was more interested in other things, would troop out to the land surrounding the water company reservoir belonging to our paternal grandfather to claim the perfect tree.

More often than not the tree we selected—perfect size and shape in the woods—was found to be crooked and too tall for the house, but that in no way detracted from the adventure of selecting it. The most fun for us was decorating the tree after our dad had strung the lights. There were no replacement bulbs to be had during these years, so if a string of lights went out (at that time when one bulb went bad, the entire set was affected), that area of the tree remained unlit.

Christmas 1946 brought me a child's electric sewing machine as well as Aunt Mary Alice's gift of a Madam Alexander doll. Princess Margaret, aka "Peggy," became one of the best-dressed dolls in town when during the next summer I learned the rudiments of sewing in 4-H Club and made a wardrobe full of doll clothes, all of which Peggy and I still have.

This Christmas, like every Christmas, was marked by the special care Mary Alice always took in selecting gifts for us. She always chose something we girls would not have ever thought to ask for and the boxes containing those gifts reflected a compendium of the finest stores: Best and Company, Marshall Field, Neiman-Marcus—wherever Mary Alice had traveled each particular year. Without her realizing it, she was familiarizing her nieces with the grand stores and fine merchandise and was setting a standard of good taste from Philadelphia and New York City to Chicago and San Antonio.

The Christmas morning ritual in many families, including ours, began with the oldest child leading the procession down the staircase. Our stairs opened directly into a large hall where the Christmas tree stood, with all its lights shining (our father having already made a trip an hour earlier to add coal to the furnace and to connect the tree lights). Mother followed, carrying the youngest child, and my father walked with the next youngest down the stairs, holding her hand. We will especially remember the Christmas that Santa left personal cards addressed to each of us!

Visiting relatives on Christmas Eve and Christmas Day were traditions that remained unbroken.

Outdoor Winter Activities

Winters were cold in the mountainous region of Curwensville from November through March, and usually there was a lot of snow, allowing for great sledding. The older girls took turns pulling Baby Nan on a sled on sunny afternoons, sometimes "the whole way up" to the tannery and back. We all loved to go sled riding (the term used rather than "go sledding") after school and into the evening. The evenings were the most fun as very few cars interfered with sled riding on Schofield Street (more because of the gasoline rationing than the street being blocked off).

Children from all the nearby streets gathered on Schofield Street because of the slope and length of its two long blocks. The slope was just right for younger children and their older siblings ordered to "mind" them, because a sled would speed the whole way to the bottom (if not side-railed in a gutter), yet the incline was not too steep for short legs to pull the sled back to the top. A block over, near the elementary school, was what seemed like an almost vertical hill (approximately a 45° slope), nearly too inclined for the children to pull their sleds up. Of course, parents forbad the youngsters to sled ride there. The older kids—teenagers—

loved it. Aside from its severe gradient the street was relatively safe because *no* cars would or could navigate it in the snow.

Upper Schofield Street also afforded a wonderful declivity, even though the danger of crossing the main thoroughfare of Susquehanna Avenue was a deterrent from sledding from the very top of Schofield Street. The children all dreamed of what a ride that would have been and suspected that the "big kids" took rides there late into the night.

However, the best part of an evening's sled riding was coming home and finding the wonderful aroma of baked potatoes being kept warm for hungry sledders. No baked potato before or since has matched that flavor and to this day baked potatoes are what evoke their memories to me of security, warmth, and love.

Another winter activity that attracted both adults and children was ice-skating on the pond between the town dump and the tannery. Perhaps "pond" was too generous a term. "Swamp" might have been more accurate, as there were no definite borders between the frozen water and the shoots of sumac and other striplings. Bramble bushes and other scrub growth, some overgrown, made the area frightening at night for young children, but provided hidden "nooks" for couples looking for a spot of privacy. Of course, there were no restrooms and if one had a need, that person just had to go home (to protective parents who often did not allow offspring to return).

Other Events

It was ice skating at this pond that Kay's natural grace was first noticed. Even at the young age of twelve she had developed a style that had first shown itself in dancing school, but the poise came with skating. While she had long given up on piano lessons and did not have a strong singing voice, she could move like no one else in town. Ice skating, roller skating, tap-dancing, and any kind of social dancing—she could perfect the steps with very little practice. In ballroom dancing she could follow any lead. She had her mother's style, but with much more confidence, some would even say chutzpa. Others said her outspokenness reminded them more of Jessie. Like her aunt, Kay developed a unique style that would seek no quarter or approval. Her manner of dress, vocabulary (particularly her apt nicknames and terms for people and situations), and her general insouciance would more and more suggest Aunt Jessie's personality, but, as was later noted, with disregard for others.

Scenes from Childhood

We younger sisters viewed Kay as sophisticated and we accepted, as children do, that as the oldest, she held special privileges. On Schofield Street prior to 1949 she had her own large bedroom, one that had been remodeled for her, complete with new hardwood flooring, a vanity table, and its own closet (the only room with such). Even though her bedroom was off-limits to her younger sisters, Kay would make up bedtime stories that engaged us girls on the few occasions that we shared a bed. One particular way she used to signal it was time to stop talking and go to sleep was an imaginary conversation in which Kay would say, "Ho Hum, Harry" to which the little sister so favored would reply, "Ho Hum, George." This would then be followed by, "Good night, Harry," and "Good night, George." and "Ho Hum, Good night." All in all, Kay spent a good deal of time with her young siblings, taking them with her when she palled around with her own friends, and creating many games and interesting pastimes to entertain her young sisters.

As children we were in awe of our dad in uniform, be it the State Guard Unit during World War II or the Firemen's Drill Team with their bright red jackets, white trousers, and shiny black leather puttees. Jo Ellen and I liked to fasten these for our dad. We also would sit on his boots once he was fully dressed in uniform and ready to leave. Jo Ellen and I would pretend we didn't want him to leave and he, in turn, would go along with the play-acting, straining and saying he couldn't lift his feet because of our weight.

1948 marked the year of the blue two-wheeled bicycle, our only new bicycle. This wonderful, but heavy as they were at that time, vehicle from Wright's Hardware was a gift from our father to be shared by Jo Ellen, age nine-and-a-half, and me, age eleven. Getting our first bicycle was a serious matter[1] and we were so thrilled we didn't even mind that only one of us at a time could make plans to go bike riding with friends. Part of the fun was learning how to kick the bike's kickstand, then spring to the seat and dash away, in one skilled movement, imitating the Saturday Matinee cowboys mounting horses.

Most of the local groceries were bought at Fox's on South Side, the A&P, or McCue's on State Street or, later, McNeel and Smith on Filbert Street. For "big orders" our dad would drive—taking us with him—to Krogers in Clearfield which was larger than any of the grocery stores in Curwensville. Krogers had specialty items such as pimento cheese spread or dried beef in a small glass jar that could later be used as a drinking glass. We preferred, but may not have voiced this preference, the glass shape with the straight, rather than curved, sides, thereby holding more when reused as drinking glasses.

---

1   Age 12 seemed to be the median age for a first bicycle and most remember their first (and likely only) bicycle as a very serious purchase.

Scenes from Childhood

Because our father was the manager of the local theatre he often was not able to attend the evening performances in which we participated. Yet there were indications of his pride in our accomplishments that we would hear indirectly from others, more often after we were adults. I don't recall his ever saying "I love you," but that would be typical for the times when affection was not demonstrated.

One day in December 1945 our father came home early to tell our mother that the Charles Wall property had been placed on the market. This was a large house on lower Thompson Street, equidistance between Josephine's home and where our grandparents and Jessie lived. Mother was familiar with the house and jumped at the chance to purchase it with help from our Grandmother Thompson whose sister Grace's home it had been. Selling their Schofield Street house for approximately $4,000 (originally purchased for $3,500), our parents paid $6,000 for the Wall property with plans to move sometime in March.

The street, which this wonderfully capacious house faced, boasted an almost perfect hill for sledding. The lower block was not heavily traveled (and not at all when there was a heavy snow), and the sledders claimed it as their own. True, it was difficult pulling the sleds up the hill, but was well worth the effort for the glorious ride down. An old, dark-green, eight-foot sled with runners, that had been left in the fruit cellar of the house, was dragged out with great excitement for its intended use. Kay and two of her friends swept off the dust of a quarter century and proceeded to position the weight of the sled and to test the guiders. The first five lucky riders boarded the sled with Cousin Noel at the helm. To the dismay of those who had carried and dragged it from the recesses of the basement to the street, as well as those anticipating a most exciting ride, the outsized sled didn't move. The other children gave the riders a push, but the sled's own bulk, along with the weight of five riders, remained impervious to their efforts. They tried again with fewer riders, but still there was no movement.

Jo Ellen ran in to tell their mother, who had warned them the large sled might not work since it was so old. While they were struggling to get it to move she had been watching from the front window and realized the problem. She put on her coat, went to the door and called to Kay to come to the porch. "Look at the runners. They may be rusty." She was right. Two were rusted and the metal strips were missing from the other two, so that even an ash "clinker" from the furnace, used to scrape the rust off the bottom of sled runners, would do no good. The found treasure was going nowhere.

During the latter childhood summers we were kept busy with 4-H, which met in the Susquehanna Grange located on South Street behind the theatre, learning to cook and sew. The biggest news that summer of 1948 for young girls, however, was the announcement that a Girl Scout troop would be forming the first week of September. From that point, scouting with all its activities and "products" became important. By the next fall, a Brownie Scout troop was formed and Nan joined her sisters in scouting. Like all youngsters, we took these opportunities to learn for granted, only in later years fully appreciating the various women whose time and patience allowed young girls to learn various skills from sewing to leadership.

At the end of May in 1949 the Bloom twins started a club they named "The Hiking Spooks" and invited Jo Ellen and Nancy Straw to join. It did not take long, however, for a rival club to be formed. This club, "The Five Follies" held its first meeting on June 8, 1949 and continued through August 1950 when its members entered the 8th grade. Careful minutes were kept of the club meetings held in the second story of the Wright family garage where the heat often reached 100 degrees. Kate had suggested that the two clubs join forces and set up a lemonade stand in the cool outer lobby of the Rex Theatre during the July Curwensville Sesquicentennial Celebration, the largest celebratory event ever undertaken by the community, which is just what they did. The lemonade stand jointly operated by the two rival girls' clubs was a great success, to the point that the girls found it difficult to keep up with the demand for their product. There were parades every day of the celebration with Kate's girls all taking part; Jo Ellen rode with Aunt Jessie on the State Bank's float, Judith on Kantar's, and Nan and Flossie Murphy, two darling little girls, stole the show on Murphy's Drug Store float.

By the fall season when dancing schools reopened, all three of us were taking dancing lessons through an arrangement Mother had made with Deloris Libreatori: use of the theatre on Saturdays for her dancing school in exchange for dancing lessons for the girls. Judith also began to study piano with Mrs. Eileen Brown, the new music teacher in town, one who had been classically trained and who took her music and her students very seriously. And by fall the thirteen-year-olds were ready to enter 8th grade and would soon be planning school social events. No more was heard of the "The Five Follies" club, soon lost in the memory of childhood much like the TDS Club of Mother's school days.

Until the "troubles," we had many happy family moments, although we did not, of course, think of them in any special way at the time. We were like most children, accepting that "whatever is, is."

By the time we were displaced from our house on 319 Thompson Street in 1952 we were past the age of playing dolls, although we did regret that the space in the theatre was to all intent and purposes lost to the equipment that had been installed for Cinemascope speakers. I recall crawling under the beamlike ducts that carried the sound, just to see what the result was. We found traces of our former years, picked up the pieces, and never went back. More importantly, by the displacement, we knew we had a bigger priority facing us: where we were going to live.

Addenda

Notes from my diaries which I began in 1949 the year I would turn 12. The diaries contain few entries relative to my father.

1949

Sunday, May 8. Today in church I sang M-O-T-H-E-R. Daddy said I sang it better than I know how.

Sunday, June 19. Father's Day. I made Daddy some fudge.

Friday, August 12. Daddy got back from Kane[2] this morning. He gave me a real nice lead pencil and some matches.

Saturday, August 13. We went to Altoona today for the Firemen's Parade. Altoona is celebrating its 100th Anniversary. It was nice.[3]

1951

June 1. Tonight the Thompson Sisters performed for the Odd Fellows and Rebekahs[4]. Harold V. Smith was the master of ceremonies. My, the way he went on about how wonderful we were. He said we were the three most talented girls in Curwensville. But, of course, he gave all the credit to "our past Grand H. V. Thompson." Jo Ellen sang "Mighty Like [Lak] a Rose." I played the piano— "Indian Love Call," "Tennessee Waltz," and "Johnson Rag." Nan, Jo, and I did "Three Little Sisters," and got a good hand.

1953

March 9. Received a birthday card from my father.

1955

March 9. My birthday. I received cards from Letha[5] and my father.

---

2   This would have been a Firemen's parade in Kane the night before. The matches would have been strictly a souvenir.

3   Kay was one of the banner carriers for the drill team and it is likely Mother would have driven to the parade with Jo Ellen, Nan, and me in tow.

4   Odd Fellows and Rebekahs were the first US fraternal organizations to establish homes for senior members and for orphaned children.

5   Letha was the housekeeper for my Grandfather Thompson.

The Theatres

Mid State Theatres

Among his other entrepreneurial ventures, including both an electric company and a water company, Howard J. Thompson started the Mid State Theatre chain in 1924. There is evidence that in 1939 he owned at least 15 of the following theatres:

- Ritz (1929)[1], Lyric (1929), and Roxy Theatres in Clearfield

- Rex Theatre (1935) in Curwensville

- Sherkel Theatre in Houtzdale

- Dixie Theatre (1935) in Coalport

- Liberty Theatre (1930s) in Madera

- State and Plaza Theatres in Bellefonte

- Valley Theatre in Weedville

- Watson Theatre in Watsontown

- Adelphi Theatre in Reynoldsville

- Academy Theatre in Meadville

- Stone Theatre in Stoneboro

- Sykes Theatre in Sykesville

- Eagle Theatre in Montgomery

- Brockway Theatre in Brockway

- Regency Theatre (location unknown)

- Others throughout the state, but mainly in central Pennsylvania.

By mid-1945 the total count was said to be ownership of twenty-three theatres.

---

1   Date of acquisition

206

Artwork by Enola J. McClincey, Curwensville, Pa.

The Rex

For obvious reasons, the lives of the Thompson family revolved around the Rex Theatre. The main negative factor was that Howard spent most evenings working and was not always able to attend evening events in which his daughters participated.

The Thompson children—along with the paying public—spent a lot of time at the theatre in a time when there were no "X" rated movies. *Frankenstein* and *The Wolfman* series were about as frightening as movies got. Theatres—and the movies shown—were safe and families knew they could drop off their children in front of the theatre and pick them up later in the evening. Parents also were welcomed to come into the theatre and go directly to where their children were sitting if the children had not emerged at the appointed hour.

Oddly enough, Judi and Jo Ellen were more frightened on their way home from the movies than they were of the movies themselves because the oldest daughter enjoyed frightening them as they walked home to South Side. Kay would fall a step or two behind Judi and Jo Ellen (ages about seven and six) moving along the shrubbery as they turned from Susquehanna Avenue to Schofield Street. She would place her hand into the shrubbery just enough to create a rustling sound that she herself would then comment upon, feigning alarm. She also made sounds—

207

behind, or having run in advance of her vulnerable young sisters—like the cry of the werewolf all three had just seen on the screen.

There was only ever one movie the girls were not permitted to see and that was by rule of the movie producers (likely because of the Hayes Act[2]) when there was a campaign to distribute "public service" health films such as (1) *Man* and (2) *Woman* with separate show times for men and women.

Under the Hays Act there were very few films not suitable for younger viewers, so the girls took full advantage of the four movies per week that were shown on Sunday-Monday, Tuesday (whose attraction was Bank Night), Wednesday-Thursday, and Friday-Saturday, with a matinee thrown in on Saturday afternoon complete with a Western serial. Various short subjects accompanied an evening's entertainment, including "The March of Time," "RKO News," "Joe Doakes Behind the Eight Ball" (remembered as inane), and the very popular "Movie Sing-along" in which the theatre audience would "follow the bouncing ball" as it directed the audience to "sing along" as the ball struck each word of the lyrics printed across the screen. Once the family moved to town and lived less than a block from the family-owned Rex Theatre, there were few films that the girls missed.

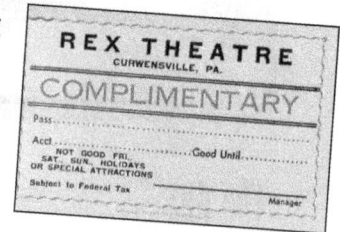

Bank Night

Bank Night, held every Tuesday at the Rex Theatre, was a promotional event that many theatres used to attract higher attendance on a week-night (with perhaps less-well-known films that would play only one night). Patrons filled in their information on cards which were deposited in a large hand-cranked clear celluloid drum. Each Tuesday a name was drawn for a modest cash prize which increased in value each week that no winning ticket was drawn. Occasionally a delighted winner would give a dollar to the person (usually one of the manager's daughters) who had pulled the winner's name.

2   The Hays Act was the common term for the Motion Picture Production Code, a set of industry moral censorship guidelines that governed the production of most United States motion pictures released by major studios from 1930 to 1968.

The Bane of Candy and Popcorn

On the negative side, within two weeks of the family's move to the Wall house, H. J. Thompson decided to install concession stands in the lobbies of his then twenty-three theatres to provide employment for his younger son Philip. At first only candy was sold, but later popcorn was added to the array of sweets, following a burgeoning national marketing campaign for soon-to-be omnipresent snacks in public places.

Because he was responsible for most of the theatre cleaning, Howard was angered because of the enormous amount of refuse these sales generated. The time required sweeping the aisles every day quadrupled and Howard had to press his daughters into service. Each was given a section of the theatre aisles to clean and each was paid proportionately. Kate usually helped them and was known for often taking their place so that they could continue in their many activities.

The little money the girls earned from sweeping the aisles of the theatre was theirs to do with what they wanted. They did not get "allowances" (and didn't know anyone who did). An allowance sounded very grown up to those who had heard of the practice and most parents simply scoffed at the suggestion of an allowance. The "earnings" from sweeping floors, therefore, became the girls' discretionary funds.

"It Comes With the Business"

One of the benefits of being in the theatre business was being able to go to the movies without paying and to enjoy visiting theatres in other towns where there were Mid State Theatres, particularly at the comparatively luxurious Ritz Theatre, one of the two theatres the family owned in Clearfield, and which boasted double seats, attractive to those on a date. The girls also gave theatre passes as birthday gifts to their friends or took a special friend "in free."

The sisters also helped to collect for the March of Dimes, an annual event sponsored by the entertainment industry. Every January containers were passed through the aisles among the theatre patrons; however, the person who was assigned to collect in the section where children sat often returned empty-handed and had to be consoled for returning with nothing collected.

A definite perk of being "in the business" was the opportunity to meet movie stars who made personal appearances. These personages were usually of the "B" movie variety; however, while James Craig was at the time the "biggest name" of the four who made a memorable appearance at the Ritz in Clearfield, it was Frank

Lovejoy and Mel Ferrer whose popularity increased in later years. The fourth actor was Jody Lawrence.[3] All signed autographs for the wide-eyed Thompson sisters who at this time still viewed their father as magic.

The End of an Era

With the advent of television, the motion picture industry began to design and promote ways in which to attract people to continue patronizing the theatres. When it soon became apparent that television was beginning to edge out movies, many new film processes were developed to attract audiences back to movie theatres. One such attempt was 3-D movies that used a two projector process, giving the illusion of depth to the screen through the use of special Polaroid glasses. While the concept had great artistic potential, poor plotlines and shoddy production prevented 3-D movies from being successful.

When the novelty of 3-D movies waned, a new film process called CinemaScope sounded 3-D's national death knell in 1953. By 1954 CinemaScope screens had been installed nationwide, including in Curwensville's small Rex Theatre where the addition of the very wide screen eliminated most of the space on either side of the theatre stage and the sound system obliterated the small dressing rooms. The wide, slightly curved screen of CinemaScope gave an illusion of depth and provided more screen space, making the picture more rectangular than square. Movies filmed by this new process were larger, clearer, and brighter than the standard, and Howard Jr. remarked that CinemaScope "brought the audiences back to the movies."

However, CinemaScope, with all its enhanced size and sound, still paled in comparison to the newly competitive motion picture projection system known as Cinerama, which used three synchronized projectors to place the picture in three sections on an extra-wide screen. This screen was deeply curved and nearly three times as wide as it was tall. The soundtrack was also broad, recorded in seven-channel stereo, unheard of in the early fifties, except for Cinerama. Only seven Cinerama films were ever shot, but those patrons who traveled to one of the theatres built in major cities especially for Cinerama never forgot the experience.

CinemaScope, however, was better than Cinerama for most viewers because of its action and wide-angle displays such as a chariot race or cavalry charge. Filming in Cinerama concentrated on places visited rather than plot or character.

---

3   Perhaps more remembered for being a foster sister to a young Marilyn Monroe when Marilyn (Norma Jean Baker) was in foster care with newlyweds Grace McKee and Ervin Goddard, the parents of their own daughter who later took the stage name Jody Lawrence.

For example, "Cinerama Holiday," the second Cinerama movie (the first was "This is Cinerama"), was nothing more than a travelogue with a weak plot of two young married couples on tour. Their predictable itinerary included such places as Las Vegas, Notre Dame Cathedral, and various universities, as well as showcasing New Orleans jazz and the intricacies of marionettes. While CinemaScope—and to a lesser degree, Cinerama—did hold the audiences for a while against the encroaching television, it soon became obvious just what a force this new television medium was becoming.

Studios began to make alliances with television producers to make TV films and, by the end of the decade, movie studios were producing the majority of TV's prime-time action-adventure series. This effort, however, was not enough to save the movie theatres, and notices such as were posted by the Rex on June 14, 1955—"From now on we'll be closed Wednesdays and Thursdays"—began to proliferate and by 1960 a fifth of the nation's theatres had closed for lack of business.

Short History of the Rex and Ritz Theatres

- **1920.** Fred and Francis Thompson purchased land upon which to build the Strand Theatre in Curwensville.

- **1924.** Howard J. Thompson began acquiring a chain of theatres that would later be known as the Mid State Theatres, Inc. a chain of as many as 23 theatres in the mid-state area by 1939.

- **1929.** Howard J. Thompson acquired ownership of the Ritz Theatre.

- **1935.** Howard J. Thompson purchased the fire-destroyed Strand Theatre that had belonged to his brothers Fred and Francis. He remodeled and renamed it the Rex Theatre.

- **1957.** Howard J. Thompson sold the Rex Theatre to Athol Rummings.

- **1961.** As the result of a lawsuit against Howard J. Thompson, Howard V. Thompson and Mary Alice Thompson Crunk were awarded several theatres. One was the Ritz Theatre.

- **1963.** Howard V. Thompson gained sole ownership of the Ritz. Upon Howard's death in 1964, ownership was retained by Elizabeth Velouci Thompson, his widow.

The Break-Up

Death Knell

The day his mother told him her illness was terminal, Howard had come home crying and upsetting the children who did not understand what was happening. In fact, because he was so grief-stricken, the children misunderstood what he was saying and thought he was announcing the imminent death of their own mother. From that day, he became more discouraged and more powerless, finally completely unable to interact with his father.

In Howard's despair regarding his mother's illness he began to drink and to withdraw from his family. Kate later reflected that she had not had the energy at that time to emotionally further support her husband. His lifelong dependency on his mother and his inability to stand up to his father had been wearing on both of them throughout their marriage, and Kate, a few years before Elizabeth's death, finally had decided she was unwilling to devote any more time in dealing with how her husband's father treated him.

Howard, already vulnerable, simply could not cope with the inevitable loss of his mother and he found further comfort in alcohol and in another woman, one considered far below his station. One day when he and Kate had words over his philandering, Howard began taking her dresses from the closet and clothing from bureau drawers, throwing them out the bedroom window to the yard below. This indignity to both his wife and his mother's final months of life made for a very stressful situation for the entire family. Adding to Kate's indignation was the day the family usurper came to the house asking for Howard. Kate, who was sweeping the porch at the time, not only ordered the woman away, but made the message clear by using the broom to sweep her off the porch, "like the trash you are," Kate said to her, as the broom bristles brushed the woman's shoes.

Downward Spiral

It was at this point the children began to notice the change in their father, and his actions eventually became an embarrassment to them. For example, shortly after it became clear that Kate had resigned herself to the fact that she could not help her husband, Jo Ellen recalls being sent to the grocery store, a responsibility always fraught with strife to her reserved, almost timid, personality. As she left the McNeel and Smith store on that particular day, carrying the bag filled with items light enough for her to carry—still with the grocery list in hand, she saw her father approach her with tearful eyes. Somewhat apprehensive, Jo Ellen wasn't sure what she should do. As she stepped off the curb, her father walked toward her. She lowered her eyes, but he came closer, saying to her, "Here, let me carry that for you. It's heavy." Even though the bag was not too heavy for the child—her mother would never send her to buy groceries that were too weighty for her to carry, Jo Ellen did not resist. As Howard took the bag from his child's arms, his breath revealing that he had been drinking, he spoke again, "There, now, run along home." He turned and started walking up Filbert Street toward their house carrying the groceries. However, he stumbled, and the bag fell from his grasp, crashing onto the sidewalk.

A similar incident that left an even stronger mark on Jo Ellen occurred one evening when this interloping woman became angered when she could not reach Howard by telephone. She went to his home and threw a rock at a window, breaking it. The noise awakened Jo Ellen, who jumped from her bed in terror, grabbed a coat and went in search of her mother, running first down the alley to the theatre, then to Aunt Jessie's. Not immediately finding either her mother or Jessie, she began to panic as she raced to Aunt Josephine's. By the time Josephine had calmed her and was preparing to walk her home and remain as long as she was needed, the telephone was ringing. Josephine answered it and heard Kate's frightened voice, worried because she had walked home a different route from the theatre and had walked into the house where she discovered the broken window and a missing child. This incident convinced Kate she would have to leave her husband for the safety and welfare of her children.

Elizabeth Bailey Spencer Thompson died on October 10, 1951 less than two years following the death of her own father, Vincent U. Spencer. Born September 14, 1880, Elizabeth was 71, twenty-five years younger than her father had been at his death. Elizabeth's husband fell asleep during her funeral service and her son added this offense to the many indignities he had suffered at the hands of his father. He continued to be inconsolable at the loss of his mother as, with her passing, he also had lost his best friend.

With this penultimate tragedy in his life, Howard, Jr. began a downward spiral that would, within the year, end his marriage and break up his family.

Homeless

In the summer of 1952, Kate vacated the house, taking the children with her. The furniture went into storage into the Water Company Building owned by H. J. Thompson. Further, Kate's father-in-law paid the legal services for the divorce she sought and offered her the position as manager of the Rex Theatre, the job previously held by her husband.

Judith, at fifteen, went to live with her Grandfather (H. J.) Thompson whose household was attended by a housekeeper. Josephine harbored Jo Ellen who remained in the home for the year and a half of homelessness. Kate and Nan, the youngest, traveled from place to place, space to space. Initially they stayed at Aunt Josephine's, then moved in temporarily with Kay and her husband Albert who were living in Albert's parents' home while the elder Brunettis spent several months in Texas visiting with their daughter. Kay was about to deliver her first baby and welcomed the help of her mother with her new baby daughter, Mavis Kim. Nan, having just turned ten, recalls leaving for the first day of school from this household.

When the senior Brunettis returned home, Kate and Nan moved in for several months with Kate's parents and her sister Jessie. Because the three bedrooms were in use and Kate would not consider displacing her parents (Jessie's room was very small, not large enough for two), Kate and Nan carved out space in the attic, much as Kate's mother had prepared the unfinished space years before as a sleeping area for Kate and her own younger sister Jean. As it was nearly spring and not bitter cold, Kate gratefully told her mother that they could manage. Nan recalls, "I remember its being cold in more ways than one."

While unvoiced, the burden Jo Ellen carried may have been the most difficult, considering that Aunt Josephine never had reared a daughter. Kate also was concerned because Jo Ellen was the most sensitive of the four Thompson sisters and earlier had suffered a bout of shingles. The only thing Jo Ellen ever mentioned—and only years later—was how much Aunt Josephine "fussed" over her high school age son, offering him seconds of everything at the dinner table and offering Jo Ellen only small portions, very likely because of inexperience with girls and because Jo Ellen would never have asked for more. Jo Ellen also later shared with Nan that she had "felt hungry" some of the time. As Nan observed, also years later, "Jo Ellen was more reserved and probably should have been the one to stay with Mother."

In contrast Judith had the best situation, living in the handsome, large light

215

tan brick house of her grandfather—a home with a private suite on the third floor which was her quarters. The only trial she had to face was silence. H. J. had always been aloof and he ignored his granddaughter almost entirely. She took her meals with him and the housekeeper. He never spoke a word to her during the meals or at any other time.

Since their grandfather and their father had been estranged for years, it was surprising that H. J. allowed Judith to live in his home (and it must have been very difficult for Kate to ask him the favor). Judith, as youngsters do, made the best of it, and in innocence rather than in boldness, occasionally invited friends to this house. She once even held a "sleep-over" (or slumber party, the term used then) in the living room for a group of six—on a school night! She also had a party or two, and one that had been planned, but canceled:

> **Diary, January 5, 1953:** "I'm so mad I could spit B-B's!!! H. J. came back tonight unexpectedly. He wasn't due back until at least Wednesday, maybe later. And I was going to have a party here tomorrow night after the basketball game! I've been helping and coaxing Lucille all day to find a way home after the party. I suppose tomorrow she'll have a solution and I won't have the party. I can't think of another place to hold it. I'm so stunned I can't think, period! What can I do? I'm desperate!"

Needless to say, the party was canceled. The other memorable escapade was the time that Cousin Bill (the son of Mary Alice and three years Judith's senior) spent the day cleaning H. J.'s Cadillac and when he was finished "borrowed" it and the two teens went for a drive.

It is impossible to second guess, but one does have to admire not only Kate's fortitude, but the kindnesses of her sisters and the families of all of those who shared their homes with Kate and her girls. No one else had a divorce in their family and, while there may have been comments made, the daughters never heard anyone criticize their mother's decision or the family's position at the time. Even more remarkable is the resilience of all.

Reunited

On July 20, 1953, after Uncle Philip and Aunt Eva had moved into their brand new house in Temple Heights, likely subsidized by H. J. Kate, Jo Ellen, and Nan moved into their very small, recently vacated apartment on the second floor of the rear of the Rex Theatre building. This apartment had been built from a large open space, formerly used as a dressing room among other purposes, a few years earlier for Philip and Eva. Exterior steps and a door allowed direct access from South Street which was the narrow street behind the theatre.

Weary, but happy to have a place to "land," Kate used the small bedroom directly off the living room as her own; Nan and Jo Ellen shared another small bedroom off the kitchen. Judith remained at her grandfather's home while the theatre apartment was enlarged with an addition of a bedroom built onto the apartment, under the direction of H. J. Judith, as the now eldest (and most in need of "her own space"), was awarded the new sun-filled bedroom, off the dining area. The summer was spent learning to live together again as a family of a mother and three daughters, two ready to enter, respectively, their sophomore and junior years of high school and one a pre-teen-ager.

Kate's divorce hearing was held on August 7, 1953 with Jo Ellen testifying, on behalf of their mother against her father, as a witness to several episodes which were considered due reason for Kate's filing for divorce. At this time divorces were still rare and "no fault" was not yet an option.

During the fall of her senior year, after a year of enjoying her spacious bedroom, Judith asked her mother if one of the dressing rooms in the basement of the theatre building (directly under the apartment) could be made into a "studio" bedroom. She made the case that such an arrangement would give her a sense of "her own place" and would free up the large bedroom in the apartment for Jo Ellen. Further, she argued, she would be heading to college and the separate quarters would be fitting for the times she was home. There was also a powder room in a separate room beside this dressing room which would result in fewer people having to share the small bathroom in the apartment.

Kate agreed, permission was given, and minor renovations began in February 1955. A plywood floor was installed along with a counter top the width of the narrow room that could serve as a vanity and a desk. In this room that contained only a small cot bed, a fiberboard clothespress, a small chest of drawers, and a chair at the counter, an older, upright piano from the theatre added the crowning touch. (Judith never told anyone of the night she was awakened by the sound of someone trying to open the locked door to the room where she was sleeping, for fear she would have to relinquish it. Fortunately there were no further incidents.)

The girls did not see much of their father during the next several years. Judith remembers sending him a graduation announcement but no one recalls if he attended the ceremony. Six years later, Judith received a post card from him,

217

mailed in Niagara Falls on July 3, 1961. The message indicates that he had received her gift, but Judith has no recollection of what this might have been. What the card's simple message does reveal, however, is that their father was recalling taking the girls to Niagara Falls and possibly hoping they would remember those trips as well as several to Atlantic City. At the time Judith didn't share the card, but later thought that what her father wrote indicates his caring for his family or at least remembering with some fondness the trips they took:

Up here over the 4th. Remember our trip here 18 years ago. Thanks for the Xmas present. Was in Philadelphia a couple of weeks ago. May get to Atlantic City next week.

Love,
Bubby

Displaced Again

In the spring of 1958 Kate and her three daughters once again were suddenly displaced from their home, in this case the apartment in the Rex Theatre building. H. J. had decided to sell the Rex Theatre (either because of the pending lawsuits or perhaps because of the decline of the viability of the theatre business or simply to divest his holdings). In any event the Rex Theatre was sold; the sale included the building and all property related to the theatre. This meant that Kate and her girls had to move from the apartment. Such news was devastating, as rental for the apartment was part of the salary Kate earned as the theatre manager. Thus, with the theatre being sold, she not only lost her current dwelling but her livelihood as well. (The details of this are told in the Story of Kate.)

Family Lawsuits

Judith's Diary Entries

None of the daughters heard much from Howard after the separation of their parents. In the fall of 1956, the first semester of her sophomore year of college, Judith made mention of him in diary entries regarding the lawsuits herein discussed.

November 1956

They told me that my dad now has a job keeping books for a distributor in Clearfield and that he is looking happier and better. I really hope things work out for him. I am beginning now to understand that H. J. is mostly at fault for my dad's being like he is.

December 8, 1956

Mother told me about my father and Aunt Mary Alice trying to settle Grandma Thompson's estate. It has been five years since her death and nothing has been settled yet. H. J., of course, is fighting it strongly. Everything is being counted and checked. H. J. called Mother to tell her he wanted the rings all of us were given by our grandmother to be returned to him to have them appraised. We have decided that we'll have them appraised, but won't give back the rings based on his request. Another thing that came out of this case is that Grandmother Thompson established trust funds for each of us grandchildren. I don't know what will come of that. But it seems so unfair for us not to get what she wanted us to have. Time and law will tell.

Lawsuits

Lawsuit # 1: Howard V. Thompson vs. Howard J. Thompson – 1959

A lawsuit by Howard V. Thompson against Howard J. Thompson was first filed in 1957 (which may have been the impetus for H.J. to sell the Rex Theatre) but was not heard until two years later in 1959. On April 26, in a letter to her daughter Judith, Kate wrote, "...I am eager for the first week of May (the date scheduled for the trial)—public sentiment is for H.V.—he must be quite sure of winning the case as he has obtained a loan and is paying me off this week (regarding the sale of the house on lower Thompson Street.) [See more on this in the Story of Kate.]

Briefly, the dispute in the lawsuit involved shares of the Curwensville Water Company that Howard, Sr. had given to his son in 1922 when the latter was attending business school in Williamsport. Howard, Jr. soon after became secretary/treasurer of the water company and in 1925 had been named manager.

Then in 1941 Howard, Jr. had been dismissed from his position without explanation. He had not been permitted to examine the books or have access to the safe where the stocks allegedly were held. When Howard Sr. decided to sell the water company the stocks were found to have been "canceled" without the knowledge, permission, or signature of Howard, Jr. In addition, it appeared that Howard Sr. had endorsed, or caused to have endorsed, checks issued to Howard Jr. but never seen by him. The court found in favor of the son.

In a similar suit, heard during the same week, Howard Jr. claimed that he had stock in the Clearfield Amusement Company. When it was reorganized as Mid State Theatres in 1942, Howard Sr. had asked his son for the Amusement stocks to be returned in order for the stock to be re-issued as Mid State. Howard Jr. returned the stock certificates to his father as requested and, without the son's knowledge, Howard Sr. wrote the word "canceled" on the certificates. New stock in Mid State Theatres was then issued to the younger son, Philip Thompson, who in 1957 turned these over to his father.

The Court again ruled in favor of Howard Jr.

The battle between father and son clearly confirmed the lack of paternal regard which had had such a sad effect on every facet of the son's life. What made it more difficult was that Howard, Jr. knew the machinations of his father would not have occurred had his mother still been living. What made the scenario more poignant is that his Great Aunt Minie (his mother's aunt) had just turned 100, another reminder of the great loss and support of his mother.

Please see Appendix A. for more detail on this lawsuit, copied from news articles in *The Clearfield Progress*. (June 1959)

Lawsuit # 2: Howard V. Thompson and Mary Alice Thompson Crunk vs. Howard J. Thompson

In December 1961 Howard V. Thompson and his sister Mary Alice Crunk acquired Mid State Theatres, Inc. from their father, with Howard becoming president. Mid State Theatres, founded by the Thompson family in 1925, included movie houses at Clearfield and seven other Central Pennsylvania communities.

Bubby • Howd • HV • Howard

In 1963, two years after the acquisition of the theatres, Howard and Mary Alice distributed their theatres between themselves with Howard assuming sole ownership of the Ritz and Lyric Theatres at Clearfield and the Regent Theatre at Reynoldville. He also became manager of the Clearfield Theatres which previously had been under the management of his brother-in-law, Bradford B. Crunk.

Mary Alice Crunk became owner of Bellefonte Theatres, Inc., and the Moshannon Valley Theatres, Inc. These included properties and theatres at Bellefonte, Houtzdale, Madera, Coalport, Sykesville, and Weedville. A theatre in Watsontown was also a part of these holdings.

Aftermath

While the division of property appeared to be amicable, it placed a strain on the relationship between Howard and Mary Alice as well as creating a rift between Mary Alice and her father who had always adored her. A nearly lifelong estrangement already existed between father and son, as Howard, Jr. never was able to earn his father's respect, approval, or affection.

Jessie occasionally ran into Howard in public but their conversations were very brief. She told her sister Kate that Howard always sounded sad.

On June 24, 1962 Judith received a letter from her father written on Hotel Fort Pitt stationery in Pittsburgh. It is included in this section because it reveals the difficulties between Howard and his sister Mary Alice:

Dear Judy

I want to thank you for your present. A little late.

Came out for Odd Fellows convention last Sunday. Went home Wednesday but came back Friday nite. I put Eliz. In Mercy Hospital Monday. She was in Clfd hospital for 12 days.

Wrote a letter to Kay tonite—long overdue.

Did Tom tell you the evening he came to the Lyric? It was the first formal meeting we had had.

Brad has taken over the theatres—put me out as Pres. Using mother's estate stock to swing the deal. I am Secy.

After estate is settled it will be different. He and Mary Alice get more money than I do.

The Story of Howard

Eliz. and I personally ran Lyric Theatre and made over $500 a week. Since Brad took over he is not making expenses. The employees hate his guts and business people in Clearfield don't like him.

You girls won't get your stock. Ask Mary Alice why. Phil lost out entirely—his own fault. I own half of the stock the same as Mary Alice after estate is settled. Also Glenn Thomson[1] has 101 shares of stock.

I called Brad a crook and it gave him ulcers or something.

Excuse the writing.

All my love, Your father

This was the last correspondence Judith had from her father

---

1   An attorney, Glenn Thomson was not related to us and we were told his name was not spelled the same as ours, but as shown.

The Death of Howard V. Thompson

Final Days

In mid-January 1964 the Thompson girls received word of the imminent death of their father. Knowing he was close to death, the girls found themselves in a dilemma. Should they return to Curwensville as quickly as possible to say their last good-byes? All were working and the question of bereavement leave, particularly for Judith in the public schools, was an issue. More than that, however, was the question of being disrespectful of their mother. She would not be comfortable with their rushing home melodramatically to see their dying father. In fact, her daughters knew they would be asked "why" they would want to chance being seen in the company of his present wife whose very existence they had chosen to ignore. Thus, each daughter needed to make her own decision, while preparing for the inevitable.

Judith chose to pay her respects by writing a profile of her father, a description that addressed the view she held of his life: sympathy with sorrow for a talent never fulfilled. Two days before his death she began her tribute, unable to express her regret at his death, rather mourning the father they all had lost years before:

"There he lies, waiting to find in death what he could not find in life…"

She then briefly reviews his life from his beleaguered youth to his failures as an adult—failure with his father even though he had won two lawsuits against him; failure because he lost his family, including his wife, his daughters, and his sister; and, worst in his mind, failure in that he had lost his best friend with the death of his mother. The tribute concludes, "A sad, wasted life. At the early stages a life with potential, but a life browbeaten and discouraged at every turn by an unloving, unforgiving father. So now this life waits for the release of death. The two things he best loved are reflected in his last wish—that he be buried in a uniform and be laid to rest beside his mother." Both wishes were honored.

Memorial Service

Howard's memorial service created an awkward situation, as the daughters had been estranged from him for a decade. Even in the small town of Curwensville the girls had seen him only rarely in the ten years following the dissolution of the family. In addition, a few years after the divorce, he had married the person who had created at least two "scenes" at their prior family home and who was not regarded as respectable in the community. The funeral home visitation was particularly uncomfortable for that reason, but all four daughters dutifully took their places among the five children of the woman married to their father, without exchanging more than a nod with her.

Together the four Thompson sisters greeted those who had come to pay their respects to a man who had had much talent but whose life had ended so sadly, a man broken in both body and spirit, before reaching his sixtieth birthday. "Bubby," as the town knew him, was buried in his Fireman's Drill Team uniform, a reflection of his long-held desire to belong to a uniformed team and a sad remembrance of the boy whose father had not permitted him to join the Boy Scouts a half century earlier.

Obituary

H. V. Thompson, Theatre Owner, Dead at 59

The Clearfield Progress, January 15, 1964

Howard Vincent Thompson of 307 East Locust Street, Clearfield, owner of Mid State Theatres, Inc., died yesterday at 5:55 p.m. in the Clearfield Hospital. He was 59.

Aside from the theatre business, Mr. Thompson, who spent most of his life at Curwensville, was extremely active in volunteer firemen's affairs on the local, county, district, and state levels.

In addition, he was a former Curwensville Borough tax collector, auditor, and minority inspector of the election board in Curwensville's First Ward.

A member of the Curwensville Methodist Church, Mr. Thompson also was a member and past governor of the Curwensville Loyal Order of Moose and held a fellowship degree.

He belonged to Bethesda Lodge, I.O.O. F., at Curwensville and headed the Odd Fellows' Building Association Committee.

He was very active as a member of the Curwensville Rescue Hose & Ladder Co., treasurer of the Clearfield County Volunteer Firemen's Association and past president of the Central District Volunteer Firemen's Association. He also was affiliated with the Pennsylvania State Volunteer Firemen's Association.

Mr. Thompson was born at Clearfield April 10, 1904, a son of Howard J. and Elizabeth (Spencer) Thompson.

In December 1961 he and his sister, Mrs. Mary Alice Crunk, then of Watsontown, acquired Mid State Theatres, Inc., from their father, with Mr. Thompson becoming president of the company.

Mid State, which was founded by the Thompson family in 1925, at that time included movie houses at Clearfield and seven other Central Pennsylvania communities.

Last spring he and Mrs. Crunk distributed their theatres between themselves with Mr. Thompson assuming sole ownership of Mid State Theatres, Inc., and Laurel Theatres, Inc.

These included the Ritz and Lyric Theatres at Clearfield and the Regent Theatre at Reynoldsville. He also became manager of the Clearfield Theatres which previously had been under the management of his brother-in-law.

Meanwhile, Mrs. Crunk became owner of Bellefonte Theatres, Inc., and the Moshannon Valley Theatres, Inc. These included theatres at Bellefonte, Houtzdale, Madera, Coalport, Sykesville, and Weedville.

Mr. Thompson is survived by his father, Howard J. Thompson of Curwensville; his wife, Elizabeth (Velouci) Thompson; and four daughters: Mrs. Robert (Kay) Walker, North Hollywood, Calif.; Mrs. Thomas (Judith) Ball, Hummelstown, Pa.; Mrs. Kendall (Jo Ellen) Lorenz, Falls Church, Va.; and E. Nan Thompson, Bethesda, Md.

Other survivors include five step-children, Mrs. Roberta Hess, Susan Maines, and Judith Bennett, all of Clearfield; Mrs. Joan Maines and Vincent Bennett, both of Curwensville; two grandchildren; and five step-grandchildren.

His sister, Mrs. Bradford (Mary Alice) Crunk of Bellefonte, and a brother, Phillip B. Thompson of Curwensville, also survive.

His mother preceded him in death in 1951.

The Aftermath

Preface

Shortly following their father's death, Kay began to obsess over her father's Will. She had earlier had a conversation with him and had asked him about his Will. At that time he had assured Kay that she and her sisters were to be his beneficiaries. Kay later visited him in the hospital a few days before his death with the intent of asking him again about the Will. However, he was in pain and not able to speak coherently, and she did not have that opportunity.

Family Letters and Conversations

The details here following are taken mainly from family correspondence and recalled conversations:

Fretting over her father's Will, Kay asked her mother to find out what she could about the duties of an executrix in Pennsylvania. Kate wrote,

> *I have found out that the executrix* (his wife) *does not have to notify any beneficiary of any bequeaths. If the lawyer were named executor, then he would notify; otherwise, he has nothing more to do than have the Will recorded, so it is up to all of you if you wish to check on it.*[1]

At the behest of Kay, her mother found herself as a reluctant intermediary in the Will situation, and agreed to meet with Glenn Thomson, the girls' father's attorney in earlier days, telling Kay that she would go to Mr. Thomson if Judith, an even more reluctant participant in Kay's quest, would go with her. Because Kay frequently indicated her struggle with ulcers and migraines, other family members found themselves trying to lessen her stress by doing the "leg work" she requested. As Kate wrote to Judith,

> *No doubt it can be done Easter vacation week-end. I'll write and tell Kay we will be working on the idea and to keep her ulcer quiet. Poor soul!*[2]

In an earlier letter to her mother, Kay had written,

> *Now I think I'm simmered down enough. I must watch my ulcers. … The place is driving me crazy, too. It is a fast paced life. I have seen myself go downhill since I came out here.*[3]

---

1   Kate's letter to the author, January 28, 1964.
2   Kate's letter to the author, February 7, 1964.
3   Letter from Kay to Kate, early February 1964.

The Story of Howard

And in March, Kay wrote to her sister Judith,

I didn't quite understand about our money. You had written on the pad $960 to each of 'our' children. Does that mean hers, too? Also it said upon our death. Maybe we won't get it until she goes? I'm still sick and depressed about the whole deal. I still can't believe it. Maybe you could talk to Dr. Bell and get his opinion if he [their father] was normal and himself when he wrote the Will. I don't like to think we haven't a chance.[4]

Kay later continued,

I don't think we have any chance to contest the Will. I really didn't think it was his wish to cut us off like that, but I guess it was. I feel badly that he felt like that, but I guess he really wanted Liz [his wife] to have it [his assets], or she convinced him that he did. … I am going to write Liz, however, and ask her where it [the money] is."[5] And Kay did, as she later noted, *I wrote to Liz re money, but no answer.*[6]

Kay continued to nag her sisters about their father's Will, still trying to nudge Judith to meet with Glenn Thomson, a chore Judith had been evading,

What do you think we should do about our money? Do you want to talk to Glenn or not? I want to when I come to Curwensville if you don't.[7]

And three weeks later was yet another reminder from Kay to Judith,

Are you still going to talk to Glenn? Maybe I'll have a chance when I come home.[8]

In October Kate wrote again to Judith on Kay's behalf,

[Kay] wants you to see Glenn Thomson and get him to work on your interests with Carl Belin [the attorney who drew up the girls' father's Will]. She is convinced there is dirty work afoot.[9]

---

4   Letter from Kay to the author, March 5, 1964.
5   Letter from Kay to the author, March 17, 1964.
6   Letter from Kay to the author, May 4, 1964.
7   Letter from Kay to the author, August 2, 1964.
8   Letter from Kay to the author, August 22, 1964.
9   Letter from Kate to the author, October 22, 1964.

This was followed by a letter from Kay to Judith,

I wanted to tell you to go ahead and go to see Glenn. I hope you did. H.V. always told me that we girls would get our share of everything and that he made Liz sign a statement that everything he had coming to him from his mother she couldn't touch. It seems to me we could prove his mind was affected if only the doctor didn't witness the Will.[10]

Through later conversations, sharing of information, and piecing together of this sad story it was said that the girls' father once had told their mother (Kate) that he was afraid of his (second) wife. Thus, it was likely that his wife had dictated his deathbed Will and that he, in his weakened condition and realizing his imminent death, simply couldn't object. An added possibility was that the nature of his illness, cirrhosis of the liver, had, in fact, affected his mind.

In late November Kate relayed another message to Judith from Kay relative to the pursuit of their father's Will,

Perhaps you can see Glenn Thomson the Monday after Xmas if you stay that long. Kay says she needs the money and is becoming fearful of not getting it at all.[11]

Finally, in December, Judith could no longer procrastinate in this unpalatable task. After Kay had written to Mr. Thomson, Judith kept the appointment and read their father's Will. Kate relayed this information to Kay by telephone and reported her oldest daughter's reaction to Judith, "[Kay] asked me what you found out from the lawyer and was dismayed anew."[12]

---

10 Letter from Kay to the author, October 27, 1964.
11 Letter from Kate to the author, November 23, 1964.
12 Letter from Kate to the author, December 30, 1964.

The Will of Howard V. Thompson

In essence, Howard V. Thompson willed to Mary Elizabeth Thompson, his estate, "whether real, personal or mixed, to my dearly beloved wife which includes, but is not limited to the following: All my stock in the Mid State Theatres, Inc. which I shall own at the time of my death and all the stock I shall own in the Laurel Theatres, Inc. at the time of my death, which theatre stock includes

- Regent Theatre in Reynoldsville to include building and contents and three apartments and two storerooms.

- Ritz Theatre to include Theatre and contents therein, Lodge Room, four apartments and the two storerooms housing the Ritz Grill and Milligan's Dress Shop.

- Lyric Theatre to include the Theatre and contents, one apartment and office, theatre office and the apartment above.

All stock in the Curwensville State Bank (which had been founded by his father; the stock presumably had been given to him by his mother).

Stock in the Mid State Theatres (330 shares) and in the Laurel Theatres (100 shares) and shares (6) in the Curwensville State Bank totaled $73,210.00, plus a loan from Elizabeth @$11,927.43 for a total of $85,147.43, minus the final expenses, thus totaling $77,203.60."

Schedule of Distribution:

Elizabeth	$ 73,210.00
To each of the four daughters, (Kay, Judith, Jo Ellen, Nan)	$ 998.40 ea.

January 3, 1964

Settled in June 1966

Kay's Actions

Early in the new year (1965) Kay still could not put the issue of her father's Will from her mind and wrote directly to her sister Judith, expressing disappointment, vowing to pursue any avenue by which his daughters could contest it.

> *I guess the first Will made you sick. It's a shame we can't do anything about it. Do you know the value of his estate? I would like an idea, wouldn't you? I wish you would give* [Carl] *Belin* [the attorney who had drafted their father's most recent and standing Will.] *a jingle. Find out what's the hold up. I still wish we would have contested it. I really would like to talk to Dr. Bell* [their father's physician] *and see if he thought he* [their father] *was normal. I still intend to when I get a chance.*[13]

Kay's sisters were uncomfortable at her brashness in seeking a way to contest the Will, but didn't express this to her. She was the oldest daughter and her father's favorite, always "his little girl," and while the three younger daughters found it repugnant to ask anyone—let alone one's father on his deathbed—about a Will, they had not openly challenged Kay's choice to have done so. Moreover, they did not share her intense interest in his Will. True, their father had finally "come into some money and property" as a result of winning the court case against his father, but the three younger sisters did not believe they had any claim on their father's estate. After all, they had remained with their mother following their parents' divorce and, out of respect for their mother, none of them had had much contact with their father since that time.

Kay, however, did not share her sisters' opinion that the daughters held no claim on what she liked to refer to as "their inheritance." She also did not accept the fact that Judith, Jo Ellen, and Nan did not share her fervor in pursuing any legal course of action. To them, a Will was a Will, not to be questioned or contested. Kay, however, could not stop thinking about what might have been, or in her own mind, what *should* have been.

In late January Kay obtained a copy of the Will filed in the Clearfield County Court and left it with Kate for Judith to read, sending this letter,

> *Did you read the complete Will when I had it home? It says in there that he* [their father] *had $207,000, so I don't know why the lawyer said $134,000. Maybe that's what the property would bring on the market. I sure would like to*

---

13   Ibid.

fight for some of that. I still don't believe it's hopeless. Joan [Kay's good friend from high school who was a registered nurse and lived in Long Beach, California] *said the hospital records could be subpoenaed and that would show his true condition and ability to make a Will. I must talk to Dr. Bell when I come in again or I'll never rest. All he did was witness the Will. He didn't say he* [their father] *was of sound mind. Also Joan said a nurse is not allowed to witness a Will. That $207,000 is eating at me. How about you?*[14]

In February, Kay again wrote to ask Judith if she had yet made an appointment with Carl Belin concerning insurance policies Kay was sure their father had established in their names. Kay wanted Judith to pursue this matter, as well as to question Mr. Belin about their father's Will, but Judith was very uncomfortable doing that, finding this pursuit inappropriate. She wrestled with the dilemma, as she wanted to do as her older sister asked, but she found the task distasteful.

Kay expressed her disappointment in Judith's reluctance to meet with Attorney Belin,

> *I know you say you don't have time to see Belin, but I come in for two days a couple of times a year and get quite a bit accomplished. You wouldn't even have your insurance policy if I hadn't gone in to get it.*[15]

And Kay was correct that Judith, Jo Ellen, and Nan would not have pursued a search for any possible insurance policies. Finally, at Kay's behest, Judith did speak with Mr. Belin.

In June 1965, Kay wrote to her two sisters on the East Coast, referring to their father as "H.V." [All of his daughters referred to him either as "H.V." or "Bubby" as it seemed to unsettle their mother when they called him by their childhood name for him, "Daddy."]

> *I assume you both received your check for $998.40 last week. Last Monday, I went down to talk to John Gates and took my "Dave"* [David Ammerman, an attorney and high school friend she had consulted] *file along with the Will and Petition for Probate. I spent about 45 minutes with him and he reviewed everything and said we didn't have a chance* [to contest the Will], *that Elizabeth* [their father's wife] *just simply changed H.V.'s mind or what was left of it.*

---

14 Letter to the author, circa spring 1965.
15 Letter to the author, February 21, 1966.

As far as Dr. Bell was concerned, his word would stick in the highest court. He [Mr. Gates] *has handled numerous cases such as ours, and with more loopholes, and still has not won. I asked him about getting the hospital records, and he didn't think I could without Liz's* [Elizabeth] *consent. I asked him about tax on our money* [from the insurance policies] *and he thought any tax that was to be paid was already taken out before we received our money.*

From there, I marched down to Carl Belin's office and was fortunate to find him in. He was very nice and said we would be getting our money soon. I must have looked as if I was after it! He cleared up the question of the $960 amount. I did ask him before, but it must have slipped his mind at the time. I then asked him if it could be the stock that Grandmother Thompson wanted us to have and then he recollected that it was. I then told him it was Mid State Theatre stock which H.V. had said was worth $95 a share. [Belin] *said the stock was worth $96 a share and H.V. said we were to have 10 shares each, so that would make the amount $960. I then told him the correct amount Grandmother Thompson mentioned was 20 shares for each of us. That shows right there that he* [Belin] *couldn't remember clearly.*

I also asked him about the difference between the amount of the estate and the final amount of distribution, which was about $73,000. The original Will listed the amount estimated at $207,000. Belin said H.V. estimated everything too high and the estate was actually worth about $134,000. He showed me the papers stating it at that amount. Of course, there is still a large discrepancy, but Belin got 3% of the gross and the debts came out of the amount and maybe they [H.V. and Elizabeth] *owned things together which would not be listed as part of his own estate.*

Kay then asked Mr. Belin how the new Will happened to be written. Mr. Belin explained that he had been contacted by Elizabeth Thompson that her husband was in the hospital and because of his medical condition desired a new Will. She asked him to come to the hospital. This he did on January 3, 1964 and, while he had never met his client prior to the call, he told Kay that her father appeared to be mentally alert. Mr. Belin relayed that Mr. Thompson had asked his wife Elizabeth to leave the room after which Mr. Thompson told the attorney what all he wanted done. Mr. Belin further explained that he had requested Dr. Bell and the duty nurse to go into the room to see if they thought Mr. Thompson was clear as to what he was doing. They both entered the room to do a sight evaluation—and perhaps engaged their patient in conversation. At any rate, both had told Mr. Belin that Mr. Thompson seemed to them to be perfectly normal.

Kay's letter to her sisters commented, *So you can't fight that.* She then asked Mr. Belin about the possibility of obtaining the hospital records and asked if she would need the consent of her father's wife. She explained, *He didn't think so, but wasn't sure. He suggested I go see her. He said if I would get her consent, he would see what he could do and handle it for me.*

The letter continued,

I next went to see Elizabeth to get her consent, saying I wanted to know his condition during his last days. She was very nice and said it was O.K. with her. I asked to see his death certificate and she immediately got that for me to read. The cause of death was listed as cirrhosis of the liver and that he had gone into a hepatic coma before death. The word must be derived from hepatitis, which he had in addition to the cirrhosis. He also earlier had hepatitis several years prior that had weakened his liver. I asked her why Dr. Bell would operate with his condition being so weak, and she told me that it was Dr. Yingling who performed the surgery after a consultation with Dr. Bell because H.V.'s hernia was so bad that he was in great pain and could hardly sit up."

I asked Elizabeth for something of H.V.'s to keep and she gave me an old I.O.O.F. tie clasp. I thought it was rather nice of her. She did give me a big line about no one could ever measure up to "your Dad." I told her that in my mind he was never the same since he started drinking and to me his mind was gone by the time he died. I further said I was the only one bothering to find out everything I could about his last days, because I remembered him when he was normal.

I feel much better and more satisfied about the whole matter now. I know Dr. Yingling personally and think he wouldn't do anything that wasn't necessary.

Kay then went on to tell her sisters what she expected the attorneys' fees to be and that if they wanted to help with these expenses she would send each of them one of the bills from Mr. Gates and Mr. Belin. She had already paid Mr. Ammerman and did not expect that Glenn Thomson would bill for his services since he previously had been their father's attorney.[16]

---

16 Letter to the author, June 20, 1966.

The Vow

This failure to gain what she felt was rightfully hers upset Kay greatly. She told her mother that they were always losing out, that their Grandmother Thompson's dying before her husband had set many unfortunate circumstances into motion. Grandmother Thompson's death had driven her son to drink, as with that death, Howard Jr. lost his best friend and his defender against a hateful father. Kay lamented that Elizabeth had ensnared her father and, while she did not say as much to her mother, she partly blamed her mother for the divorce and subsequent downslide of her father. Still believing that the Will should have been contested and smarting at her perceived loss of an inheritance, Kay resolved that if ever a similar situation should arise she would be ready.

Addenda

1920 Diary of Howard Vincent Thompson

Memoranda

1919

People I gave Presents to:

Mama – Casserole and handkerchief
Papa – Linen Handkerchiefs
Sister – Writing paper and cologne
Brother – comb
Mama Spencer – Pyrex dishes
Papa Spencer – cigars
Pauline – box of candy
Aunt Grace – Talcum powder
Aunt Maude** – Writing paper
Cecil* – book
Kenneth* – puzzles
Mable Musser – table set
Mrs. Heverly – cards
Arthur* – whistle
Richard* – tool set

Christmas Presents Received:

Aunt Grace – book
Cecil – tie
Kenneth – handkerchiefs
Mama – slippers, shirts, stockings, gloves
Papa – pair of shoes
Sister (Mary Alice) – tie
Mrs. Heverly – silk handkerchief
Aunt Maude – book and handkerchief
Uncle Francis – pocket book
State C. El. Co.[1] – pair of plyers
Papa Spencer – fountain pen[2]

* Cousins, the sons of his Aunt Grace Spencer Wall, sister to his mother Elizabeth
** Sister to his father

Cards

Cousin Anna	Mark Hunter	Uncle Francis (Thompson)
Bobby Custer	Louise Miller	Andrew Runkle
Mrs. Allen Wrigley	Minot Willard	Miss Marion Harm
Audrey Hyde	Foster McGovern	Lois and Doris Young

---

1   Likely the Pennsylvania Electric Company, since Howard worked for his father who owned the local electric company in Curwensville, and earlier in Bellefonte.
2   Howard's first fountain pen which I still have. Fountain pens were just then coming into fashion despite the criticism of them by President Wilson.

1920 Diary of Howard V. Thompson

1922 Sophomore Class (1919-1920)

> President – Linn Bodle
>
> Vice-president – Joe Parrish
>
> Secretary – Alice Whitaker
>
> Treasurer – Elizabeth Williams

Contests between the Reds & Blues, 1920

> Reds 878 points; Blues 1018 points
>
> Total amount for A.A. $474.00

1922 Junior Class (1920-1921)

> President – Joe Parrish
>
> Vice-president – Andrew Runkle
>
> Secretary – Raymond Brooks
>
> Treasurer – Mark Hunter

Information

> (1) Area of Rect. = length x breadth
>
> (2) Area of Rect. divided by length = breadth
>
> (3) Area of Parallelogram = base x altitude
>
> (4) Area of Triangle = base divided by ½ altitude
>
> (5) Area of Triangle divided by base = ½ altitude
>
> (6) Area of Trapizoid = Sum of π x ½ A. sides
>
> (7) Circumference of a circle = Diameter x π
>
> (8) Circumference of a circle divided by π = diameter
>
> (9) Area of a circle = πR^2 or circle x ¼ diameter

On the next two pages are the basket ball[3] games and scores from Bellefonte High School where he attended until his junior or senior year when the family moved to Clearfield, the high school from which he was graduated. Also included are the Preliminaries and Finals at State College.

The following page is titled "Things I need and want." Recall he was 15 at the time.

> Need measurement folder (OK)

> [It should be noted that he most likely wanted a handy guide as he also did work for his father's water company.]

Next in the Memoranda section is a list of "People I owe" and "People who owe me." The amounts have been erased with the exception of "Mama" to whom he owed $5 reduced to $2.

---

3   Throughout the diary, Howard spells basketball as two words, according to the form at that time.

1920 Diary of Howard V. Thompson

The next several pages are filled with maps of the continents.

The last page of Memoranda lists the following birthdays:

> Mama – September 14
> Sister – November 21
> Papa – January 12
> Howard (self) – April 10
> Anna Rich – September 7
> Louise Miller – August 31
> Margaret Bower – March 18
> Pauline Sasserman – August 29

Entries begin with three of the last four days of 1919:

DECEMBER

Sunday – Useful information:
> 1 gal water weighs 8 lb.
> 7 ½ gal = 1 cu. ft.
> 1 cu. ft. of water weight 62 ½ lbs.

Monday – Pressure of water in tank equals the no. of ft. in depth times 434.

Tuesday – C. Building and Loan Stock
> -2-Series 28 –Mat. 400
> Got on Aug. 21, 1916

JANUARY

Beginning now in January 1920

1. Took inventory of old plants in morning. Awful cold. Tubby and Dave helped. Sorted cards.

2. First day collected, took in over $412. dollars. Coldest weather. We beat Hollidaysburg by a close score. School on Monday.

3. Collected money today. Went to pictures. [movies] Mama Spencer coming home tomorrow. Took her (P.S.[4]) home from pictures.

4. (Sunday) Took bath in morning. Went to Sunday School and Church. Missed papers as they were gone after church. Played games.

5. First of school since Dec. 19. Paid $18.10 for 2 weeks work. Cold and clear. Worked after school.

---

4   Likely Pauline Sasserman.

6. Worked in morning till 11 when I went to Latin. Bad cold. Mama Spencer home. Worked also after school.

7. Worked in morning. Through (sic) collecting money. Got $760.90 for December. Have sour (sic) throat bad. Took R. B. Taylor's meter out. But he paid and it was put back in.

8. Raining icy and slippery out. Papa and Papa Spencer went away to Millersburg. I'm doing P.S. work. Fixed pump chart.

9. Trouble on Port H/W/M line so I missed school; was there all day, no dinner. Basket ball game Friday BHS Girls – 7; L.H. [Lock Haven] H.S. – 31.

10. Worked at office. Went to pictures in evening. Friday the BHS Boys beat L.H. HS, 36-25. Saturday they beat LH. Normal School 31 -19. Cold and icy.

Sunday January 11. Went to Sunday School. 30 above. Fixed pump chart. Fine dinner. Went out on Howard [name of a small town nearby] line in afternoon. Papa and Papa Spencer came home.

12. Went to school. MT 1st and 2nd periods; 3rd vacant; 4th Latin. Have History, English, Latin and Algebra to make up by Tuesday.

13. Snowing. Made up all my lessons. 5th period Alg; 6th, vacant; 7th History; 8th English. Snowing and blowing in evening. $13.60 for ½ month pay.

14. Clear & colder. Went to school. First, second & third periods vacant on all Except Mon. & Thurs. Got reports All C's except one B.

15. Went to school. MT 1st & 2nd periods. Game and dance tomorrow night. Got hair cut after school. Card Party at our house.

16. Went to school. Snowing out. Mid-year examinations 28, 29, & 30th of this month. First three periods vacant.

17. Didn't work at office but I cleaned the old plant walls. Went to pictures in afternoon. Loafed in eve.

Sunday January 18. Went to Sunday School. Went to Mussers with his paper. Had chicken for dinner. I helped pick it.

19. Went to school. Went to dentist in afternoon after school. Got my pay. Deposited $10 for suit in Spring.

20. Worked in morning rangering (?) service. $.50. Went to school. Got tickets to sell for Athletic Association at .15 each.

21. Business Men's meeting this evening. Going to put up a big silk mill where Crixxx(?) planing mill was situated.

22. Went to school Got off from 1:45, on account of the death of Mrs. Dr. Locke. Went sled riding. Played basket ball.

23. Went to school. Latin 4th period, Algebra 5th, vacant 6th, History 7th, English 8th. Snowing out. Went to basket ball game in eve.

24. Shoveled walks. Went to dentist. Went to pictures in afternoon. Xxx box candy. We beat Mt. Union 19 – 41 on Friday.

FEBRUARY

February 1, Sunday. Went to Sunday School. Got papers. Stayed home in afternoon & evening. Studied for examinations in evening.

2. Had Algebra exam in A.M. Had English exam in P.M. Sorted cards after exam was over. Got out at 3:30 p.m.

3. Manual Training exam in morning. History in P.M. Collected in evening. Studied this morning after exam.

4. Had Caesar exam in morning. Collected after exam and in afternoon as I was through. Played in snow in eve.

5. Been snowing all day yesterday & today. Got 33% in Manual Training exam and 95% in Algebra. Collected money.

6. Collected money in morning. Went to school. Finished collecting in evening. Tubby got more than I did. Mr. Coldern was helping.

7. B. H. S. beat Army & Navy, 33-17 and beat Renova 33-21, the last being the hardest game this year. Worked at office in morning. Went to game in evening.

February 8, Sunday. Went to Sunday School. Home the rest of the day. Philip in high chair part of the time. Went to bed early.

9. Went to school. Through working for a while. Dance, game, and social Friday the 13th. Have cold. Regular lessons.

10. Went to school. Regular lessons. Snowed some last night. Flunked Caesar and M.T.[5] so far. Made up lesson today.

11. Went to school. Got no more marks yet. Everybody has the Flu. Got last period in morning for receiving health inspection.

12. Lincoln's birthday. Last period in the afternoon had speech by Dr. McKinney about Lincoln. Went to dentist in evening.

13. Went to school; had dance and social in the evening at high school. Pauline has the Flu. So I hadn't any girl.

14. Worked at office today. Payroll goes in on Monday. I have $4.60 coming. Went to pictures this afternoon. Helped clean a chicken.

February 15, Sunday. Went to Sunday School. Had fine dinner. Lights were out last night. They fixed them this morning. Awfully cold out. Studied in eve.

---

5   Manual Training

16. Went to school. Sec. Lansing resigned as Sec. of State.[6] People say Wilson isn't all there. Cold at school, registers 58 (inside).

17. Went to school. Weik (?) still home. Pauline still sick. Had speeches in English in auditorium. She missed me.

18. Went to Opera House tonight to see "Mutt and Jeff," fairly good. Worked some at office this eve. Had homemade ice cream.

19. Went to school (Weik back and things running smoothly). It is at the end of the 3rd period that I'm writing this. I sit in seat B-A in school.

20. Went to dentist. Went to concert last night at high school. Regular lessons. Papa went away yesterday.

21. Went down to Tubby's in morning gotten it (?) fixed. Went to pictures last night. Took M.B.[7] home. Put up wireless aerial in afternoon. Cleaned chicken in eve and shoveled snow.

Sunday, February 22. Went to Sunday School. In afternoon Tubby, Margaret and Sara came up and we went for a walk & took pictures.

23. Went to school. Go to Centre Hall to read meters tomorrow. Reg. lessons. Joe Katz said 50 lines before the school today.

24. Went to Centre Hall on 6:00 train. Had easy day of it. Dave helped me. Had dinner at a restaurant.

25. Went to school at 11:00 a.m. for Caesar. I flunked Caesar and Manual Training. Went in P.M. and read meters.

26. Sister went to Philipsburg today. Read meters in afternoon. The girls play PA over there today.

27. Went to school. Read meters. Went to game tonight between B. H. S. Boys & Girls and Huntingdon. Boys score 20-40 our favor and Girls score 7-19 their favor.

28. Went to Port Matilda in morn and Unionville afternoon reading meters. Went to pictures and eve.

Sunday, February 29. Went to Sunday School. Sorted cards in afternoon. Had ice cream for dinner. Studied lessons in evening.

---

6   Having been appointed counselor to the Department of State by President Woodrow Wilson in 1914, Lansing took over as Secretary of State in June 1915 following the resignation of William Jennings Bryan. Lansing was involved in various initiatives, including interventions in Haiti, the Dominican Republic, and Russia. Wilson asked for his resignation following Lansing's convocation of a cabinet meeting—without Wilson's approval—during the period in which Edith Wilson presided over her husband's affairs.

7   Likely Margaret Bower

MARCH

Monday, March 1. Went to school. Re-examinations rest of week. Tubby thinks he is sick today. Had lines for History.[8]

2. Went to school. Had Caesar re-exam in morning. Collected money in evening. Said lines in history tonight.[9]

3. Collected in morning. Went to school. Collected in evening. Very near through. RR passed into private ownership Monday.[10]

4. Finished collecting this morning. Tubby back on deck. Went to school. Made up Algebra today.

5. Went to school. Had Spelling Bee between Freshmen Boys and Girls. 2 games tonight. Boys and Girls play Tyrone. Lois and Doris Young are staying at our place.

6. Got 100 in M. Training re-exam Friday. We beat one game and lost other last night. Boys score 13-31; Girls 6-3.

Sunday, March 7. Lois and Doris are going home this evening.[11] Tubby took some pictures today of the girls. I went to the train with them.

8. Went to school. Made up History in evening. Took some negatives up to Mallory's to get developed.

9. Went to school. Made up Caesar at noon. Got 67 in my Caesar re-examination. Tubby up to my place in eve.

10. Went to school. Regular lessons. Now 11:12 or the 3rd period. Got pictures from Mallory's[12] Stayed home in evening.

11. Went to school. Mama has trouble with her eyes. I don't know what. Elizabeth is able to be around now.

12. Got off at 3 to see Basket ball team go to Mt. Union and Huntingdon. High water at the Plant. has over 5 ft of water.

13. Street lights off last night and Bellefonte crested. Fixed bicycle in morning. Rain yesterday and snow today. Rode bike in snow. Went to pictures. Good.

Sunday, March 14. Went bicycle riding in afternoon. Water has gone down. Snow melting some. We won both games. Mt Union 30-32; Huntingdon 24-26.

15. We are ahead of the league. Boys are getting pictures taken today. Only 2 more league games and the States on 9 & 10 of April to play for the championship.

8   Likely Tubby was not prepared for his recitation.

9   Possibly rehearsing an assignment to memorize a passage.

10   The Transportation Act, 1920, commonly known as the Esch–Cummins Act, returned railroad to private operation after World War I, with much regulation. Passed on February 28 and went into law March 1, 1920.

11   A separate notation lists their home as in Howard, PA.

12   Mallory Studio in Bellefonte; evidence of its operation found up to the mid-1930s with the possibility of as late as 1942.

16. Went to school. Bad day. Raining out. Had byke out after school. Got re-exam marks. M.T., B. Latin, D.

17. Went to school. Streets dry. Cloudy out. Snow about all-gone. Yea! Snowed some at noon. Went to dentist after school. Studies in eve.

18. Went to school. Mr. Menold talking of starting a class in cement. Nice day. Sun out. Going to take Baby's picture at noon.

19. Boys having game with Hollidaysburg tonight. Party and dance given by Junior Class at school tonight. I went and had a good time.

20. Boys got best of Hollidaysburg 22-40. First league game lost this year. Tonight we played Lock Haven Normal and beat them 30-20. This was a hard game.

Sunday, March 21. Went to Sunday School. Went to Milesburg on bike in afternoon. We are still ahead in the league. Game on Fri.

22. Went to school. Don't feel very good. This is the 2nd day of Spring. Sun out and everything bright. Got basket ball picture.

23. Went to school. Took 4 pictures of the baby[13] at noon. We play Lock Haven High Thursday night. Nice day.

24. Another nice day. Took pictures of Milesburg Plant yesterday. Then working on aerial last night. Trying to study Caesar now.

25. Reading meters in Bellefonte. Nice day. Helen Jack are moving next door today. Basket ball game tonight with Lock Haven High.

26. We beat LHHS last night 19-15. Game tonight B.H.S. girls and Philipsburg girls. Reading meters. Another nice day.

27. The girls got beat 4 to 9 today by PHS. I went to Port Matilda and Unionville to read meters on train. Walked back to Bellefonte from Unionville.

Sunday, March 28. Went to Sunday School. We got our reports on Friday. English, B; History, B; Algebra, A; M.T., B; Caesar, C. Went to Milesburg in afternoon.

29. Read meters before school. Dr. Beach is teaching History. Got pictures of Basket ball team. Read meters in eve.

30. Read meters in morning. Nice day. Renova challenged BHS to play them for the championship of Central Pennsylvania to be played at Lock Haven.

31. I don't think we will play them. Through reading meters. We play Houtzdale Fri. day or nite.

---

13   His brother Philip, younger by 15 years.

1920 Diary of Howard V. Thompson

APRIL

Thursday, April 1. All Fools Day. My day! Went to school. Get off Fri. Kids bringing Hoopstar contributions today. Nice day.

2. **Good Friday.** Worked collecting all day. Went to the last game of the season tonight. BHS won from Houtzdale 38-30.

3. We get the championship of the Mountain High School League of Central Pennsylvania. Went to pictures. Worked in morning. Got my first suit of long trousers today. Cost $40. Got hat also.

Easter Sunday, April 4.

Easter Sunday. Went to Sunday School. Raining. Had my new suit on. I like it. Stayed home this afternoon.

5. Finished collections today. Went to school. Friday and Saturday we go to States to decide the championship of Pennsylvania.

6. Wearing my other good suit to school. New girl started to school. Freshman and pretty. Snowed last night. Cold today.

7. Snowed hard this morning. 2nd period (10:09) just now. Getting our winter coal now. Baby got his 1st pair of shoes and stockings today.

8. First champion game played Fri. night. Admission 25. There are going to be 14 teams play. Cold today. No English teaching today.

9. Snowed again today. Dick Herman is sick; don't think he can play. Didn't have a lesson all morning. Going to State.

10. Went to State on Friday eve. We played Williamsport and got beat. 19-18, a close score. Lost championship. Harrisburg Tech won the Championship. Went to Katcha Koo at Opera House.

Sunday, April 11. Went to Sunday School. Saw P. [Pauline] in afternoon. Took her home from church. Bellview played Harrisburg Tech and got beat 34-38.

12. All the boys that played are back home. Now in 3rd period. New fellow started to school.

13. Sun was shining. Boys get Football picture taken this afternoon. Getting new girl to work for us. Base Ball season began yesterday.

14. Orchestra and Girls BB team got pictures taken also. Getting some pictures of the baby at noon. Went for a walk with P. last evening. Nice day.

15. Started to make concrete walk along side of commons. Went to B.Ball practice last eve. Went down to see P. last eve. Nice day. P. not at school.

16. Raining today. Went to Base B. practice last eve. Staid home in eve. Went to dentist tonight. Didn't have practice tonight. Raining.

17. Bad day. Worked at office. Went to pictures this eve. Didn't see P. tonight. Two B.B. games next week, State College & Huntingdon.

Sunday, April 18. Went to S. School. Went down to plant in afternoon to see then start new turbine. P. S. came up to my house to see Baby in eve.

19. Went to school. Nice day. Put Cannas in. Went down to dentist. Stayed in in evening. Play ball at home.

20. Went to school. Raining this afternoon. Played ball some. School closes on June 3, yea. Now 2nd period in afternoon.

21. Went to school. Baby six months old yesterday. Took P.S. home from pictures. Worked around house after supper. Got paid.

22. Went to school. Boys going to play Lock Haven Normal today. We got beat 7-0. Nice day. Going to dentist this evening. Read meters Monday.

23. Went to school. Worked around house in evening. Went to dentist. Go again Wednesday. Was out for half an hour tonite.

24. Worked at office in morning. Went to game in afternoon between B.H.S. and State College H.S. We won 19-4. Went to pictures in eve…P. home.

Sunday, April 25. Went to Sunday School. Took pictures of plant after dinner. Saw P.S. Walked home with her in evening. Nice day.

26. Went to school. Nice day reading meters in Bellefonte. Going to start concrete walk tomorrow morning along side of school.

27. Read meters till 11:15. Went to school. Bad day. Raining. I am reading Book 3 in meters. First time I read it. Now 2nd period in P.M.

28. Read meters in morning. Went to school. Cold out but not raining. Started to make my English notebook. Went to dentist.

29. Went to school. Worked on concrete walk. Nice, cold windy day. Get Friday off. Worked reading meters tonight. Cold.

30. Went to school in morning. Had English examination on Book. Went to Unionville in afternoon to read; supposed to go to dentist.

MAY

May 1. Finished reading meters today. Didn't work in afternoon. Went to pictures early. Didn't take P. home.

Sunday, May 2. Went to Sunday School. Sorted cards in afternoon. Took a walk. Went to church in evening. Took P. home from church tonite.

3. Finished sorting cards today. Went to school. Worked on cement walk. Getting along fine. Studied in evening.

4. Collected money till 11:00. Went to school. Collected money after school. Stayed home and studied lessons.

5. Collected money. Went to school. My check hasn't come yet. Got off tomorrow to work on walk in afternoon.

6. Worked on walk all morning and all afternoon. Went to school. Got home to eat after we were through.

7. Went to school. Collected money today. Went to High School Play, "Green Stockings" at Opera House tonight.

8. Fooled around home all morning. Went up to Pointe McCoy in afternoon with Ly, Margaret, Edna, Bobby, Pauline, Alice and May. Went to pictures in eve. Took P. for a walk and then home.

Sunday, May 9. Went to Sunday School. Cecil came over and I went for a walk with him. Kept baby in eve. P.S. came up after church.

10. Went to school. Didn't work on walk, but on my drawing. School will soon be over. Stayed home in evening. Arthur stayed.

11. Went to school. Worked on walk three periods. Raining today. Stayed home this evening also. Too bad!

12. Went to school. Worked on walk 2nd period. Talked to P. after school. Went down to her house in evening. Took Bobby Stevenson home. Yea!

13. Worked on walk all morning. They are getting ready for the Junior reception. Mama and sister went to a social.

14. The juniors put their flag up and the seniors took it down.* Went out in the evening with Porter and Joe Katz. We were with six girls—E, M, A, S, H., M. Got half brick of ice cream at Jr reception.

15. Worked around home today. Wasn't allowed to go downtown in evening as was out too late last nite. *Dave Newcomer took it down. [Dave is the one who took down the Junior Class pennant—which is what these class flags typically were called.]

Sunday, May 16. Went to Sunday School. Went for a walk in afternoon. Went to church in evening. Took P. home from church. Yea Bo!

17. School will soon be over. Worked in garden tonight. Went to dentist after school. Working on my English notebook for exhibit.

18. Went to school. Worked on concrete all day. Got off at 3:00 to go to game. We were beat by Lock Haven Normal 7-8.

19. Went to school. Seniors are having final examinations. Worked on walk in morning. Worked on notebook in evening.

20. Don't have to study much. Finished MJ sheet. Mama had a party in evening. Worked in garden. Put in beets and peas.

21. Worked on walk and finished it. I put last load of concrete in. My last regular day at school. No English or Algebra today.

22. Worked on bike. Went over to Philipsburg in afternoon. Had strawberry shortcake for supper (first). Came home eve.

Sunday, May 23. Went to Sunday School. Saw P. in afternoon. Went to church in evening. Took her home from church.

24. Read meters at Centre Hall and Pleasant Gap. Put 11 hours in. Final exams begin tomorrow.

25. Read meters in Bellefonte all day. I had no examinations today. Worked on notebook tonight.

26. Read meters in Millersburg this morning. Found jam on John Shultz's meter. Had Latin exam this afternoon.

27. Had History examination in morning. Read meters in Bellefonte in afternoon. Then down to [not legible] in evening.

28. Had English exam in morning. Went to Unionville in afternoon to read meters. Took P. home from last day of school.

29. The whole family went away for Decoration Day. Worked in the office all day. Xxx Took P. home in eve. She was up to my place in eve for a while.

Sunday, May 30. Fixed pump chart. Got dinner at restaurant. Good. Went out and saw them put circus tents up. Turned on lights.

31. This is circus of Memorial Day. Fixed chart. Worked in garden. Saw part of parade. Went down to P. tonight. Mama and family came home

JUNE

June 1. High School picnic today. I went at 10 a.m. and home at 7 p.m. Took Pauline. Went down there in the evening.

2. Went to work on Beech Creek line putting guys up (as in guy wire). Pretty hot work. Went to concert at high school in the evening. Go to dentist.

3. Worked on line today. Went to Commencement exercises this evening. I got $5. From A C. Mingle (?) for the best history exam paper.

4. Worked on line today. New fellow working. He is just learning to climb. We are now in Eagleville.

5. Worked in Bellefonte. Collected money in afternoon. Went to pictures. Took P. home this evening.

Sunday, June 6. Took bath. Didn't go to Sunday School. Went to Church in evening. Took Pauline home from church. Last time I went with her.

7. Worked around Bellefonte today. Worked on gutter job in the evening. Bought some clothes. Gave Mama $5. to pay what I owed her.

8. Worked around Bellefonte today. Saw Marion Marn; Weik is working for State—Center as meter man.

9. Worked around town. Went down to band concert this evening. I was going to take Pauline home but Cryder Rockey took her home.

10. Worked around town today. Mama went to Beechcreek to see Uncle Francis. Went to bed.

11. Worked today (early). Put in transformer at Milesburg Brick Plant. Finished my concrete curb.

12. Worked around town. Worked in office in the evening. Went to pictures. Not very good ones.

Sunday, June 13. Worked all day at Center County line on putting in substation. Didn't get done till 9 o'clock. Had supper there.

14. Worked on Beechcreek line. I was groundman for a new lineman learning to climb. He is slow as molasses.

15. Worked same place. Was climbing some after work. Mama Spencer came home. She said Cecil made $5. a day for 2 weeks. [Not sure of some of the words.]

16. Raining out. I don't feel good. Have bad cold and cough. Not working. Was climbing a little this morning. Went to doctor.

17. I worked on the Beechcreek line and around Bellefonte all summer.

18. I got 25¢ an hour. I drove the Ford truck a lot the later part of the summer.

19. Worked on the Centre Hall line up in the mountains. Worked on line across from Hof's (?).

Sunday, June 20 and June 21. I did a little climbing. I cared for street lights, brought in meters to be tested, read meters all over the territory. I was not away from home all summer. I did most any kind of work around.

22. Kept track of all material laying along Beech Creek and Center Hall line. Tubby Runkle was working, too.

23–26. I worked some of the time with Tubby, Johnie Bunny, Sam, John, Bill, and Marxxx. I've plugged pot holes, anchor holes, put up xx, stripped poles, tied in wire, distributed material, put in meters, pulled out wire. I know everything a lineman needs to know. I could almost build a pole line, I think. In fact, I enjoyed my vacation very much. I made quite a lot of money, but spent almost all of it.

There are no entries from this point until August 29th except for a listing of football scores with only three games (with Williamsport, State College, and Lewisburg) noted, all of which Bellefonte scored nothing. A fourth game—with Lewistown—has a line through it with the notation "Cancelled." This is followed by the message (in print which is what Howard used for lists of games and scores):

"Football season closed because Edward Miller had his leg broken in practice."

Two entries on Basketball are noted, along with the list of opponents and scores of games, but it is not likely that the entries are subject specific to these dates:

Wed, August 4: "Hollidaysburg game was forfeited to BHS 2-0 because they had illegal players." [not uncommon in those early years of high school football]

Thurs, August 5: "Mt. Union won the championship of the League. Bellefonte is tied with Tyrone for 2nd place."

AUGUST

Sunday, August 29. Pauline was up in the evening. Last time I was with her. I gave her a box of candy. Her birthday.

SEPTEMBER

Wednesday, September 1, 2, 3, 4. (Each entry has only the notation "10 hrs.," presuming this was hours at work before school resumed.)

Sunday, September 5. Mama and Papa went to Curwensville. Loafed around all day. Made some candy this evening.

6. Loafed around all morning. Went to Hecla (Likely Hecla Park in Mingoville near Bellefonte [1894—mid-1950s]) in afternoon. Went to skating rink in evening. Had good time.

7. First day of school. It starts at 8:45. I take English II, American History, Health, Ins. M.T., Plane Geometry, Caesar, and Chemistry.

8. School Today. Haven't got all my books. Nice day. Started to study, 1 ½ hrs. this eve., oh, boy!

9. Rained in afternoon. Family went to Granger's Picnic. Aunt Grace and Uncle Charley are here. 1 hr. [study time?]

10. Sit in E-7. Have my books. State College E(lectric) Co. sells out Merchandise end today. Rode in new truck this eve.

11. Worked on Beech Creek line. Finished it up today. Drove truck (Ford) all of 10 hrs. the time there.

Sunday, September 12. Went to Sunday School. Went for ride with Uncle Charley to Hecla Park. Family went over to Curwensville today[14]

---

14 The family moved to Clearfield, then to Curwensville, owning theatres in both, and the water and electric companies in Curwensville. These visits are likely preparatory. (However, they might have moved to Curwensville and Howard chose to attend Clearfield because of the curriculum.)

13. Sorted out Book 2 & all ready for new ledger. Got nail cut. Foot bad. Practice started. (2 hours.)[15]

14. I gave Mama box candy and playing cards for birthday. Nice day. Drove truck to Milesburg this eve (1 hr.) Mama's birthday.

15. Seat E-7. Nice day. Weik gave experiments in Chemistry. Went to pictures. Great! Class meeting after school about things. (1 ½ hr.)

16. Rain in morning. Had experiments today. Mama & Papa & the baby came home tonight. May Crider was over then. 1 hr.

17. No English today. Miss Taylor is sick. Went to skating rink this eve. Mr. & Mrs. Wall and daughter Alice, Mr. & Mrs. Conklin were here.

18. Trimmed arcs today. Drove Ford to Howard [nearby town] with Mr. Weik to fix meter. Went to pictures. Got check for $16.75. OK. (9 hrs.)

Sunday, September 19. Went for a ride to Penn's Cave for dinner, then to State College and home. Had nice time. Studied in evening.

20. Have bad cold. Nice day. Went to pictures. "Male & Female." Good pictures, best I have seen for a while.

21. Mama went away this eve for Middleburg with Philip. Sister went to pictures. I went to bed early.

22. Feeling better. Fixed bike up and started to fix sister's. The IOS had a meeting at our house tonite.

23. Start chemistry experiments Monday. Nice day. Went to Opera House tonite. "Jim's Girl" was on. Pretty good show.

24. Went to pictures and then to skating rink to see the fancy skater. Mama and Papa came home with a new Franklin car.

25. Read meters in Centre Hall. Went to skating rink. Got pictures I took last Sun. (9 hrs.)

Sunday, September 26. Went to Sunday School. Rally Day. Went for ride in new car after supper. Got my lessons.

27. Read meters after school. Mr. and Mrs. Heberly were up in the evening. I read magazines, etc. (1 ½ hrs.)

28. Start school at 8:40 now. Have 1 hr. training. Nice day. Read meters in evening. Sprinkled some this eve. (1 ½ hr.)

29. Mama and Papa went to Curwensville today. Nice day. Recited in Caesar for the first time. Read meters. (2 ½ hrs.)

30. Read meters in morning. Raining out. Start M.T. today. Tubby got fired at the office. Still reading (3 hrs.)

---

15 I believe these hours here are hours worked a particular day.

1920 Diary of Howard V. Thompson

OCTOBER

Friday, October 1. Still reading meters. Cold, dreary day. Went to pictures this evening. Cold out. (1 hr.)

2. Read meters in Port Matilda and Unionville. Walked home from Unionville. Went to show tonight. "Polly and her Pals" was on. Good.

Sunday, October 3. Got up at 10 o'clock. Got papers. Went for a walk to Fairyland as it is called with Phil, Ray, Jimmie Mayer.

4. School again. Nice day. Have cold. Rained in eve. Loafed around after school. Ran around. Went to bed early. (1/2 hour)

5. Contest at school to raise money for a A.A. Reds and Blues. I am a Red. Mama & Papa came home this evening. Pd. $8.25

6. The Blues won. I worked around the house after school. Studied my lessons in eve. Did my Chem. experiments today.

7. Had chem. exper. Took Mama's checks around this eve. Got $2.00 from Mama this mo. I didn't feel good. (1/2 hr.)

8. Have bad headache. No History today. Game at State College tomorrow. Sold my xx and went to Dr.

9. Worked at Mussers' on xxx with Harold. Went to State in afternoon. Saw last half of H.S. game. We got beat. Saw State beat Dartmouth 7 to 11. Went to pictures.

Sunday, October 10. Sunday School, papers, etc. Stayed home in afternoon. Got my lessons in evening. Sister made candy.

11. Nice day. Still have headache. I went to Dr. on Fri. eve. Some of the Football players are quitting on account of nothing.

12. Cut grass in evening. Watched Football scrimmage. Studies in evening. Went to bed early.

13. Hauled wood after school for Papa Spencer. Put lights on. Studied lessons in eve. Don't know what to write about.

14. Had Chemistry this morning. I wrote a good English story. Handed in my time for first half 13 hrs.

15. Started political campaign in high school. Nevin Robb, chairman of Republicans and Foster McGovern, chairman of the Democrats.

16. Worked trimming arcs in morning. Had academy boy helping me. Worked up at [????] in afternoon. Pictures in eve. Mr. Musser time 3 hrs.

Sunday, October 17. Run around town for Papa in morning. Worked at plant in afternoon fixing boiler. I was used inside hot as the dickens. (9 hrs.)

18. Democrats had three speakers this morn. Mary Sebring, Musser Gelting and Mary Yorks. Kept in for being late at noon. (Muser, 1 hr.)

19. Republicans had 3 speakers this morn. Thomas Mench, Harold Wion, and Mary Dale. Bought Philip a comb for birthday.

20. Got paid $4.20 total. Democrats had platform today. Mary Sebring and Malve Decker spoke. Not very good. Philip's Birthday.

21. Rep. had platform. Mary Chambers, Marjorie Hill, and Warren Cobb spoke. Sister went to club meeting tonight.

22. Had forum today. Dr. Brech and Mr. Stoche spoke. Going to vote now. Harding won in the straw vote. (Howd saved a commemorative coin from this election, now in the possession of Judith.)

23. Went on 6:00 train to Center Hall and read meters. Came home at 4:30. Went to pictures at Opera House this evening. Good. We got beat in football by Lewisburg, 13-0. (11 hrs.)

Sunday, October 24. Went to Sunday School. Counted money. Walls came over after dinner. Mama and Papa went to Curwensville when they did. (1 hr.)

25. Went to school. English re-exam this morning and mathematics this afternoon. Read meters some in the evening after school. (1 hr.)

26. History re-exam this morning and French and Latin this afternoon. I took Latin exam. It was hard. Read meters. Went to pictures. (1 hr.)

27. Raining this morning. Read meters in evening. Wrote short story for content this morning. Raining out. (1 hr.)

28. Cold day. Had test in Chemistry. Edward Miller had his leg broken in practice this evening. Read meters. Went to pictures eve. (1 ½ hr.)

29. Cold day. Built fishing (?) decorating for party tonight. Went to party. Read meters in eve. Going to Port M. in morn. (1 ½ hr.)

30. Read meters in Port Matilda and Unionville. Cold day. Mama & Papa came home today. Went to pictures in eve. State beat Penn 28-7 and Penn State Freshmen really beat Academy 27-0.

31. Bummy and I trimmed arcs early in morning. I stayed at home in afternoon. Sister made fudge. Mr. and Mrs. Heverly (?) were here. (9 hrs.)

NOVEMBER

Monday, November 1. Read meters. Big time in evening parade. I dressed up fancy. Didn't get home till 11 o'clock. (3 hrs.)

2. Election Day. Finished reading meters. Papa going away. Went downtown till 10:30 in evening to get returns.

3. Papers say Harding won. Worked putting in meter and fixing street light after school. Cold day. Stayed home in eve. (1 ½ hrs.)

4. Nice day. Had chemistry experiments. Had to stay in for being tardy. Big parade tomorrow nite for Harding. $15.30.

5. Nice day. Chemistry experiments. Went to pictures in eve. Rep. parade this eve. Pretty good. Papa came home. (1 hr.)

6. Went to Eagleville to work putting in meters. I put in 13 and (name) put in 14. Went to open house in evening. (10 hours)

Sunday, November 7. Worked at Beech Creek sub-station today. It rained in afternoon. I have 25 lines to say on Tuesday morning. (9 hrs.)

8. School today. Football men handing in uniforms today. Ordering hooks, pliers, and dinner pail from State-Central. (1/2 hour)

9. Said lines this morning. Bad day. Papa went away. School was closed second period because a girl had scarlet fever.

10. School again. Chemistry experiments this morning. Track and Basketball meeting after school. Worked reading meters after school.

11. Had school half day, marching with B.H.S. in parade. Armistice Day. Went to football game. Army and Navy 7 and American Legion was 0.

12. Chemistry experiments today. My report sent home by mail. Fixed arc after school. Worked in cellar in the evening. (1 hr.)

13. Trimmed street arc with Stock. Cleaned up arc room and took out meters for Weik. Got my report. Papa came home. Chemistry, B; English, C; Dept. C; History, D; Geometry, D; MT, D[16] (9 hrs.)

Sunday, November 14. Went to Sunday School. Stayed home in afternoon. Sister made candy. Studied lessons in evening.

15. Snowing hard all morning. Wore long pants to school for first time[17] Handed in time (35 hrs.). Lights off about 5 o'clock.

16. School. Snowing today again. Stayed home in evening and studied.

17. Papa went away today. Capt. Richard Hobson talked in the morning at school. Ran some errands in eve.

18. Not snowing today. Had music this afternoon but I didn't take it. Helped fix street lights this evening. (1 hr.)

19. School only in morning. Local institute in afternoon. Fixed street lights all afternoon. Went to bed early. (4 hrs.)

20. Went to work at 6:15 a.m. Went to Beech Creek and put in 34 meters. I put in 12. Mr. Wiek and Stock helped. Went to picture. Bought new suit: $50 reduced from $75.00. (10 hrs.)

16 Did anyone consider that work and absences for work could be a cause? My mother told me Howard was very bright and his heart was broken when his father would not send him to Penn State, only Williamsport Business School.

17 Most young men were wearing knickers.

Sunday, November 21. Went to Sunday School. Got papers. Gave sister a dollar bill for present. Studied in eve. Mary Alice's Birthday.

22. School again. Freshmen and Sophomores are training for game on Thanksgiving. Studied in evening.

23. Have examinations today. We had test in History today and have another tomorrow. Oh, ye gods and goddesses!

24. Had chemistry exam this morning. Kept in for Clubs this eve. Papa took out insurance for me. Cleaned up cellar in evening.

25. Went up to game between Freshmen and Sophomores. Sophomores winning 19-0. Went to pictures 2 times. (1 hr.)

26. Read meters at Center Hall. Got up at 5 o'clock. Stayed home in evening and studied. Bad day. Raining out. (11 ½ hrs.)

27. Trimmed stree arcs. Johnie helped me. Went up and read meters at Port and Unionville. Snow, sleet and rain; bad day. Went to skating rink in evening. (10 ½ hrs.)

Sunday, November 28. Went to Sunday School and got papers. The Johnson boys were there. I stayed home rest of day. Ate dinner at M.S.'s.

29. Have chemistry vacant period today. Kept in for not having problems. Handed in experiments in both. Read meters in evening. (1 ½ hr.)

30. School Chem. Ex. 3 periods this morning. Went to Star Course Entertainment. Very good, funny. (1 ½ hr.)

DECEMBER

Wednesday, December 1. Three reading meters. No experiments today. Dentist about two weeks from now.

2. Loafed around after school. Basket ball practice has begun. We are in the Mountain High School League again.

3. I went to basket ball practice tonight. After that I went to pictures at Opera House. Pretty good.

4. Paid $12.30. (10 hrs.) Went to work at Beech Creek. I patrolled line from Howard to Beech Creek in morning putting on notices. Nice day.

Sunday, December 5. Worked on street system today. There was a ground on it. Other fellows worked at Howard sub-station. Studied in evening. (10 hrs.)

6. School today. Saw in paper where Clearfield High beat Tyrone High 45-21. Rebecca Rhoads house burned down today.

7. Have three vacant periods today. Elected 2 basket ball managers for boys and 2 for girls

today. Have lines to say. Don't know them.

8. Didn't say lines. Studied them in evening. Mama went to pictures in evening. The lights were low this morning.

9. Said lines this morning but have to say them again because I didn't know them. Made H-Cl acid today. Basket ball game.

10. Said lines this morning. Boys Basket ball uniforms are bright red pants and jerseys. We beat Houtzdale, 29-18.

11. Went to Beech Creek to finish up. They have lights now and we put in meters etc. The street circuit was off all evening. I worked till 9.30 on them. (Christmas party)

Sunday, December 12. Patrolled street system in morning. Found a lot of bad places. Some of the lights—about 257 were out tonight again. (9 hrs.)

13. The line crew fixed up the street lights today. They cleaned the post lights on Allegheny and Linn Streets.

14. Basket ball team have special practice tonite. Play Tyrone Friday. Start in Caesar tomorrow in Latin.

15. George Showers got a job reading meters, etc. at office last night. "Fifi's" is on at the Opera House tonight.

16. Snowing again today. The ground has frozen. Class going to Fifi's tonight. On Jan. 3rd we have 1st class at 8:40.

17. Snowing today. I got 95 in Chemistry exam. Last day of school this year. Seniors give presents this eve.

18. Boys team got beat at Tyrone last night. Worked at Julian today. (9 hrs.) Helped raise some 20 & 25 foot poles and distributed up as far as Materson's farm.

Sunday, December 19. Went to Sunday School. Got mail and papers. Went up to Mussers. Went to church in evening.

20. Worked around office today. Getting ready to take inventory. Other fellows at a line. (8 hrs.)

21. Worked around office today. Went to dentist yesterday and today. Have another date for tomorrow. (8 hrs.)

22. Still working around town. Went to dentist. Finished except cleaning. Went to pictures tonite. (8 hrs.)

23. Trimmed street lights and washed shades today. Finished at dentist. I am to stop in at Easter vacation. (7 hrs.)

24. Read meters in Centre Hall today. Charged new rate of 11¢ for first 100, 9¢ for next kw. Went to pictures in eve. (11 hrs.)

25. Worked changing meters in the morning. Went to pictures in evening. Got a lot of presents. (1 hr.)

Sunday, December 26. Went to Sunday School. Got papers. Went to church in evening. Snowed some.

27. Read meters in Pleasant Gap all day. Went to picutres in evening. Showers working in Bellefonte. (11 hrs.)

28. Read meters in Milesburg all day. I came out $3. short. Went to pictures this evening again. (10 hrs.)

29. Read meters around town, Coleville, American Line, Center Count, etc. Went to BB game tonight[18] at State College & BHS. We beat 28-4.

30. I hurt my knee last night at playing basket ball. Read Port (Matilda) and Unionville. Bad day for me not feeling good. (9 ½ hrs.)

31. Read meters in Bellefonte. Mr. Stock was back yesterday. Basket ball team got beat at Philipsburg, 29-31. (9 hrs.)

January 1, 1921. Took inventory of old plant all day. Went to pictures in evening. 9 ½ hrs.

Next are listed several telephone exchanges.

The following page includes his class schedule.

In the inside cover of the back is written

> Catherine S. Pifer
> 411 Thompson St.
> Curwensville, Pa.
>
> Saturday, June 30, 1923[19]

[Mother's name address and date in 1923 – the entry struck me as sad for some reason. Perhaps the unexpectedness of finding this information, then the thought of their being young and just meeting and having hopes and dreams and such.]

---

18 Spelling of "tonight/tonite" is inconsistent throughout.
19 One can only surmise that he had kept this diary on hand and it was the closest place in which to write my mother's name and address, along with presumably their first date. This and the first Valentine Howard sent my mother are the only two mementoes left of their young romance.

Jury Decides Son is Owner of Stock

Clearfield Progress, June 2, 1959

It took a Clearfield County jury just 40 minutes yesterday to decide that Howard V. Thompson of Curwensville is the rightful owner of 10 shares of stock in the Curwensville Water Company which his father, H. J. Thompson, recently sold to the Pike Township Municipal Authority for $392,500.

The findings returned by the jurors yesterday afternoon ended a dispute over the ownership of the stock which began in 1957 when the younger Mr. Thompson said he learned his shares, received as a gift in 1922, had been marked canceled and without his permission nor endorsement had been turned back to his father.

The younger Mr. Thompson who had served as secretary and treasurer of the Curwensville Water Company from 1925 until he was removed in 1941 began a suit in equity to determine the ownership of the disputed 10 shares. He claimed that his father had refused to let him look at the shares of stock—kept in the water company office—until he obtained a court order.

When negotiations were started a few months ago by H. J. Thompson, owner of the remaining 540 shares, to sell the company to the Pike Township Authority, his son petitioned the court to restrain the sale. The deal went through, however, with the Authority taking control of the water company April 28.

The Thompson case was a suit in equity, usually heard only before a judge and not by a jury unless there is a dispute between the parties over the facts of the case. In such suits, the jurors determine the answers to questions presented by both sides. Yesterday's jury had two questions to answer:

1. Did H. J. Thompson make out a stock certificate and deliver it to the possession of the plaintiff, Howard V. Thompson?

2. Did Howard V. Thompson at any time thereafter give up or return the said stock certificate to H. J. Thompson, the defendant?

The jury answered the first question in the affirmative and the second in the negative, thus deciding that Howard V. Thompson was a rightful shareholder in the company.

Jury Decides In Favor of Son for Second Time

Clearfield Progress, June 3, 1959

Howard V. Thompson of Curwensville yesterday won the second suit he brought against his father, H. J. Thompson, also of Curwensville, for stock in a company the elder Mr. Thompson heads.

This suit—one in equity—concerned shares in Mid-State Theatres, Inc., formerly known as the Clearfield Amusement Company.

It had originally been brought against Mid-State Theatres, Inc., H. J. Thompson, and Miss Mae Shively of Curwensville and Frank G. Smith of Clearfield, directors of the company. However, since neither Miss Shively nor Mr. Smith own any stock in the company, they were both dismissed by the court as defendants.

The plaintiff—Howard V. Thompson—had claimed that he was the owner of 220 shares of stock in the Clearfield Amusement Company. Twenty of the shares had been given to him by his mother, Mrs. Elizabeth Thompson, now deceased, and the other 200 shares by his father.

In 1942 when the name of the theatre firm was changed to Mid-State Theatres, Inc., Mr. Thompson said he was notified by his father that all stock was to be turned in for stock in the new company. In compliance with this request, he went to the Curwensville Water Company where his stock was kept in the company safe, endorsed the stock certificates in blank and gave them to Mrs. Lottie Bennett, water company bookkeeper, now deceased.

After requesting in 1956 to see his stock and being refused, Mr. Thompson obtained a court order to examine the records of the theatre company. He learned then that his stock had been cancelled although he had never given any permission for such a transaction and believed that it had been exchanged for stock in Mid-State Theatres.

Testimony, based on company records and presented during the two-day suit, showed that after the plaintiff had endorsed the stock, it had been transferred to his brother, Philip B. Thompson, also of Curwensville. In 1957 the shares were transferred to H. J. Thompson who now holds them.

Since the suit was one in equity—heard only before a jury when there is a dispute over the facts involved—the job of the jurors was to listen to the testimony and to answer written questions prepared by both sides after the completion of this testimony.

260

Yesterday's jury had only one question to answer:

> "Did Howard V. Thompson deliver stock certificates Nos. 49 and 53 to Lottie Bennett, at the request of his father, and in reliance upon a statement from his father that the name of the corporation was to be changed to Mid-State Theatres and in pursuance of a resolution of April 18, 1942, of the corporation directors that all of the outstanding stock was to be turned in and stock in the new name, Mid-State Theatres, would be issued therefore?"

The jury deliberated 40 minutes before returning with the answer, "Yes."

The suit was the second court victory this week for the younger Mr. Thompson. Earlier in the week a jury decided he was the rightful owner of the 10 shares of stock in the Curwensville Water Company which his father recently sold to the Pike Township Municipal Authority for $392,500.

The Thompson cases were the only ones heard at this week's special session of Civil Court held to take care of cases adjourned from the regular May term. Three other cases [unrelated to the Thompson cases] were settled without going before a jury.

Charles Wall, 91
Long-Time Director of George Washington's Home

Charles Cecil Wall (June 21, 1903 – May 1, 1995) was an American self-taught historian and preservationist, who spent nearly 40 years as resident director of George Washington's estate at Mount Vernon on the banks of the Potomac River, where he endeavored to keep the home and its surroundings in much the same state that it existed when the First President resided there.

Wall grew up in Curwensville, Pennsylvania. A graduate of the Wharton School of the University of Pennsylvania, Wall began a career in business in New York City. With no prior interest in Washington's life, he accepted a job as assistant superintendent at Mount Vernon in 1929, taking the place of a cousin who had died in a drowning accident. During his first years as assistant superintendent, Wall and then-resident superintendent Harrison Howell Dodge rotated turns sleeping as guard in the manor house.

Wall became resident director of Mount Vernon in 1937, succeeding Dodge, who had served in the position for 52 years. Owned and operated by the Mount Vernon Ladies' Association since 1858, Wall was responsible for supervising a staff of 85 and lived on the site in an approximation of the lifestyle available to Washington in his time. His office was the same one used in the 18th century by Washington himself.

He would ride on horseback to inspect the grounds, used a boat to oversee the estate's frontage on the Potomac River and planted greenery consistent with what

was used in the 18th century in addition to overseeing restoration at the site. Wall was the first superintendent to reside in a director's house that was constructed on the grounds of the estate. In 1974, a campaign he organized was successful in preserving as parkland areas in Maryland across the

Potomac River from Mount Vernon, as part of an effort to retain the bucolic vista from the home. During his tenure he became an expert in all things related to Washington, much of which was included in his 1980 book *George Washington: Citizen Soldier*. Charles Cecil Wall also served as worshipful master in the Alexandria-Washington Lodge No. 22, the same lodge of which George Washington was a founder, in Alexandria, Virginia in 1944.

Charles C. Wall

In addition, he planted the kind of flowers Washington had planted. And when Washington's original greenhouse buildings were re-created with fireproof materials that allowed use of their fireplaces, he kept the fires lit in the fall and the winter just to exult in the authentic aroma of wood smoke drifting over the hilltop.

Mr. Wall supervised considerable restoration at Mount Vernon, which has been owned by the Mount Vernon Ladies' Association since 1858. His crowning achievement was leading the campaign that resulted in 1974 in Federal legislation creating a park on the Maryland side of the Potomac to preserve the view from the famous Mount Vernon portico.

Cecil Wall, front left, escorting British Royalty as well as Eleanor Roosevelt, second from the left, through the grounds of Mount Vernon.

Available Generational Photographs

List of identified (but not verified) photos in the album currently housed with Judith:

1st Generation (including Matilda's father, Robert Smith, and her Aunt Rose)
- Uncle Will Clark
- Rose
- Robert Smith

2nd Generation (Matilda's Smith Pifer's)
- William (Will) Shields and Daughter Catherine Princetta
- Ella Smith Jordan
- One of Matilda's sisters (identified as Ella)
- An unidentified sister
- Ella Smith Jordan
- Identified as Lennie Smith Heighes, father Robert, daughter Margaret, Baby Helen
- Matilda's brother Robert
- Identified as Jake Heighes
- Identified as Jessie and Jake Heighes, Hazel and Robert
- Ella, dated 1913. Identifies age as 21
- Robert Clark, son of Agnes and Will Clark
- Rosanna Smith Stormer and son, Edward, Jr., born March 9, 1914, and her prized mahogany piano
- Lennie and a daughter or granddaughter, possibly Margaret
- Hugh Pifer (brother of John) and Hugh's son (probably Hal, the first born son)
- Hugh Pifer (likely)
- King Pifer, second cousin to John and newspaper editor
- Margaret Pifer Jourdet and husband Bert
- Hal and Earl Pifer, sons of Hugh
- Identified as Hugh Pifer (but does not resemble the photos above identified as Hugh (He resembles Joseph from my point of view) If Hugh, then it is wife Carrie with children Hal and Viola.

3rd Generation (Offspring of Matilda Smith Pifer and her sisters. Generation of Kate, her sisters, and cousins)

- Hilpa Heighes
- Robert Heighes
- Josephine Smith Pifer, graduation 1914
- Clark Heighes, son of Jessie and Jake Heighes
- Margaret Pifer Jourdet's son Don (cousin to Kate)
- Inez Heighes, oldest daughter of Lennie (cousin to Kate)
- Margaret Heighes, daughter of Lennie
- Mary Heighes Patterson (daughter of Lennie) and Mary's daughter Margaret
- Margaret Longwell (daughter of Lennie)
- Identified as Henry Shields, son of Kate and Will
- John Shields, son of Kate and Will (notation on back of photo that John was gassed in WWI)
- John Shields, son of Kate and Will

4th Generation (Offspring of Kate Pifer Thompson and her sisters and of the Pifer Girls' cousins, who were the children of Matilda's siblings; a few others)

- John Wayne, son of Ruby
- John Wayne
- John Wayne on his horse Babe
- Eugene Chester Bloom, son of Margaret Jean Pifer Bloom
- Tommy Wayne, son of Ruby
- Tommy and Johnny Wayne
- Elizabeth Bailey Spencer Thompson
- Elizabeth Bailey Spencer Thompson
- Howard Vincent Thompson (baby)
- Mary Alice and Howard Thompson (children)
- Kate and Will Shields
- Mary Alice Thompson
- One of the Wall boys
- Snapshot of Mary Alice and Bubby
- Possibly Kate in a group photo of a school class
- Ruby (baby)
- Ruby (approximately 8 years of age)
- Howard, 1912
- Howard, Miss Taylor's room, 1918
- School picture of Margaret Jean Pifer

Other Books by Judith T. Witmer

Loyal Hearts Proclaim: A Historical Compendium
of Lower Dauphin High School, 1960–2010

Growing Up Silent in the 1950s
Not All Tailfins and Rock 'n' Roll *

Bicenquinquagenary
Hummelstown Celebrates 250 Years (Editor)

All the Gentlemen Callers
Letters Found in a 1920s Steamer Trunk *

Jebbie: Vamp to Victim, The Truth about Miss Pifer *

I Am From Haiti: The Story of Rodrigue Mortel, MD

Je Suis D'Haiti: Par Rodrigue Mortel, MD

Moving Up! A Guide for Women in Educational Administration
(2 editions)

Team-Based Professional Development
A Process for School Reform

The Keystone Integrated Framework: A Compendium

A Style Manual for Publications

How to Establish a Service-Learning Program

* Family History

Yesteryear Publishing

Yesteryear Publishing is pledged to honor and validate the past through research-based history and attributed personal accounts, providing the skill to combine history and memories and the integrity to indicate the difference.

Yesteryear Publishing was founded under a different name fifteen years ago and recently changed identity to reflect its focus on (1) discovering, rescuing, and publishing accounts of personal histories set in accurate timeframes; (2) providing a venue through which to explain the origin of traditions relative to families, small towns, school life, and friendships; and (3) dispelling myths of 20th Century life as it was lived. We offer writing, editing, design, and publishing services in all areas of the written and spoken word, not limited to the 20th C.

Judith Witmer, the principal of Yesteryear Publishing, holds a B.A. in English Literature from Penn State, an M.S. and Doctorate from Temple, and both graduate and post-doctoral credits from Harvard University. She is an accomplished author, skilled in historical narratives, biographies, texts, journal articles, reports, profiles, speeches and other creative endeavors.

Her professional passion is historical research as evidenced by her publications. In addition to the number of books she has written, she has published numerous articles in professional journals, a cover feature in *Penn State Medicine*, newspaper columns, monographs, national speeches, book reviews, and a play.

E. Nan Edmunds, managing editor and page designer of Yesteryear Publishing, has served as a managing editor of Penn State Hershey Medical Center's publications (circulation ranging from 6,000 to 12,000) and is a skilled editor as well as a creative designer, writer, and publisher in her own right. She has worked in publications for more than twenty years.

www.ingramcontent.com/pod-product-compliance
Lightning Source LLC
Chambersburg PA
CBHW081147090426
42736CB00017B/3223